Kerry
Best Wishes
Peter Hadreas

A PHENOMENOLOGY OF LOVE AND HATE

Using phenomenology to uncover the implicit logic in personal love, sexual love, and hatred, Peter Hadreas provides new insights into the uniqueness of the beloved and offers fresh explanations for some of the worst outbreaks of violence and hatred in modern times.

Topics discussed include the value and subjectivity of personal love, nudity and the temporality of sexual love, the connection between personal, sexual love, and the incest taboo, the development of group-focused hatred from individual-focused hatred, and prejudicial discrimination. The work encompasses analysis of philosophers and writers from ancient times through to the present day and examines such episodes as the Oklahoma City Federal Building bombing and the Columbine High School massacre.

ASHGATE NEW CRITICAL THINKING IN PHILOSOPHY

The *Ashgate New Critical Thinking in Philosophy* series brings high quality research monograph publishing into focus for authors, the international library market, and student, academic and research readers. Headed by an international editorial advisory board of acclaimed scholars from across the philosophical spectrum, this monograph series presents cutting-edge research from established as well as exciting new authors in the field. Spanning the breadth of philosophy and related disciplinary and interdisciplinary perspectives *Ashgate New Critical Thinking in Philosophy* takes contemporary philosophical research into new directions and debate.

A Phenomenology
of Love and Hate

PETER HADREAS
San José State University

ASHGATE

Published by
Ashgate Publishing Limited
Gower House
Croft Road
Aldershot
Hampshire GU11 3HR
England

Ashgate Publishing Company
Suite 420
101 Cherry Street
Burlington, VT 05401-4405
USA

Ashgate website: http://www.ashgate.com

British Library Cataloguing in Publication Data
Hadreas, Peter J., 1945-
  A phenomenology of love and hate. - (Ashgate new critical
  thinking in philosophy)
  1. Love 2. Hate 3. Phenomenology
  I. Title
  128.4'6

Library of Congress Cataloging-in-Publication Data
Hadreas, Peter J., 1945-
  A phenomenology of love and hate / Peter Hadreas.
      p. cm. -- (Ashgate new critical thinking in philosophy)
  Includes bibliographical references.
  ISBN 978-0-7546-6146-7 (hardback : alk. paper) 1. Love. 2. Hate. 3. Phenomenology.
I. Title.

  BD436.H255 2007
  128'.46--dc22

                                                                    2007001497

ISBN-13: 978-0-7546-6146-7

Printed and bound in Great Britain by Antony Rowe Ltd, Chippenham, Wiltshire.

Contents

For Cathy

πάντων ξύννοιε τῶν ἐμῶν
ψυχήν, ξύντροφ᾽ ἀηδόι

Acknowledgements

There are thoughts in this book that have been germinating ever since my first studies in philosophy. As such, it is fair to acknowledge those who set me on the path. I think first of Professor Wallace Matson whose remarkable lectures on the history of philosophy made the study of philosophy a compelling pursuit. Also from years long gone by, I must acknowledge Professor Hubert L. Dreyfus who first guided me, along with many other graduate students, through the vagaries of phenomenological interpretation. Well-known as a phenomenologist in his own right, Hubert Dreyfus is a tireless teacher, often expending his extraordinary energies and critical intelligence upon novices. There is, I think, still much truth in Aristotle's declaration that there is no adequate return possible for those who have introduced one to philosophy. These are debts that can hardly be repaid, except perhaps by lasting gratitude.

More recently, many colleagues at San José State helped this book along both with administrative and moral support. Even on a short list I am grateful to Karin Brown, Thomas Leddy, Tommy Lott, Rita Manning, Bo Mou, Barbara Scholz, William H. Shaw, and Anand Vaidya. Richard Tieszen read over the book in manuscript form. I've also befitted from his own work in phenomenology. (And, as I write this, I am sure there are others at San José State I've forgot who deserve to be mentioned.)

Professors David Cousins Hoy, James R. Mensch, Robert C. Solomon, and Anthony J. Steinbock kindly offered me publication advice. John Drummond, beyond the call of duty, supplied me with a translation of Husserl's manuscript, *Gemeingeist* I & II. They cannot be held responsible for whatever arguments I advance in this book, but their goodwill helped it to arrive at the publisher's door and attests to their generosity of spirit.

Peter Eggenberger has for years been a formidable foil in philosophical argumentation. He unfailingly helps to put into perspective whatever philosophical theory I'm trying out.

Last, I cannot express thanks enough to my son, Thomas Harada, and my wife, Cathy Luchetti. Tom listens supportively to my ideas, rarely offering criticism, but when he does, he does so with subtlety and exactitude. Cathy read over all the chapters of the book, sometimes more than once. Her extremely quick eye for catching stylistic solecisms is extraordinary and her emotional support in this project has been bountiful and constant.

Introduction

Why *A Phenomenology of Love and Hate?*

> The syntactical forms enter into the essence of the emotional acts themselves ...
>
> (Husserl, *Ideas I*)[1]

The Logical Underpinnings of Love and Hate

Love and hate develop in accordance with logical forms. Unwittingly, lovers and haters in the progress of loving and hating are constrained by this hidden logic presumed in the act of conceptualizing.[2]

Why a phenomenology of love and hate? First, because phenomenology, and especially Husserlian phenomenology, provides the background for understanding the foundations of love and hate, in the sense of their implicit logical forms. And, unraveling the logical underpinnings of love and hate answers a number of perennial questions: How does personal love – the cherishing of another person – enable the discovery of the irreplaceable uniqueness and source of value of the beloved? How is the allure of nudity different from nakedness? Why is the incest taboo an essentially human, or possibly a primate, proscription? How is generalization implied in an individual's hatred of another person? How does the generalizing alter with violent 'us-them' hatred? In detailing the logical underpinnings of love and hate, answers will be offered to these questions and others.

As will be detailed, there are logical 'underpinnings' to love and hate in several respects. They may be suggested by considering the various senses of 'underpinnings'. First, logical forms shape a person's feelings. They pin together beliefs, desires, and evaluations, producing distinct types of love and hate, as one might pin together pieces of cloth or paper. Antoine de Saint-Exupéry notes: 'Life has taught us that

---

1 Edmund Husserl, *Ideas Pertaining to a Pure Phenomenology and to a Phenomenological Philosophy, First Book* (Dordrecht, 1982), § 121, p. 289. [Die syntaktischen Formen gehen in das Wesen der Gemütsakte selbst ein, ...] Husserl, *Ideen zu einer reinen Phänomenologie und Phänomenologischen Philosophie, Erstes Buch*, Husserliana, vol. III, 1 (Den Haag, 1976), p. 279.

2 I am referring to logic here in keeping with the notion of 'transcendental logic' which is programmatic for Kant and whom Husserl follows in this regard. 'Transcendental logic' refers not to a *general* or *formal* logic, but to a logic which has to do, as Kant puts it, 'with the laws of the understanding and reason ... insofar as they are related to objects *a priori* ...' Immanuel Kant, *Critique of Pure Reason* (Cambridge, 1999), A57/B81–2, pp. 196–7. In this study, the objects in question are 'the loved' and 'the hated'.

love does not consist in gazing at each other but in looking outward together in the same direction.'[3] Implied here is a distinctive manner of pairing that arises with personal love. But what is the manner of conjunction in this pairing? In the section on personal love, we'll draw upon little-discussed phenomenological concepts to describe this manner of pairing.

A second sense of underpinning emphasizes how logical forms, like pricks of a pin, spur on the development of these passions. Stendahl, in *The Red and the Black*, has Julien Sorel recall as he sets out to capture Mme de Rênal's affections: 'Love does not seek equals; it creates them.'[4] Again a manner of pairing, a kind of affective conjunction is implied, but increasingly it urges on a relation between lover and beloved that resists differences in rank and status. Again, the affective conjunction of personal love is at work, but in this case, in effect, it wears down inequalities.

Third, as we'll consider, personal love is founded upon an empathizing with the beloved's strivings. Husserl notes in a late manuscript that we love a person who 'takes the trouble to strive ...'[5] Again, the pairing of personal love operates but here it grounds itself upon an understanding of the beloved that, the lover feels, is more subtle and truthful than a less devoted friend or relative might perceive. In this third sense, the logic of personal love underpins lasting affection as a building's foundation underpins its structure.

Personal love, *sexual* love and *violent group-targeted* hatred, as we'll suggest, are not *elemental* passions. They're not 'simples' by which complex passions may be analyzed. But, however varied our reasons for pursuing or avoiding another person may be, increasingly, as love and hate unfold, they become shaped by their logical complements and the basic types of love and hate emerge.

Consider the 'progress' of hatred. First, there is a degree of generalization. So, for example, with simple 'individual-focused' hatred, Medea arrives at what is generally hateful about Jason and then about men in general, 'shamelessness'.[6] Second, an exclusive '*or*' also enters into all types of hatred. Jason is at once both a husband and an enemy to Medea. Medea's conflict is that she is wedded, in one man, to both.

As hatred develops, increasingly more intense degrees of generality and 'either-or' opposition appear. A limiting case of hatred emerges when groups of people are believed to be monolithically *necessarily* worthy of harm and blame. This especially destructive human disposition is unfortunately all too recurrent. In making Arabs, Americans, Jews, Bosnian Muslims, Chechens, Tutsis, Chinese, Japanese, etc., into sub-humans, who, allegedly, by their essential nature, seek to undermine and destroy the home-group, this type of hatred arrives at a kind of perfection. It is not denied that the development of such a hatred has a multi-factored causality. It may be abetted by longstanding blood-feuds, and political propaganda as well as by the opportunity

---

3   Antoine Saint-Exupéry, *Wind, Sand and Stars* (New York, 1992), Chapter 9.6, p. 215.

4   'L'amour /Fait les égalités et ne les cherche pas.' Stendahl (Marie-Henri Beyle), *Le Rouge at Le Noir* (Paris, 1964), Book I, Chapter xiv, 'Les Ciseaux Anglais,' p. 107.

5   Husserl, Ms. E III 4, p. 20 [Aber wie ich den einzelnen Menschen, 'der streben sich bemüht', liebe ...].

6   Euripides, 'Medea', *Euripides in four volumes*, vol IV (Cambridge, 1912), lines 469–72.

hatred provides for avoiding self-doubt, fear and humiliation. Even so, the same logical components increasingly unfold in the development of hatred. In extreme violent group-hatred the logically exclusive '*or*' emerges in decision-making as a choice between two, and only two, violently opposed actions. It typically reaches a limit, as individuals believe that they must act violently against some hated group or face the immanent destruction of their own home-group.

New Resources Made Available by Recent Husserlian Scholarship

There are additional reasons why it is timely to apply phenomenology, and especially Husserlian phenomenology, to the topic.

Husserlian phenomenology has undergone changes in the last few decades and these changes provide new resources that urge this approach. As has been expressed by current scholars of phenomenology, by the end of the twentieth century, 'a new Husserl' has emerged.[7]

Many students of twentieth century philosophy were taught that phenomenology was a school of philosophy founded by Edmund Husserl (1859–1938) but largely developed by his colleagues and students. Husserl's own contribution was often depicted as constrained by his methodology, as narrowly conceived. His own positive doctrines were regularly characterized as an elaborate development of the Cartesian discovery that one has certainty about one's own consciousness. According to this standard account, it was the work of those whom Paul Ricoeur referred to as the 'Husserl-Heretics'[8] – Heidegger, Scheler, Merleau-Ponty, Sartre, Levinas, and Derrida – that brought phenomenology to fruition and critical maturity.

But this portrayal has turned out to be largely myth. Dan Zahavi, in a recent revisionist introduction to Husserlian phenomenology, describes the methodical misreading of Husserlian phenomenology as promulgated throughout most of the twentieth century.[9] Not only was Husserl's own account of consciousness erroneously taken to be solipsistic, foundationalist, and idealist. The breadth of his philosophical investigations was left largely in the dark.

The slow erosion of the dominant interpretation of Husserlian phenomenology came about largely through the protracted publication of the volumes of *Husserliana*. The appearance of these volumes continues throughout the second half of the

---

7   Donn Welton fittingly titles his recent collection of Husserlian studies: Donn Welton, (ed.), *The New Husserl: A Critical Reader* (Bloomington, IN, 2003).

8   Paul Ricoeur, 'Sur la phénoménologie', in *A l'école de la phenomenology* (Paris, 1987), p. 156.

9   As Zahavi explains, Husserlian phenomenology was not taught during the Nazi era (1933–1945) on account of Husserl's Jewish origin. So, 'an entire generation of German philosophers was trained in Heideggerian phenomenology instead'. Dan Zahavi, *Husserl's Phenomenology* (Stanford, CA, 2003), p. 141. After the war, Husserl was most often read, 'through the eyes of Heidegger'. Ibid., p. 141. This situation endured with little change well into the 1960s and 1970s. It wasn't until the 1960s that young philosophical scholars took Husserl's research manuscripts seriously enough to make them the subject of doctoral dissertations. Zahavi mentions in particular Held and Claesges. Ibid., p. 142.

twentieth century and into the twenty-first. (Volume XXXIV appeared in 2002. More are on the way.) These publications slowly have corrected the view that Husserl was exclusively concerned with descriptions of consciousness, as pursued from an expanded Cartesian perspective.

The *Husserliana* volumes, largely collated from Husserl's lectures as well as the extensive body of his research manuscripts, show a remarkable deepening of Husserl's philosophical investigations.[10] Husserl's investigations take on the full breadth of philosophical topics. He returns repeatedly to the topic of intersubjectivity, taking numerous approaches. He offers extended investigations of ethical issues, develops a manner of 'transcendental sociology',[11] based in an encroachment of 'home' and 'alien' cultures, as well as repeatedly returning to considerations of the teleology of human consciousness, as fully realized in a human community.

Along with the correction of Husserl's role in the history of phenomenology, recent scholarship also has more sharply depicted Husserl's own personality.[12] The publication in 1994 of Husserl's correspondence shows Husserl to be driven throughout his career by a grand philosophical mission that, in large measure, was accomplished, if his research manuscripts are taken into account. In letters, Husserl refers to 'his awesome life-task' (*ungeheure Lebensaufgabe*).[13] Writing to family friends he goes so far as to say his work involves: 'a complete transformation of the whole style, of the necessary way of posing the problems of the entire philosophy of the millennia and, included therein, a complete reform of the sciences.'[14]

In the last years of his life Husserl saw that his own work lay largely in his unpublished research manuscripts. Because of their immense volume, he doubted that much of his life's work would come to light.[15]

---

10 Recent scholarship has also supplanted the previously dominant account of Husserl's own intellectual development. Husserl's intellectual development had been characterized by 'a series of decisive ruptures'. Zahavi, *Husserl's Phenomenology*, p. 143. Since insufficient attention was paid to the research manuscripts that indicated a growth of ideas, built upon reworkings of previous solutions, it appeared that Husserl's intellectual development involved various breaks and turn-abouts. Husserl's career now shows a consistency in the development of his thinking that hitherto remained concealed. Ibid., p. 143.

11 Edmund Husserl, Ms C 8 (1929), 11a: 'We pass over from transcendental Egology to transcendental sociology ...' [Treten wir nun von der transzendentalen Egologie in die *transzendentale Soziologie* über ...] Cited by Steinbock in *Home and Beyond*: *Generative Phenomenology after Husserl* (Evanston, IL, 1995), pp. 303–4, n. 7.

12 The publication of Husserl's letters attests to the habits of a thinker driven to complete a monumental project. Husserl realized what he sometimes called his 'awesome life-task' with the help of cigars and strong coffee to the extent that, on several occasions, he was hospitalized because of nicotine poisoning. Edmund Husserl, *Briefwechsel* (Husserliana Dokumente III), in ten volumes, Karl Schumann and Elisabeth Schuhmann, (eds) (Dordrecht/ Boston/London, 1994), vol. II, p. 200; vol. X, p. 40, vol. IV, p. 366.

13 Edmund Husserl, *Briefwechsel*, vol. IX, p. 46, as quoted by Barry Smith in his 'Book review of Husserl's correspondence', *Husserl Studies*, 12 (1995): 101.

14 Husserl, Ibid., vol. IX, 78, as quoted by Barry Smith, Ibid., p. 101.

15 In a letter to Adolf Grimme dated 5 March 1931, Husserl writes: 'Indeed the largest and, as I actually believe, the most important part of my life's work still lies in my manuscripts, scarcely manageable because of their volume.' [In der Tat, der grösste und wie ich sogar glaube,

An additional reason for writing *A Phenomenology of Love and Hate*, then, lies in the resources provided with the emergence of 'The New Husserl'. *A Phenomenology of Love and Hate* draws particularly on Husserl's middle and late research manuscripts[16] along with the recent scholarship that is based in little discussed themes in the manuscripts. In particular, the work of James R. Mensch and Anthony J. Steinbock must be cited even in an introduction. Mensch's detailed account of Husserl's research into the pre-objective instinctual striving, which persists pre-consciously,[17] along, of course, with Husserl's own manuscripts concerning personal love, will be elemental to our first part on personal love. Steinbock's examination of Husserl's many texts and monographs concerning the mutual encroachment of a 'homeworld' and 'alienworlds' will be elemental to our part on violent hatred.[18] We'll also return to Scheler's writings as they concern personal love and hatred. But Scheler's acute insights take on a quite different sense and depth as elaborated by Husserlian manuscripts, which have been applied rarely, if at all, to the topic.

Phenomenology is Suited to Handling Cross-Disciplinary Topics such as Love and Hate

A final reason for a phenomenology of love and hate lies in the general suitability of phenomenological methods for approaching inter-disciplinary topics, such as love and hate. Love and hate extend across the tessellations of personal, interpersonal, social and cultural interrelations. Consider the complexity of various explanations for violent hatred as they appear in an especially well-known extremely violent hate crime.

Eric Harris and Dylan Klebold, in opening fire at Columbine High School on 20 April 1999 enacted the worst case of high school violence in US history up to that time. According to tapes made by these two teenagers, their actions were driven by rage, humiliation, and hatred.[19] In one of the videotapes, Harris refers to what he

---

wichtigste Teil meiner Lebensarbeit steckt noch in meinen, durch ihren Umfang kaum noch zu bewältigenden Manuskripten.] Edmund Husserl, *Zur Phänomenologie der Intersubjektivität, Dritter Teil: 1929–1935*, Husserliana XV (Den Haag, 1973), p. lxvi. See also similar remarks from a letter to Paul Natorp, dated 1 February 1922, in Edmund Husserl, *Zur Phänomenologie der Intersubjektivität, Zeiter Teil: 1921–1928*, Husserliana XIV (Den Haag, 1973), p. xix.

16 The middle period, as understood here, runs roughly from 1916 to 1928, the year of Husserl's retirement; the late period from 1928 to Husserl's death in 1938. During his later years, Husserl remained especially productive.

17 Particularly pertinent are James R. Mensch, 'Freedom and Selfhood', *Husserl Studies*, 14 (1997): 41–59; Mensch, 'Instincts – A Husserlian Account', *Husserl Studies*, 14 (1998): 219–37 and Mensch, *Postfoundational Phenomenology: Husserlian Reflections on Presence and Embodiment* (University Park, PA, 2001) especially chapter two, 'Instincts'.

18 Anthony J. Steinbock, 'Generativity and generative phenomenology', *Husserl Studies*, 12 (1995): 55–79, and Steinbock, *Home and Beyond: Generative Phenomenology after Husserl* (Evanston, IL, 1995).

19 Klebold and Harris left five videotapes in which they expressed their motives. Nancy Gibbs and Timothy Roche, 'The Columbine Tapes', *Time*, 20 December 1999, pp. 40–56. See also Matt Bai, 'Anatomy of a Massacre', *Newsweek*, 3 May 1999, pp. 25–31.

saw as his continual ridicule.[20] But, by the time they arrived at the deadly decision to take action, Klebold's and Harris's hatred flowed into accommodatingly well-worn channels of racism, anti-Semitism and homophobia.[21]

The rage and hatred of Klebold and Harris cannot be adequately explained by psychopathology alone. There is little doubt that the two teenagers' individual psychologies and, likely, neurobiologies, were 'disturbed'. Harris stopped taking anti-depressant drugs to intensify his anger.[22] Even so, appealing to psychological and neurochemical explanations alone tends to result in a 'tunnel-visioned' epistemology. As is well known, in the US, gun violence, especially the gun violence of children towards other children, statistically, is significantly higher as compared with other post-industrial nations. It has been argued that the violence of US minors is caused by the ready access to firearms in the US. But the social causes are clearly more complex. There are, for example, more guns per household in Canada than in the United States but Canadian minors are far less violent. Sociologists often point to correlations between the frequency of exposure by the media to violent events and violent acts by minors.[23] However that may be, there's little question that socio-cultural factors played a role in the Columbine tragedy.

How to relate the relevant psychological, and perhaps neurobiological, abnormalities of Harris and Klebold to sociological and cultural factors? A methodology that can take into account neurobiological, psychological, social and cultural factors must be one that has a conceptual basis sufficiently broad enough to consider love and hate from both an individual and a social perspective. Phenomenology, including hermeneutical phenomenology as represented influentially by Heidegger in *Being and Time*, does provide the conceptual foundation for investigating the complexity of human concerns connected with our topic.

We need to review two basic contributions of phenomenology to consider why phenomenology is especially capable of dealing with topics, such as love and hate, which require an inter-disciplinary perspective.

First, the notion of the world as 'horizon' or a 'field' is elemental to Husserlian[24] and post-Husserlian phenomenology[25] and this notion paves the way for an integration of psychological and socio-cultural points of view.

---

20 'My face, my hair, my shirts', Harris says. Gibbs and Roche, Ibid., p. 44.

21 Harris says on the tapes: 'More rage. More rage ... Keep building it on.' Gibbs and Roche, Ibid., p. 44. Klebold says: '... n---rs, spics, Jews, gays, f---ing whites.' '... I hope we kill two hundred and fifty of you.' Gibbs and Roche, Ibid., p. 42.

22 Harris indicates on the tapes that he stopped taking the antidepressant drug, Luvox, to spike the intensity of his rage. Gibbs and Roche, Ibid., p. 44.

23 Roy F. Baumeister, *Evil: Inside Human Violence and Cruelty* (New York, 1999), pp. 277–81. Eric Harris and Dylan Klebold were obsessed with violent video games and films. Gibbs and Roche, Ibid., p. 44.

24 Husserlian scholar, Donn Welton, recently writes that characterizing the world as 'horizonal' is: 'Husserl's most enduring and promising insight.' Welton, (ed.), *The New Husserl: A Critical Reader*, p. 223.

25 Welton observes that the Heidegger of *Being and Time* on the topic of worldly horizons is 'within the same field of discourse' with Husserl regardless of their otherwise philosophical differences. Welton, Ibid. On this issue, Merleau-Ponty was also in agreement.

The fundamental method of phenomenology remains for Husserl to the end of his career the so-called transcendental phenomenological *epochē*, or the transcendental phenomenological reduction.[26] The *epochē* attends to a 'transcendental' field, not a 'psychological' field.[27] In performing the transcendental phenomenological *epochē*, phenomenologists bracket not only their belief in the existence (as well as the non-existence, possibility or probability) of objects in the field; they also bracket their individual psychological self. In effect, the psychological point of view is also bracketed. What remains is a field that is given within a horizonal structure, irreducibly 'worldly' in the sense of being irreducibly intersubjective. It is hence 'transcendental' in the sense of being presupposed by any point of view whatsoever. Every perceptual object, an apple, a tree, or an automobile, is given as having insides and backsides, which are presumed as 'there' but which remain indeterminate. Further, these backsides or insides are open to *other* perceivers.[28] Every discourse, and this includes explanations concerned with the neurobiology of violent hatred, also presumes a context that is open to further investigations, revisions and corrections

---

Merleau-Ponty notes that the extraordinary contribution of Husserlian phenomenology lies in conceiving the world as a transcendental *field*. The notion of a transcendental field implies a 'horizonal' structure, that is, a world partially individually determined while at the same time partially open to the perspectives of others, both as individuals and as social persons. Maurice Merleau-Ponty, *Phenomenology of Perception*, (London, 1989), p. 61.

26 Husserl writes in *The Crisis of the European Sciences*: '... it is only absolute freedom from prejudice, [freedom] gained through the unsurpassable radicalism of the full transcendental *epochē*, that makes possible a true liberation from the traditional temptations ...'. Husserl, *The Crisis of European Sciences and Transcendental Phenomenology*, (Evanston, IL, 1970), p. 263.

27 Husserl's view of how the psychological field fits into the transcendental field, here as well, involves some long-standing misinterpretations, in this case, sustained by some of the most influential writers in the phenomenological tradition. Davidson and Cosgrove point to the influential figures who endorsed this position: H. Drue, J. Kockelmans, Maurice Merleau-Ponty, Paul Ricoeur, and Jean-Paul Sartre. L. Davidson and L. Cosgrove, 'Psychologism and Phenomenological Psychology Revisited, Part II: The Return to Positivity', *Journal of Phenomenological Psychology*, 33, 2 (2002): p. 145.

Again, relying on Husserl's earlier publications alone fosters a misconception of the role of the transcendental field in psychological investigations. Husserl, earlier in his career, specifically in the *Logical Investigations* and *Ideas I*, strove to separate phenomenology from empirical psychology to escape from a naïve psychologistic approach to logical and epistemological issues. By contrast, in his later works Husserl emphasizes the transcendental Ego as witness to a full range of intentionalities, active, passive, and long-standingly sedimented, including those involving complex intentional relations between peoples, singly and collectively, in traditions that, in some cases, extend over millennia.

28 'Thus anything objective that stands before my eyes in an experience, and primarily in a perception, has an apperceptive horizon – that of possible experience, my own and foreign. Stated ontologically, every experience that I have is from the beginning a member of an open, endless, although not explicitly actualized, range of possible appearances of the same [objective thing], and *the subjectivity of these appearances is the open intersubjectivity*.' Husserl, *Ideas Pertaining to a Pure Phenomenology and to a Phenomenological Philosophy, Second Book*, (Dordrecht, 1989), p. 298. Cf. Husserliana IV, §51, p. 195; Husserliana XIV, p. 274; Husserliana XV, pp. 33 and 497.

by other researchers. Backgrounds and contexts together are already implicit in the horizon of the world.[29] Saying the world is horizonal means that the world is, from the beginning, a '*concrete interconnection*'[30] as conveyed by the term, *field*.

Because phenomenology conceives of the world as one with open horizons that encroach one upon another, phenomenological investigations from the beginning presume the interconnection between individual psychological and socio-cultural perspectives. It, as well, establishes the locus from which scientific explanations may be abstracted. However sorrowful the perspectives of Klebold and Harris may have been, they still were lived out in a world that is also our world. Further it is that one world that may be investigated even to detecting Klebold's and Harris's motivations, as well as intersubjective sociological perspectives and historical 'sedimentations'.

There is a second primary phenomenological doctrine that provides a method for relating *physical* sciences with *psychological and socio-cultural* explanations. It concerns the notion of an essence or *eidos*. Husserl never ceased maintaining that, if phenomenology is to be an exact science, it must be based in the determination of 'essences', for which Husserl coined the term the *eidos*.[31] Even so, the *eidos* is perhaps among the most misunderstood of phenomenological notions. Husserl's description of an eidetic reduction, through which one 'sees' essences, the so-called *Wesenshau*, surely did not help to dispel the belief that essences were fixed, determinable universals, regardless of the emphasis Husserl placed, especially in later writings, on the *genesis* of the essence.[32] Merleau-Ponty rightly observed that Husserlian essence exists neither: 'in a heaven of ideas or in a *ground* (*fond*) of meaning – it is neither above nor beneath the appearance but at their joints; it is the tie that secretly connects an experience to its variants.'[33] In time, children come to distinguish the real objects around their beds from the dreamed or fantasized objects that they imagine beneath them. In so doing they acquire an essential or, if you like, an *eidetic* distinction, without which the child cannot distinguish dream from reality.

Key for the purposes of connecting neurobiological with psychological and sociological explanations is the genesis of an *eidos* that transpired over centuries allowing the hammering out of the distinction between the physical and human sciences. In late works, Husserl details how the physical and human sciences came

---

29   So Husserl writes in the *Crisis*: 'Natural life, whether it is prescientifically or scientifically, theoretically or practically interested, is life within a universal unthematic horizon.' Husserl, *The Crisis of European Sciences and Transcendental Phenomenology*, p. 145.

30   Husserl so describes the situation in which 'each consciousness and its intentional object actually stand'. Husserl, *Formal and Transcendental Logic*, (Den Haag, 1969), p. 316.

31   'Phenomenology rigorously and systematically carried out, ... is divided into eidetic phenomenology (or all-embracing ontology) as *first philosophy*, and as *second philosophy*, [it is] the science of the universe of *facta*, or of the transcendental intersubjectivity that synthetically comprises all *facta*.' From 'Phenomenology', written for the *Encyclopaedia Britannica*, reprinted in Edmund Husserl, *Shorter Works* (Notre Dame, IN, 1981), p. 33.

32   'Throughout all this, the "static" description of essences ultimately leads to problems of genesis, and to an all-pervasive genesis that governs the whole life and development of the personal "I" according to eidetic laws [*eidetischen Gesetzen*].' Husserl, 'Phenomenology', p. 26.

33   Merleau-Ponty, *Phenomenology of Perception*, p. 116.

to be separated. The dichotomy between the physical and human sciences follows upon the eidetic understanding of the corporeity of things.[34] The interconnection between the neurobiology that played into Klebold's and Harris's tragic acts and those explanations proffered by the human sciences finally lies in the basing of explanation purely on the abstraction, 'physical bodies' as contrasted with whole persons or psycho-physical beings. This is not to presume that phenomenology provides a completed system for interconnecting the role of neurobiology, psychology, sociology in accounting for love and hate. In fact, any philosophy that purports to do so must overreach what can be accomplished by any ordering of the sciences, since the very distinction between physical and human sciences is based in essences that are subject to historical reformulations.[35] Nonetheless, the notion of a historically imbedded *eidos*, namely that of the corporeity of physical bodies, enables a researcher to discern the grounds on which the physical and human sciences are distinguished and to interrelate them accordingly.

In sum, primary phenomenological methods, the *epochē* and the eidetic reduction, provide lasting philosophical contributions: the notion of the world as a 'field', and the grounds for sequestering the physical sciences from psychology and sociology through the abstraction, 'physical bodies'. These doctrines provide the conceptual foundation for investigating topics as broad as love and hate. Researchers may fill out positive accounts for love and hate more or less adequately. But if one begins with a method that adequately makes room for the complexity of the subject, as phenomenology does, the descriptions and explanations offered will not suffer from the narrowness of a purely psychological, or for that matter a purely neurobiological or sociological, approach. Husserl, duly with humility, understood the role of future phenomenology in writing: 'Accordingly, phenomenology demands that the phenomenologist forswear the ideal of a philosophic system and yet as a humble worker in a community with others, live for a perennial philosophy [*philosophia perennis*].'[36]

---

34 Husserl proposes in *Crisis* that the path of modern physical sciences relies on abstracting the corporeity from things, regardless of whether they be natural objects, artifacts, animals or persons. 'Through such an abstraction, carried out with universal consistency, the world is reduced to abstract-universal nature, the subject matter of pure natural science. It is here alone that geometrical idealization, first of all, and then further mathematizing theorization, has found its possible meaning.' Husserl, *The Crisis of European Sciences and Transcendental Phenomenology*, p. 227.

35 Husserl discovered as much in his own working out of essences. As Merleau-Ponty observed: 'It is nonetheless clear that Husserl himself never obtained one sole *Wesenshau* that he did not subsequently take up again and rework, not to disown it, but in order to make it say what at first it had not quite said.' Maurice Merleau-Ponty, *The Visible and the Invisible* (Evanston, IL, 1968), p. 116.

36 Husserl, 'Phenomenology,' in *Shorter Works*, p. 35.

An Explanation of the Book's Plan

Before beginning the discussion of love and hate in detail, it may be helpful to explain the book's organization. Ordinarily, the terms, 'love' and 'hate' cover a multitude of dispositions and passions. Even on a short list, love is romantic, erotic, libidinous, compassionate, friendly, and sympathetic, although seldom all at once. Hatred sometimes focuses on an individual, sometimes on general manners, and sometimes on groups, monolithically conceived. But the logical underpinnings of love and hate suggest that there are distinct *ideal* types of love and hate, in the sense of distinct *perfections* of loving and hating. These types can be distinguished through their complementary logical forms. As children or even young adults, our loving and hating may be relatively amorphous. But, the logical underpinnings of love and hate, and the consequent opportunities they provide for their full expression, instill specific lines of development. This development increasingly leads us to experience certain basic types of loving and hating. This book is organized accordingly into chapters concerned with *personal* love, *sexual* love, a chapter on hatred that arrives at *violent group-targeted hatred* as its ultimate expression, and a conclusion that details further the logical foundations of love and hate.

In Chapter 1, we consider how 'personal love' carves out a deep distinctiveness from other kinds of love. It is *in* and *through* this kind of love that the uniqueness of another person comes to be discerned. It relies on a history of subtle interactive empathetic responses with the beloved's strivings and endeavors. As James Thurber put it: 'Love is what you've been through with somebody.'[37] Personal love builds upon a history of empathetic calls and responses, which subtly couple the lover to the beloved. This coupling is an affective and volitional analogue to the conjunctive '*and*'. Uncovering the 'affective and volitional *and*' of personal love also yields the *perfection* of personal love: the discerning of persons in general, individually and universally, as bearers of immeasurable value.

Sexual love is the topic of Chapter 2. As we'll argue, it's not by chance that we refer to sexual 'parts' or that English slang, dating from the fourteenth century to the present, designates both sexual intercourse and a sexually attractive person as a 'piece'. As we'll consider, the language of wholes and parts, and the logic of the relations between wholes and parts, enable the unraveling of many of the curiosities of sexual love. We'll consider how these distinctions fit the ways people, in the throes of sexual passion, describe their partners and how they reveal a shift in our everyday perceptual organization. It will also become forthcoming how the intractability of the incest taboo emerges as a special case of the conflict between personal and sexual love.

Again, the point is not that the conscious experience of sexual desire involves an awareness of distinct logical forms. Rather, the distinction between sexual desire, as a kind of passion, and other kinds of love has a logical foundation, which extends deeply enough to constitute the manner of organizing the loved and the hated.

Chapter 3 maps out the progress of hatred through its various degrees of generality. Its *perfection* arrives, as violent group-focused hatred stereotypes Chinese, Jews,

---

37 James Thurber, quoted in *Life* magazine, 14 March 1960.

Arabs, Blacks, women, Americans, Japanese, and so on, as the necessary cause of the home-group's thwarted destiny. This full-blown hatred is markedly different from individual hatred, as well as from the civil hatred that, arguably, is socially useful extending as it does to community menaces such as serial killers and child molesters. It is also contrasted with philosophical misanthropy, as expressed in the anti-human diatribes of Diogenes and Nietzsche. Here, not a specific stereotyped group is targeted, but generalized human hypocrisies and faults.

A last chapter, the Conclusion, provides summary considerations of the logical underpinnings of love and hate. There, the limits and conflicts of personal and sexual love are discussed, along with considering ways of arresting group-focused violent hatred.

One final explanatory note regarding the book's use of literary examples and scientific experimentation. To illustrate phenomenological concepts, sometimes elusive in their abstraction, we'll rely upon honored literary sources. They include: Homer, Euripides, Catullus, Apuleius, Shakespeare, George Eliot, Dostoyevsky, Mark Twain, Chekhov, Proust, Yeats, and T.S. Eliot. Not only do these literary artists provide illustrations, they often offer insights that presage or fill out phenomenological explanations offered. As needed, we'll also rely on the work of current literary figures, for example, E.L. Doctorow, Marguerite Duras, Adrienne Rich and Chuck Palahniuk. Sometimes studies as drawn from psychology, sociology and anthropology will be considered. As indicated previously in this introduction, a major strength of the phenomenological approach is the notion of a transcendental field from which, as an ongoing philosophical project, the inter-working of phenomenology with the human and physical sciences may be understood. In this regard, the use of studies from physical and human sciences does not mark a departure from the general phenomenological approach to love and hate.

Chapter 1

Personal Love

> It has been hard, I know, my daughters, but one word alone/ wipes out all of the hardships/ love [*agape*]...
>
> (Sophocles, *Oedipus at Colonus*)[1]

> And when there is love, you can live even without happiness.
>
> (Dostoyevsky, *Notes From Underground*)[2]

To reach out in personal love to another person is to be more exactly aware of the other's behavior. Husserl, like Leibniz and William James, came to found 'consciousness' on a subtle level of strivings, urges, and endeavors. Leibniz knew these subliminal helps and hindrances as *petite perceptions*.[3] James understood these pre-conscious 'tendencies', as 'fringe' promptings of 'furtherance' or 'forbearance'.[4] Husserl sometimes refers to the level of pre-objective strivings simply as 'life'.[5] Husserl's investigations into this world of pre-objective strivings, in particular, reveal the level at which personal love operates. As we'll consider, personal love, in reaching out on this subtle level of strivings, urges, and endeavors, establishes both the uniqueness of the beloved as well as provides an irreducible foundation for value.

We'll introduce phenomenological notions in this part that are little discussed in phenomenological investigations, let alone philosophical discussions in general. First, the notion of '*contact*'. To 'make contact' or to be 'in contact' with another person, is to establish a consensual openness to affect and be affected by the other person. We can't deliberately terminate a contact, as we can a lovers' tryst, a marriage or a friendship. Personal love begins with 'contact' and, like personal love, contact endures as a 'pre-objective' opportunity.

A second notion, little discussed in Husserlian circles, marks the developments of personal love as based in interactive empathy. Departing from ordinary German

---

1 Sophocles, *Oedipus at Colonus*, ll. 1615–17 [my trans].

2 Fyodor Dostoyevsky, *Notes From Underground* (London, 1972), 2.6, p. 90.

3 See, for example, G.W. Leibniz, *New Essays on Human Understanding* (Cambridge, 1996), pp. 53, 115, 164 and 194.

4 William James, *The Principles of Psychology* (Chicago, 1952), pp. 161–87. Husserl was aware of the kinship between his notion of 'horizon' and James's notion of the 'fringe'. Husserl notes as much in *The Crisis,* Husserliana VI (Evanston, IL, 1970), p. 264.

5 Ms. A VI 26, p. 42a: 'All life is constant striving, all satisfaction is transitory.' [Alles Leben ist unaufhörliches Streben, alle Befriedigung ist Durchgangsbefrieigung.] Cited by James R. Mensch, in 'Instincts – A Husserlian Account', *Husserl Studies*, 14 (1998), p. 220, p. 231, n. 5.

usage, Husserl coins the term *Nachverstehen* 'understanding one after another', to this purpose. In building *Nachverstehen*, we conjoin empathetic understandings. One person's empathy follows upon the empathy of another. This conjoining of empathies transpires 'pre-objectively' even without a conscious judgment of the other person. The personal love built through such interpolated empathies may or may not be erotic. But as indicated by its designation, it is *personal* just inasmuch as the very notion of 'person' comes to be constituted through the adjoining of empathies.

Before we begin, one further note. To say that love is *personal* is to say that it is more than *individualized*. Individualization ordinarily implies a determination of a man's or woman's uniqueness as marked by proper names or definite descriptions. The 'planet Mercury' and 'the planet whose orbit is nearest to the Sun' are locutions that have one and only one referent. Quite differently, personal love establishes the uniqueness of the beloved as a singular subject, with a unique and characteristic physiognomy and style of endeavor. The uniqueness of the beloved arises because the beloved is understood through acts of empathy that, from the beginning, are joined with our own interaction. The singular style of walking, posture or vocal inflection is unique because added on to it is the lover's own empathy.

Husserl on 'Pre-Objective' Strivings

Husserl came to investigate how consciousness is founded upon pre-objective strivings in his later, so-called, 'genetic' phenomenological studies. They were the product of the remarkably creative last two decades of his life.[6]

---

6   In developing transcendental phenomenology, Husserl distinguishes two programs, an earlier *static* methodology and a later *genetic* one. Husserl, *Analyses Concerning Active and Passive Synthesis* (Dordrecht/Boston/London, 2001), pp. 624–34. *Static* phenomenology encompasses the phenomenological program from the pre-transcendental *Logical Investigations* (1900/01) through to and beyond his discovery of the transcendental *epochē* and the methodology of the phenomenological reductions as published in *Ideas I* (1913). *Genetic* phenomenology emerges in later writings. Although Husserl often employs genetic methods from 1917 to 1921, the earliest date for an explicit acknowledgment of the genetic methodology is likely 1921. Steinbock, *Home and Beyond: Generative Phenomenology after Husserl* (Evanston, IL, 1995), p. 37.

The work of static phenomenology is primarily descriptive, focusing on manners of intentionality. Husserl scholar, Ulrich Melle, fittingly compares the 'static' approach to the uncovering of geological strata. Ulrich Melle, 'Husserl's Phenomenology of Willing', in Hart, J.G. and Embree, L., (eds), *Phenomenology of Values and Valuing* (Dordrecht, 1997), p. 192. As with geological strata, in static phenomenology, the lower stratum of consciousness shapes the structures of the higher levels. The most fundamental stratum of consciousness is representation and judgment, which Husserl calls the '*doxic*' level. Next is the evaluative stratum of feelings and values or the 'axiological' level. Following the geologic comparison, last and 'uppermost' is the volitional or practical level. The structures of the axiological and practical strata are responsive to the fundamental doxic level of representation and judgment and, as such, exhibit structures analogous to the most foundational level.

In genetic phenomenology, Husserl investigates the developmental processes, which yield the structures described by static phenomenology. Husserl, for example, repeatedly

The ordinary experience of respiration provides a ready example for witnessing pre-objective strivings. The impulse to breathe is not so much a desire as a tendency, an urge, a prompting. It is not directed towards a conscious object or goal. Yet it has an *élan,* what James calls a 'furtherance'. An uneasiness prompts inhalation, resulting in a passing satisfaction. But, again, there is ordinarily no distinct reflection on taking pleasure in the inhalation. It is pre-reflective and the satisfaction, rather as Leibniz described, is 'a semi-pleasure'.[7] Exhalation similarly begins as a hiatus, a momentary pause, which turns into an urge to exhale.[8] All this takes place pre-objectively inasmuch as it involves no intentional or conscious *desideratum.* However, once we have difficulty breathing, we shift attentively into subject-object relations. Catching a breath is a profoundly sought after goal. And, in our desperation to breathe, we emerge as a self-consciousness ego. Of course, the shift from normal pre-objective respiration to troubled, near-asphyxiated breathing, focusing upon an object, is not reflected upon. Although not reflecting on the shift, persons struggling for breath nonetheless shift to the orientation of the 'objective world'. Struggling for breath, they single-pointedly try to throw off the smothering pillow or to swim their way to the lake's surface to gasp for air.

In manuscripts, Husserl points to the complexity of instinctual 'unfulfilled intentionality' through the example of an infant's 'desire' to breast-feed:

> When the smell of the mother's breast and the sensation of moving one's lips occur, an instinctive directedness towards drinking awakes, and an originally paired kinesthesia comes into play ... If drinking does not immediately occur, how does it happen? Perhaps the smell alone awakens something else, an empty apperception, so to speak, which has no 'conscious' goal. If touching occurs, then the way to fulfillment is first properly an ongoing instinctive drive, which is an unfulfilled intention. Then, in fulfillment, [there are] the movements of swallowing, etc., which bring fulfillment, disclosing the instinctive drive.[9]

---

revisits the phenomenological *epochē* formulating the conditions, which must pre-exist so as to enable its enactment. When Husserl declares, for example, that there is a standing underground of flowing that founds the structure of the ego, he proposes a genesis, in the phenomenological sense, of the *epochē.* Husserl, *Zur Phänomenologie der Intersubjektivität, Dritter Teil,* Husserliana XV, p. 598. It is within the program of genetic phenomenology that Husserl uncovers the pre-objective world of strivings, urges and endeavors that found the acts of consciousness.

7   G.W. Leibniz, *New Essays on Human Understanding,* Book II, chapter xx, §1, p. 166.

8   Husserl also uses respiration to exemplify pre-objective strivings: 'It [Respiration] is not a mere process, rather in playing itself out it is a relaxation of tendencies and a new exertion, a blind drive that works itself out and does so without involving my will.' Husserl, Ms. A VI 12 I, p. 130b. Cited by Melle, Ibid., p. 189.

9   Husserl, Ms. C 16 IV, p. 36b. [Sowie der Geruch der Mutterbrust und die Lippenberührungsempfindung eintritt, ist eine instinktive Richtung auf das Trinken geweckt, und eine ursprünglich angepaßte Kinästhese tritt ins Spiel ... Kommt es nicht alsbald zum Trinken, wie ist es da? Etwa der Geruch allein weckt ein Weiteres, sozusagen eine Leerapperzeption, die doch kein 'bewußtes' Ziel hat. Tritt dann Berührung ein, so ist der Weg zur Erfüllung aber erst recht fortgehender instinktiver Trieb, der unerfüllte Intention ist. Dann in der Erfüllung Schluckbewegungen etc., als Erfüllung bringend, als den instinktiven Trieb enthüllend.] Cited and trans. by Mensch, Ibid., p. 232, n. 8.

The talk of 'an apperception ... which has no "conscious goal"' casts the infant in the role of a subject who has yet to formulate the world of consciously desired objects. Husserl's breast-feeding infant is also ensconced in the pre-objective world of striving, urges and endeavors.

In his later investigations, Husserl goes so far as to refer to 'life' (*Leben*) itself, in general, as a confluence of subjective strivings in face of worldly resistances or accommodations.[10] And it is on the level of 'life', in the sense of the level of strivings, urges, and non-reflected upon satisfactions, that personal love operates. So Husserl writes in a 1921 manuscript titled, 'Love' (*Die Liebe*): '... lovers bind themselves in a loving partnership' so that '... all the striving of one enters in the striving of the other ...'[11] Personal love arises from a bundling together of striving subjects, who take 'security-in-one-another'.[12] It depends upon intersubjective 'contact' and an 'understanding after one another'. Personal love consists in 'a striving not only for the richest possible exercise of this joy, but for personal "contact" with it and for a partnership in living and striving ...'[13] To understand how personal love reaches out to the beloved, we need to consider the notion of 'contact' and 'understanding after one another' in more detail.

---

10 Husserl, Ms. A VI 26, p. 42b: 'Life is striving in the manifold forms and contents of intention and fulfillment; in the broadest sense, [it is] pleasure in fulfillment; in the lack of fulfillment, [life is] a tending towards pleasure as a pure striving that desires or as a striving that slackens off in the realization that fulfills it and that accomplishes its purposes in the process of the realization of the life-form of pleasure with its release of tension.' [Leben ist Streben in mannigfaltigen Formen und Gehalten der Intention und Erfüllung; in der Erfüllung im weitesten Sinne Lust, in der Unerfülltheit Hintendieren auf Lust als rein begehrendes Streben oder als sich im erfüllended Realisieren entspannendes Streben und sich erzielend im Prozeß der Realisierung der in sich entspannten Lebensform der Lust.] Cited and trans. by Mensch, Ibid., pp. 231–2, n. 6.

11 Full quote from which above is taken in ellipsis: 'First off: they [lovers] do not merely mutually communicate with one another; they do not merely construct a communal understanding by their common surroundings, and so on. Rather, because they have bound themselves in a loving partnership, it is implied, that in a universal way, all the striving of one enters into the striving of the other, or rather, once and for all, one has entered into [the other] and conversely. [Vorher: Sie machen einander nicht bloss wechselseitige Mitteilungen, betätigen nicht <bloss> Gemeinschaft der Kenntnisnahme, hinsichtlich ihrer gemeinsamen Umgebung u. dgl. Sondern darin, dass sie sich zu einer Liebesgemeinschaft verbunden haben, liegt, dass in universaler Weise alles Streben des einen in das Streben des anderen eingeht bzw. ein für allemal eingegangen ist und umgekehrt.] Husserl, *Zur Phänomenologie der Intersubjektivität*, Husserliana XIV, p. 173.

12 Full quote from which above is taken: 'But what matters then for the type and intimacy and this partnering is the range of security-in-one-another of the I and the You, the range of the partnering of strivings and of further [strivings] at various other points.' [Aber es kommt dann für die Art und Innigkeit dieser Gemeinschaft an auf den Umfang der Ineinander-Geborgenheit von Ich und Du, auf den Umfang eben der Gemeinschaft des Strebens und des weiteren auf verschiedene andere Punkte.] Husserl, Ibid., p. 172.

13 [Ein Streben nicht nur nach möglichst reicher Betätigung dieser Freud, sondern nach personaler 'Berührung' mit ihr und nach Gemeinschaft im Leben und Streben ...] Husserl, Ibid., p. 172.

The Notion of 'Contact' and its Relation to Personal Love

In a section of the 1921 manuscript that accompanies Husserl's description of kinds of love,[14] titled, 'The I-You Relation', Husserl refers to the 'mutually and simultaneously accomplished empathy' which brings oneself and another into a manner of 'contact'.[15] The term, 'contact', a translation of the German word *Berührung*, means literally 'touch' or 'touching'. English idiom similarly enlists 'touch' in such phrases as 'keeping in touch with someone', 'losing touch with someone', and so on.

The 'contact' or 'touch' Husserl sets out to distinguish is unlike an intentionally arranged appointment or meeting. Upon 'contacting' another person we need not share their motivations. In fact, motives of all sorts may lead two people into contact. But regardless of their motivations, 'contact' occurs whenever two subjects are drawn into empathetic relation with one another.[16] When they contact one another, they open themselves to an interaction, to an openness of two striving wills.

Contacts can be trivial, as with a telemarketer. They can be ephemeral and passingly appealing, as in the dinner party small-talk. Contacts can also mark the beginning of a profound inter-personal relationship that subsequently alters the direction of two individuals' lives. The key feature to Husserl's notion of 'contact' is that it consists in an open-ended receptivity to another person. Making contact may befall two people by chance, but henceforth they share a horizon of possible interaction.

Contacts have their own manner of inauguration and dissolution that operate outside of the deliberate intentions of the communicating parties. When, for example, a shipwrecked crew 'makes contact' with a rescue team by radio, their contact establishes a mutual consent to communicate. But, the ship-wrecked crew may 'lose contact' with the rescue party or their contact may 'break off'. Even so, their losing contact may have nothing to do with the deliberate intentions and interests of the crew and the rescue party.

---

14 Besides titling one section, §5, 'Love' [*Die Liebe*], he titles another section, §6, 'Ethical Love' [*Die Ethische Liebe*], and another, §7, 'Love and Love-Partnership' [*Liebe und Liebesgemeinschaft*], Husserl, Ibid., pp. 172–5.

15 Husserl, *Zur Phänomenologie der Intersubjektivität, Zeiter Teil*, Husserliana XIV, pp. 166, 168. Husserl explains 'contact' in a manuscript dating from 1921: 'So I influence the other, and not only in general but rather in the framework of the mutually and simultaneously accomplished empathy which brings [the] I and You into "contact"; and in the special way that my influence (i.e., my will or my instinctive striving to "determine" the other, to "move" him mentally, to determine his striving or willing) should be noticeable to the other and itself belong together with the "way", with the means of determination.' [Ich wirke dabei also auf den Anderen ein, und nicht nur überhaupt, sondern im Rahmen der wechselseitig und gleichzeitig vollzogenen Ich und Du in 'Berührung' bringenden Einfühlung; und zudem in der besonderen Weise, dass mein Einwirken (d. h. mein Wille oder mein triebhaftes Streben, den Anderen zu 'bestimmen', ihn geistig zu 'bewegen', ihn zu einem Streben oder Wollen zu bestimmen) dem Anderen merklich sein soll und selbst mitgehört zu dem 'Wege' zum Mittel der Bestimmung.] Husserl, Ibid., p. 168.

16 Cf. Husserl, Ibid., p. 168.

In fact Husserl's discussion of 'contact', as a foundation of human interpersonal communication, is a typical topic that has been missed even by particularly astute earlier readers of Husserl. In this regard, it is clearly part of the 'new Husserl'. In particular, Jacques Derrida, in his highly influential criticism of Husserl's theory of communication in *Speech and Phenomena*, might well have altered his critique of Husserl if these later texts were taken into account.[17] They presume an inter-personal horizon for communication in which the intentions of the speaker need not be specifically acknowledged by the auditor. Derrida does not entertain that Husserl considered such a possibility.[18]

Anton Chekhov's short story, 'The Kiss', illustrates how the experience of 'contact' opens the possibility of interaction without a specific agenda. In the Chekhov story, Ryabovich, a stooped, shy, and socially maladroit member of a reserve artillery brigade, is invited with his comrades to the manor house of a local land-owner for tea, followed by dancing and billiards. But Ryabovich has never been to a dance and never played any game but cards. Not invited to billiards, Ryabovich struggles to

---

17 Jacques Derrida's influential criticism of Husserl on communication presumes that Husserl's account of communication in the *Logical Investigations* is altogether representative of Husserl's position on the topic. Jacques Derrida, *Speech and Phenomena* (Evanston, 1973). But as Mensch details, several scholars have shown how Derrida's analysis fails to take into account Husserl's later work, especially the work of the 1920s. Derrida overlooks Husserl's later concepts of association and kinesthesia, notions elemental to genetic phenomenology. Mensch, *Postfoundational Phenomenology: Husserlian Reflections on Presence and Embodiment* (University Park, PA, 2001), pp. 122–6, notes: 4, 5, 7, 9, and 10. Mensch cites in particular the work of Mulligan, Seebohm, and Evans on this topic. Kevin Mulligan, 'How not to Read: Derrida on Husserl,' *Topoi*, 10 (1991), pp. 199–201; Thomas M. Seebohm, 'The Apodicity of Absence', in *Derrida and Phenomenology*, W. McKenna and J. Evans (eds), (Dordrecht, 1995), pp. 185–200; J. Claude Evans, *Strategies of Deconstruction* (Minneapolis, 1991).

18 Husserl had held in *Logical Investigations* that communication requires: 1) that the intentions of a speaker be directed to an auditor; 2) that they are conveyed by means of indications; and 3) that the intentions of the speaker are acknowledged by the auditor. Husserl, *Logical Investigations* (New York, 2001), esp. §7, 'Expressions as they function in communication', pp. 189–90. Derrida, in *Speech and Phenomena*, discusses Husserl's theory of communication in *Logical Investigations* inasmuch as communication is conveyed by a means of indication that presumes an *ideality of meaning*. Derrida argues that the notion of ideal meaning rests on the false belief in a self-identity of meaning. The illusion of self-identity of meaning is exposed when one realizes that it consists in no more than the possibility of repeating the same expression. Derrida defends the position that there is no reason to suppose an identical one-in-many sense. Communication, as Husserl theorized, does not exist because the auditor cannot acknowledge the self-same intentions of the speaker. Consequently, there are no selfsame meanings upon which to anchor the means of indication, for both the speaker and auditor. As Derrida writes: 'But this ideality, which is but another name for the permanence of the same and the possibility of its repetition, does not exist in the world, and it does not come from another world; it depends entirely on the possibility of repetition.' Derrida, Ibid., p. 52. But 'contact' as an inter-affective venue for communication allows for communication to take place as a reciprocal apprehension of the other's strivings. This apprehension of the other's strivings may proceed pre-objectively and as such need not acknowledge the other's intentions, or indeed a 'self-identity of meaning'.

find his way back to the drawing room, but he becomes lost in a labyrinth of rooms. Resolutely, he opens a door and walks into to an absolutely dark room. He hears hurried footsteps, the rustling of a dress and a breathless feminine voice saying, 'At last!'[19] Unmistakably fragrant arms clasp him about the neck, a warm cheek presses against his, and he's kissed. The unknown lover then utters a faint shriek and springs away, 'as it seemed to Ryabovich, with disgust'.[20]

Because it is a kiss, Chekhov's story illustrates how erotic 'contact' sets up the possibility of amatory interaction. But, because the kiss comes from an anonymous lover, whom Ryabovich can never identify, Chekhov focuses upon a case of contact as stripped away from the follow-up of further acts directed toward a specific object, a specific beloved.

The kiss transforms Ryabovich for some months. For the first time, Ryabovich sees himself as someone who might have a love affair ending in marriage. Curling up in bed, Ryabovich tries to gather the flashing recollections that come into his mind, the hurried footsteps, the rustle of skirts and the sound of a kiss so as to 'combine them into a whole'. But as Chekhov notes, 'nothing came of it'.[21] In phenomenological terms, Ryabovich never constitutes an 'intentional object' as the focus of his desires. The kiss, rather, installs a generalized prospect of promise, an 'intense baseless joy'.[22] It is this manner of human interaction that introduces personal love. If love is to be extended to another person, as a *person*, and not merely someone who satisfies our interests or merely someone whose manners or looks please us, we must be willing to enter into a relation with the other person that will allow us to understand the other person, on *their* terms. The joy of personal love requires entering into a reordering of ourselves and the other person that cannot be foreseen in advance.

For Ryabovich, the promise of the love affair inaugurated by a kiss is dispelled only when Ryabovich, months later, his heart-racing, returns to the garden gate of the manor house hoping to encounter his anonymous lover. He finally realizes that the 'kiss' was an accident, '"How stupid, how stupid!" thought Ryabovich ... the incident of the kiss, his impatience, his vague hopes and disappointment, presented themselves to him in a clear light ... he would never see the girl who had accidentally kissed him instead of someone else; on the contrary, it would have been strange if he had seen her ...'[23]

'Contact' in its very open-endedness, inaugurates the possibility of a mutual reordering, for the unique prospect of an, as yet unknown, interaction. It implies an altogether less determinable set of expectations from social engagements, business negotiations, personal friendships or romantic encounters. And its manner of termination is altogether different. We may cancel social engagements, conclude business negotiations, 'break off' friendships, and fall out of love. But 'contacts' cannot be so terminated. So it is with the Ryabovich of the Chekhov story. For

19 Anton Chekhov, 'The Kiss', in *The Portable Chekhov* (New York, 1977), pp. 163–4.
20 Chekhov, Ibid., p. 164.
21 Chekhov, Ibid., p. 169.
22 Chekhov, Ibid., p. 168.
23 Chekhov, Ibid., p. 179.

Ryabovich's would-be anonymous lover, there was contact, but with a stranger. The lady in the dark room, hoping to meet her lover, immediately recognized her mistake, uttered a faint shriek and sprang away. She made contact with someone, but fled as soon as she realized he wasn't her lover. Still there *was* contact. Without this initial contact, Ryabovich could not have embarked on his misguided pursuit.

The Notion of 'Understanding-Following-After-Another' and the Development of Personal Love

Personal love requires far more than mere contact. But it is a beginning. For the development of personal love we must turn to a second notion Husserl discusses in manuscripts.

In a section of the 1921 manuscript mentioned above[24] Husserl describes an 'I-You relation', as a relation in which two striving subjects come to be related to each other, one after another, in mutual interactive affecting and being affected.[25] In this manuscript we find three times in just three lines, that striving subjects interact, 'one after the other' (*aufeinander*).[26] In fact, here, we have a fundamental condition of the development of personal love.

Personal love requires what Husserl calls 'understanding-following-after-another' (*Nachverstehen*), which, as mentioned, is a Husserlian neologism.[27] It is

---

24 The manuscript in question is titled: 'The attainment of personal self-consciousness in the I-You relation' [Die Gewinnung personalen Selbstbewusstseins in der Ich-Du-Beziehung]. Husserl, *Zur Phänomenologie der Intersubjektivität, Zeiter Teil*, Husserliana XIV, pp. 170–72.

25 The full passage (Husserl, Ibid., p. 171) runs: 'I, as a subject of motivations, enter now into the proto-social I-You relation not only beside the other as other, but also I motivate him and he motivates me; and in the manifest relation, which through social acts, produces the I-you-relation, lies a unity which encompasses both striving or specific willing subjects, in which both are related mutually, one to the other, in the actual consciousness, one to "affect" the other as mutually striving subjects, that is, to determine the other in the directed striving to an activity, or to a forbearance.' [Ich als Motivationssubjekt trete nun in der ursozialen Ich-Du-Beziehung nicht nur neben den Anderen als Anderen, sondern ich motiviere ihn, er motiviert mich; und in dem ausgezeichneten Verhältnis, das die Ich-Du-Beziehung, die durch soziale Akte, herstellt, liegt eine beide Subjekte umgreifende Einheit des Strebens oder spezifischen Wollens vor, in der beide wechselseitig aufeinander bezogen sind im aktuellen Bewusstsein, aufeinander als Strebenssubjekte wechselseitig zu 'wirken', das ist, einander im strebend aufeinander Gerichtetsein zu einem Tun zu bestimmen bzw. zu einem Erleiden. In dieser Gemeinschaft strebt nicht nur jeder, sondern jeder ist auch sich selbst als Strebender gegenständlich, er ist nicht nur, als das, sich selbst vorgegeben, sondern sich gegenständlich gegeben.]

26 Husserl, Ibid., p. 171.

27 As published through the website database GTH, Glossary-Guide for Translating Husserl, (www.filosoficas.unam.mx/~gth/dat-n.htm), Dorion Cairns renders 'Nachverstehen' as 'to follow and understand', 'to understand in following', 'to follow in understanding' and 'to understand regeneratively'. He renders 'Nachverstehen' as 'following and understanding' and 'understanding-in-following-another'. Dorion Cairns, *Guide for Translating Husserl, Phaenomenologica*, 55 (The Hague, 1973).

this empathetic understanding 'of one person following after the other' which makes the interrelationship with another person impossible to objectify. The beloved person remains more than can be collated into an object.[28] Scheler well understood this in writing: ' ... the personal in man *can never be disclosed to us as an "object"*'.[29] 'The

---

Although we are focusing here on *Nachverstehen* as applied to serial inter-empathetic reactions, Husserl also so terms cognitive reappropriations. For example, in the 'The Vienna Lecture', philosophy, as an 'ideal structure of *theōria*', from Thales onward is so described. Husserl, 'The Vienna Lecture', in *Crisis of the European Sciences*. The German text is reprinted as an *Abhandlung*, titled, 'Die Krisis des Europäischen Menschentums und die Philosophie' in *Die Krisis der europäischen Wissenschaften*, Husserliana VI. See pp. 277, 286 and 287 for the use of *Nachverstehen*.

28 A person, as is disclosed through personal love, is a unique and substantial subject. It needs to be distinguished from the notions of person and personal as they appear in post-transcendental works and meaning an individualized acculturated point of view. This second sense of the personal is fundamental to *Ideas II* and is reflected in the book's basic divisions. *Ideas II* is divided into three sections: 1. The Constitution of Material Nature; 2. The Constitution of Animal Nature; and, 3. The Constitution of the Spiritual World (*der geistigen Welt*). The constitution of the spiritual world in general is defined by 'the personalistic attitude' (*die personalistische Einstellung*). We attain the personalistic attitude in the establishment of a cultural world. Husserl, *Ideas Pertaining to a Pure Phenomenology and to a Phenomenological Philosophy, Second Book* (Dordrecht, 1989), esp. §51, 'The person in personal associations'.

In *Ideas II*, Husserl understands that to see someone, *as a person*, one needs to acknowledge the individual's capacity to have an idiosyncratic apprehension of cultural objects. The personal point of view arises in relation to cultural objects because cultural objects are not given in-themselves but for us, thus enabling the marking of individual personal differences. Husserl, Ibid., p. 196. As Husserl states: 'And a person is precisely a person who represents, feels, evaluates, strives, and acts and who, in every such personal act, stands in relation to something, to objects in his *surrounding world.*' Husserl, Ibid., p. 195.

In *Cartesian Meditations*, Husserl expands this sense of 'person' to the constitution of 'human existence as such', (*menschliches Sein also solches*) Husserl, *Cartesian Meditations: An Introduction to Phenomenology* (Den Haag, 1973), p. 135. Further, as is evident in later writings, the notion of person and the personal may be adjusted accordingly to the breadth and character of a community. Thus as late as the 'Vienna Lecture', delivered May 1935, Husserl writes: 'Personal life means living communalized as "I" and "we" within a community-horizon, and this in communities of various simple or stratified form such as family, nation, supranational community.' The 'Vienna Lecture' in *Crisis of European Sciences*, p. 270.

But Husserl distinguishes the sense of another person as arises in personal love from the notion of the personal, which is borne out of an idiosyncratic apprehension of cultural objects. 'The valuing of a person is not in that sense, i.e., [the sense] of a mere propensity for enjoyment, but rather its "true value" arises because of what is loved ...' [Die Werte der Person, <nicht> in dem Sinn derjenigen, die sie als blosse Bereitschaften des Genusses hat, sondern die ihren 'wahren Wert' ausmachen, diejenigen, um deren willen sie geliebt wird, ...] Husserl, *Zur Phänomenologie der Intersubjektivität, Dritter Teil*, Husserliana, XV, p. 406.

29 Max Scheler, *The Nature of Sympathy* (Hamden, CN, 1970), p. 167 [Scheler's emphasis].

Scheler's notion of the person in *The Nature of Sympathy* explicitly departs from Husserl's doctrine of how a personal point of view is established: 'We therefore count it the gravest of metaphysical errors in any theory ... that it should seek to construe persons ... as modes or function of a universal spirit; ... a transcendental absolute consciousness (Husserl) ... Again,

person of another can only be disclosed to me by my joining in the performance of his acts, either cognitively, by "understanding" and vicariously "re-living", or morally, by "following in his footsteps".'[30] As Scheler understood, this is made evident in the case of those spiritual and moral leaders whose 'person' we understand by following in empathetic understanding of their lives. Consequently, the persons of Jesus, Krishna,[31] Confucius and Socrates, for example, are conveyed not by biographies that describe the features or aspects of their characters, but by a 'following in the footsteps' of their lives. So Plato, in the *Phaedo*, discusses the immortality of the soul through argument. But Plato acknowledges the limits that argument bring to this topic, finally adding, '... you will, I think, follow and agree with the argument, so far as it is possible for a human being to do so.'[32] Plato conveys the sense of Socrates' soul by drawing his readers into an empathetic 'understanding-following after another'. He carries the reader through the events of Socrates' last hours of life, his actions and reactions with his interlocutors. And so, the reader follows in the footsteps of Socrates' life. Plato thereby offers us a chance to discern Socrates' person.[33]

---

we do not define personality by reference to the quality of its acts or the content and objects thereof; nor by the temporal coherence of its experiences, in memory or in any other aspect. On the contrary, this whole quality and continuity of the stream of consciousness already owes its peculiar content to the peculiar *character* of the intrinsically individual personalities to whom it belongs.' Scheler, Ibid., p. 75. In a manuscript dating from 1924, Husserl in turn questions whether Scheler's theory of empathy deserves to be called phenomenological: 'In this respect, Scheler's theory of empathy is the opposite of a phenomenological theory.' [In dieser Hinsicht ist Schelers Theories der Einfühlung das Widerspiel einer wirklich phänomenologischen Theorie.] 'One is not yet a phenomenologist if one cites "empty presentations" and refers back in the explanations to intentionality.' [Man ist noch nicht Phänomenologe, wenn man 'Leervorstellungen' anführt und in den Erklärungen auf Intentionalität rekurriert.] Husserl, *Zur Phänomenologie der Intersubjektivität, Zeiter Teil*, Husserliana XIV, p. 335. Husserl questions here if Scheler is a proper phenomenologist, inasmuch as Scheler in the 1913 *Nature of Sympathy* explains that love and, in general, moral consciousness 'contain an intentional reference to other moral persons ... without implying that such persons must already have been encountered in some sort of experience ...' Scheler, Ibid., p. 229.

But, in view of the primacy Husserl later assigns to the 'person' as a source of value, Husserl's criticism of Scheler would seem to be open to revision. By the time of writing the text quoted above from Husserliana XV (November 1931), the notion of personhood would seem to be irreducible to an idiosyncratic cultural apprehension. Even more, it would seem irreducible to the intentional acts of a transcendental Ego.

30 Scheler, Ibid., p. 167.

31 *Bhagavad Gita* (Cambridge, MA, 1944), ix.34; xii.8; xii.6, 7; x.10; xiv.26.

32 Plato, *Phaedo* (Cambridge, MA, 1914), p. 107B.

33 Cf. Scheler, *The Nature of Sympathy*, pp. 122–3: 'The more we come to know of men in whom the spiritual element operates freely, unhampered by the needs and necessities of *life*, through having acquired that mastery of life and its demands which is the characteristic mark of genius, the more individual and definite does our picture of such men become. But from this marginal case we must also conclude that the spiritual person, such as it exists in *every* man, is equally individual in itself, and that it is only because it is more deeply hidden

The character of Confucius is discerned through the collection of bits of conversations known as the *Analects*. In the *Analects*, Confucius' sayings are mixed with the sayings of his disciples, such as Tzengtse, Tsehsia, Yutse and Tsechang. The personalities of these disciples are well-known in the Confucian tradition. Tsengtse was especially philosophical; Tsehsia, literary-minded; and Yutse, a practical politician. So, as with Socrates, the Confucian scholar follows Confucius as he encounters different types of interlocutors.[34] The person of Confucius is disclosed through such interactions.

Philosopher Robert C. Solomon recently noted: 'A sense of history, for example, "what we've been through together", is perhaps one of the most important reasons for love, although it is all but absent in the initial enthusiasms of love.'[35] For personal love such a history is not only a reason, it is a necessary condition.

Unquestionably, personal love requires *more* than an empathetic 'understanding-following-after'. As Husserl writes: 'Not every partnership is a reciprocal partnership and not every reciprocal partnership is a partnership of love.'[36] One can surely have empathetic understanding-following-after-another without personal love.[37] 'Love entails an interest in assisting the other.'[38] But the collation of the empathic understanding of one person after the other is also a condition of personal love. Without understanding how personal love is borne out of an empathetic following-after-another, the circumstances are missed by which the other person becomes a source of value and an altogether unique, irreplaceable beloved.

That the development of love depends upon an interworking of empathies has not been lost on literary artists of various stripes. George Eliot writes in *Daniel Deronda* of Deronda's love for Mirah: 'For what is love itself, for the one we love

---

through its more laboured mode of activity, and also because of our lack of interest, or love, that it appears less individual to us, and merely an example of some general type.'

34 Lin Yutang, *The Wisdom of Confucius* (New York, 1994), p. 155.

35 Robert C. Solomon, *About Love: Reinventing Romance for Our Times* (New York, 2001), p. 159.

36 Husserl, *Zur Phänomenologie der Intersubjektivität, Zeiter Teil*, Husserliana XIV, p. 172: [Nicht jede Gemeinschaft ist wechselseitige Gemeinschaft, und nicht jede wechselseitige ist Liebesgemeinschaft.]

37 In a supplement to the section we have been discussing, titled, 'THE INFLUENCE OF EGO-SUBJECTS UPON EACH OTHER' [EINWIRKUNG VON ICHSUBJEKTEN AUFEINANDER], Husserl considers the following cases: Suppose someone wants to harm another and sets out to do so. Suppose also the second person sees through the first's harmful machinations and avoids him or takes preventative precautions. Add that the first person detects the second's suspicions and backs off from his plans. In so saying, Husserl constructs an example where two people 'read' the motives of the other. One tries to stab the other in the back, the second sees it coming, dodges, and the first backs off. This is a case of understanding 'one-after-the-other' that does not involve explicit communication in the sense that one party sets out to make his intentions known to the other. Thus, it broadens the notion of communication proposed in the *Logical Investigations*. (See footnote 18 above.) On the contrary, the back-stabber wants to hide his intentions from notice. There is nonetheless 'contact' and, furthermore, self-awareness through empathetic 'understanding-in-following-another'. Husserl, Ibid., Beilage (Appendix) XXIII, pp. 184–5.

38 Husserl, Ibid., p.166: 'Die Liebe bestimmt ein Interesse der Fremdförderung ...'

best? An enfolding of immeasurable cares which yet are better than any joys outside our love.'[39] Byron: '... all who joy would win/ Must share it, – Happiness was born a twin.'[40] Yeats: 'A pity beyond all telling/ Is hid in the heart of love.'[41] The basic insight again is conveyed by James Thurber, 'Love is what you've been through with somebody.'[42]

The mutual concatenation of empathy is portrayed by Shakespeare in *Othello*. Recall that Desdemona's father invites Othello to his house, where he recounts his life from his boyhood, to his experiences with floods and in battle, through hairbreadth escapes, enslavement, and manumission. These experiences overlayer Desdemona's empathy. Othello says Desdemona would 'devour up my discourse'.[43] In the phenomenological terms discussed here, Othello and Desdemona establish 'contact' through her father's invitation to Othello. But their meeting is mere happenstance, at least at the beginning. Othello does not enter Desdemona's father's home, seeking to woo Desdemona, at first. Nor does Desdemona seek Othello as a suitor. Their personal love arises from the mutual empathetic 'understanding-following-after-another'.[44]

> She loved me for the dangers I had passed,
> And I loved her that she did pity them.[45]

Chekhov, in particular, would seem to be occupied with detailing the development of personal love. Chekhov describes it especially in his well-known story, 'The Lady with the Pet Dog'.

Anna, the lady with the pet dog, elicits the empathy of Gurov, her suitor. She is a poignant figure: 'there was something touching about Anna Sergeyevna.'[46] Even her eponymous pet dog calls forth empathy. The white Pomeranian trotting behind her marks the absence of, and stands in for, children, family, and friends. It is an emblem of its mistress's loneliness and vulnerability.

Chekhov details the recurrent overlaying of occasions for mutual empathy: 'Then they met every day at twelve o'clock on the esplanade, lunched and dined together, took walks, admired the sea. She complained that she slept badly, that she

---

39 George Eliot, *Daniel Deronda* (London, 1903), p. 578.

40 Lord Byron, *Don Juan* (London, 1906), Canto II.172, p. 130.

41 W.B. Yeats, 'The Pity of Love', in *The Rose*, from *The Collected Works of*, vol. I., *The Poems* (New York, 1989), p. 40.

42 Thurber, James, quoted in Life magazine, 14 March 1960.

43 Shakespeare, *Othello*, from *The Complete Works of* (London, 1980) I.3:110–70.

44 Iago's machinations succeed in blinding Othello to the 'person' of Desdemona as here understood. But even in the act of murder, Othello does not lose altogether Desdemona's uniqueness. She is 'the cunningst pattern of excelling nature' (*Othello*, Ibid., V.2.11), which is of course irreplaceable: 'I know not where is that Promethean heat/ That can thy light relume' and so on. (*Othello*, Ibid., V.2.12–13).

45 Shakespeare, *Othello*, Ibid., I.3:167–9.

46 Anton Chekhov, 'The Lady with the Pet Dog', from *The Portable Chekhov* (New York, 1977), pp. 417–18.

had palpitations, asked the same question, troubled now by jealousy and now by the fear that he did not respect her sufficiently.'

When a letter comes from Anna's husband saying that he has eye trouble and Anna must return to him, Anna and Gurov assume they will part forever. But what is key is that before their separation Chekhov establishes that: 1) Anna is an affecting figure, entreating an empathetic response; 2) Gurov's behavior has altered because of his empathy for Anna; and, 3) Anna's behavior is further altered in response to Gurov.

At first the *roué* Gurov sees himself deceiving Anna, indeed, through this interaction of empathies. After Anna's train pulls out, he reflects:

> She had constantly called him kind, exceptional, high-minded; obviously he had seemed to her different from what he really was, so he had involuntarily deceived her.[47]

Gurov's indulgences *are* deceptive given his rakish history of short-lived affairs. But the deception fades, as the 'deceptive' role that he has played with Anna provides the vehicle for lasting endearment. During the months when Anna and Gurov believe they will never see each other again, Gurov seems to grow a second self: 'He had two lives: an open one, seen and known by all who needed to know it, full of conventional truth and conventional falsehood, exactly like the lives of his friends and acquaintances; and another life that went on in secret.'[48] This second self grows out of his reaction to Anna, his reactions to her reactions, and *vice versa*.

The well-known story implies the impossibility of reducing the *Nachverstehen* of personal love to the mere sum of the individualized empathies of each partner. As indicated, Anna is a figure that invites empathy. The empathy she elicits brings out behavior in Gurov that, at first, departs from his normal behavior. Anna responds to his 'deceptive' behavior, which in time leads Gurov to find in his former deceptiveness the chance for lasting affection. And here lies the transformative potential of *Nachverstehen*. Like the wedge-shaped *voussoir* or keystone of a Roman arch, seemingly defying gravity, serial empathetic interactions establish a communality which, although based upon the individuality of each of the lovers, encompasses an identity that is, strictly speaking, neither's. Husserl describes this remarkable mutual creation in writing: 'As a lover, I know that what I always think, feel, strive for, and do, all this is necessarily "in the sense" of my beloved ...'[49] This 'sense of the beloved' is precisely the result of the mutual creation of *Nachverstehen*. It is a communality built upon empathetic interaction. In the case of Anna and Gurov, Chekhov describes accordingly the transformation:

> ... and it was as though they were a pair of migratory birds, male and female, caught and forced to live in different cages. They forgave each other what they were ashamed of in their past, they forgave everything in the present, and felt that this love of theirs had altered them both.[50]

---

47 Chekhov, Ibid., p. 422.
48 Chekhov, Ibid., p. 430.
49 Husserl, *Zur Phänomenologie der Intersubjektivität, Zeiter Teil*, Husserliana XIV, p. 173.
50 Chekhov, Ibid., p. 433.

In her collection of essays, *Words That Must Somehow Be Said*, Kay Boyle offers the following anecdote:[51]

> My friend, a French painter and Resistance fighter, was put in a concentration camp by the Nazis. Every evening during his long incarceration, he and two or three of his fellow prisoners ... entirely by means of conversations and gestures ... dressed for dinner in immaculate white shirts that did not exist ... They drank Château-du-Pape throughout the meal and Château d'Yquem with the dessert pastry ... There were certain restaurants they did not patronize a second time because the lobster had been overcooked ... On the evenings that they saw themselves as men of letters, they quoted from the great poets while they dined.

One prisoner pantomimes the savoring of the Château-du-Pape. The other seeing him, surely aware that the first's imbibing is an illusion, nonetheless empathizes with his pantomime. But, the third and fourth prisoners also empathize with the second's empathy. The third and fourth, then, have one foot in the world of illusion of the first man, but another foot in the non-unreal empathetic reaction of the second. In their imaginary banquet, these resistance fighters engage in a kind of *Nachverstehen* that creates a unique communality. And the focus of their enjoyment becomes ineradicably unique since it depends on inter-subjective creations that they mutually enjoy and which cannot be subtracted from the additions of their fellows. The reactions of the prisoners supply additional meaning to the champagne mime, which in turn the simulated drinker responds to and further elaborates. As they build upon each other's empathetic reactions, they create a world of their own that is unique and inviolably *theirs*. It defies their oppressors. It is a creation into which their oppressors cannot enter.

It is perhaps then not so surprising how personal love conveys a uniqueness of the beloved that cannot be conveyed apart from the act of loving. In a late manuscript Husserl declares: 'Love, loving, loses itself in the other ... and [is] not at all hedonic although it establishes joys, "high" joys.'[52] It is not the potential satisfaction of our interests that establishes personal values. But rather, '..."true value" arises because of what is loved ...'[53]

---

51 Kay Boyle, *Words That Must Somehow Be Said: Selected Essays of Kay Boyle* (San Francisco, 1985), p. 88.

52 Husserl, *Zur Phänomenologie der Intersubjektivität, Zeiter Teil*, Husserliana XIV, p. 406: [Die Liebe – liebend sich im Anderen verlieren, im Anderen leben, sich mit dem Anderen einigen, ist ganz und gar nicht hedonisch, obwohl sie Freuden, 'hohe' Freuden begründet.]

53 Husserl, *Zur Phänomenologie der Intersubjektivität, Dritter Teil*, Husserliana, XV, p. 406. The full text runs: 'The valuing of a person is not in that sense, i.e., [the sense] of a mere propensity for enjoyment, but rather its "true value" arises because of what is loved, so with all specifically "mental" (*geistigen*) values, [they] arise from entirely different sources, the sources of love in the full sense of the word.' [Die Werte der Person, <nicht> in dem Sinn derjenigen, die sie als blosse Bereitschaften des Genusses hat, sondern die ihren 'wahren Wert' ausmachen, diejenigen, um deren willen sie geliebt wird, so wie alle spezifisch 'geistigen' Werte, entspringen aus ganz anderen Quellen, den Quellen der Liebe im prägnanten Wortsinn.]

Scheler stressed that through love persons are ascertained in their individual personality:

> It is characteristic, however, of individual personality that we can only become acquainted with it *in* and *through* the act of loving, and that its value as an individual is likewise only disclosed in the course of this act.[54]

The uniqueness of *things*, as borne out of person's 'here' and 'now', is altogether derivative and banal as compared with the uniqueness of a person.[55] But although Scheler was correct in stating that individual personality is disclosed in the act of loving, he missed that the uniqueness and the manner in which the other person becomes a source of value arises through *Nachverstehen*.

Scheler's description of the progress by which persons arrive in their 'full individuality', overlooks the requisite interaction that establishes uniqueness. Scheler explains that, from the beginning, a person is presumed a 'concrete whole'.[56] 'This hypothesis' concerning the person's real character is thereafter tested, verified and corrected by observation, real and abstract. But it is guided by a 'blue-print', as Scheler puts it, of the true and essential nature of a person.[57] As the knowledge of the individual increases, the hypothesis becomes 'ever more individual, ever harder to put into words (*individuum est ineffabile*) – yet at the same time ever more certain'.[58] Since it is love that drives this occupation with another, love: 'necessarily fastens upon the individual core in things, the core of value ... which can never be wholly resolved into values susceptible of judgment, or even of distinct apprehension of feeling.'[59] 'The more deeply we penetrate into a human being, through knowledge and understanding, guided by personal love, the more unmistakable, individual, unique, irreplaceable and indispensable does he become in our mind.'[60]

Even though Scheler rightly finds in personal love the passion that allows us to find how the loved person is 'ever more individual' and 'ever harder to put into words', the process he describes might as well apply to any physical object that we explore and better understand by formulating hypotheses that we confirm or discard. Scheler's explanation finally leaves unsolved the puzzle by which the loved person is a unique person and a source of value. The beginning of personal love is not the intuition of a 'blueprint' made 'ever more individual'. Rather, initial 'contact'

---

54 Max Scheler, *The Nature of Sympathy*, p. 166. Here Scheler joins with the Augustinian tradition according to which 'one does not enter into truth except through love'. Augustine, *Contra Faustum* (Grand Rapids, MI, 1956), lib. 32, cap. 18: 'non intratur in veritatem, nisi per charitatem.'

55 Scheler, Ibid., p. 123: 'Indeed in the inanimate world, it is rather the category of the "individual" which ceases to have real meaning on the metaphysical plane.' Scheler further explains, Ibid., p. 123, note 1: 'Even in physics and chemistry the "things" of everyday life lose their individual character.'

56 Scheler, Ibid., p. 122.

57 Scheler, Ibid., p. 122.

58 Scheler, Ibid., p. 122.

59 Scheler, Ibid., p. 149.

60 Scheler, Ibid., p. 121.

opens the possibility of building inter-reactive empathies. When both parties remain actively involved they co-create a weave of interaction. Just because it is the product of mutual interest, which cannot be reduced to the activities of either lover, the other person becomes 'ever more individual', 'ever harder to put into words' ... 'yet at the same time ever more certain' as seen through the lens of their love.[61] The certainty we have of the beloved's person does not come from proposing, refining, and verifying a hypothesis through repeated interaction with the other person. It is rather a uniqueness, which from the beginning is inviolable, because it is the creation of interactive loving that is irreducible to the cognition, feelings and volitions of either lover alone. As such, the certainty comes from the fact that love penetrates to the core of the creation of interactive empathy. There is thus a manner of self-evidence that is known as 'adequacy'[62] in the phenomenological tradition. This self-evidence is based in a remarkable feature of personal love, namely, that the same mode of access to the entity, that is, loving the other person, is also that which makes possible the sense of the other person. Thus love 'awakens' the unique personhood of the beloved, but it does so through recalling the conjoined interactions with the other person that the inter-empathetic experiences propelled by love establish in the first place. Scheler, then, was correct in asserting that it is characteristic of individual personality 'that we can only become acquainted with it *in* and *through* the act of loving...'[63] But he missed that we become acquainted with the uniqueness of the other's person 'in and through the act of loving' because, from the beginning, loving builds the possibility of an interactive conjunction of personal meanings.

Because the uniqueness of the other person is established through the lovers' *Nachverstehen*, the uniqueness of the beloved person has none of the atemporality of empirical generalizations or essences. It is not based in the generalization of particulars, nor in universal features presumed to be necessary for any particular. The personhood of the beloved arises rather as the *truth* of the other person. The inter-empathetic collations consist in a dovetailing of worldly confrontations, impasses, passings, openings, and freedoms that we know of through our history with the other person. We know this person's *truth* by knowing their history of conflicts and confrontations.

Personal Love and the 'Truth' of the Beloved

How does knowing the history of other's conflicts and confrontations allow us to have a sense of the truth of the beloved? The dominant conception of truth since Aristotle makes truth a property of judgments or statements. But, as Michel Foucault observed, there are far older approaches to truth. A long-standing sense of truth is based in what Foucault called the *l'épreuve*, that is, the test, trial, or ordeal. The *épreuve*, Foucault tells us, appears in 'propitious moments' and 'privileged places'

---

61 Scheler, Ibid., p. 122, cited above.

62 The notion of 'adequate' evidence, as justification for the complete or 'perfect givenness' of a thing is discussed by Husserl in *Ideen, Erstes Buch*, Husserliana III.1, §§142–4.

63 Scheler, Ibid., p. 166, cited above.

where a ritualized 'ordeal' takes place.[64] The Delphic oracle that incited Socrates to set on a lifelong quest for truth is a privileged place. So too are the desert caves where Christian ascetics, such as Saint Anthony, would go to battle with the Devil, so as to test their faith. For 'propitious moments', Foucault specifies the 'crises' that early physicians saw as revelatory of the outcome of a disease, the ordeals of torture and public pageants, tournaments and ceremonial war games. These rituals were not a way to establish truth through an examination of the participants. Rather, the ordeal provided a venue for a precarious balancing of scales. As determined by ritual, the stage was set for the gods to disclose the cosmic will by abetting the victor or abandoning the vanquished.

This notion of truth appears currently in the 'race of truth' (*l'épreuve de vérité*) as it is called in the Tour de France. To succeed at the 'race of truth', the cyclist must maintain extraordinary stamina, enough to average a speed of 30–31 mph for from sixty to eighty minutes. (The average cyclist can sustain 30–31 mph for about three minutes.) In 2005, Lance Armstrong was again victorious in this ordeal. As implied by the race's title, the sense of truth associated with his win departs from the mere attribution of 'first-place' ordering of contestants. The race is offered also a trial and a proof.

Understanding a person's uniqueness as their *truth* involves understanding their trials. The other person's strivings and struggles are key.[65] The concatenation of empathies of the other person is myriad. They might involve being stymied by a particular educational system, by the unique admiration of a father, by the hopes for romance with a particular love, by the death of a child, by the pride taken in a spouse's accomplishments, and so on. In reality, the person of the beloved is established through conjoining with the striving of the other person. And this uniqueness requires, as a lens, love for the other person, for on the condition of love for the other person the conjunction of such empathies arises. Thus the love opens onto the uniqueness of the other person, not as the verification of a hypothesis, but as a recollective opening to another's personal truth.

---

64 Michel Foucault, 'La maison de fous', in *Les criminels de paix* (Paris, 1980), pp. 145–60. Saint-Exupéry proposes a comparable alternative notion of personal truth borne out of self-fulfillment: 'Truth is not that which can be demonstrated by the aid of logic. If orange-trees are hardy and rich in fruit in this bit of soil and not that, than this bit of soil is what is truth for orange-trees. If a particular religion, or culture, or scale or values, if one form of activity rather than another, brings self-fulfilment to a man, releases the prince asleep within him unknown to himself, then that scale of values, that culture, that form of activity, constitutes his truth. Logic, you say? Let logic wangle its own explanation of life.' Saint-Exupéry, *Terre des hommes* (New York, 1992), Chapter ix, p. 175.

65 Kierkegaard in particular hits upon the notion of personal truth as 'personal striving' in an exegesis of the Scriptural (John 14:6). Kierkegaard writes: 'Truth in its very being is not the duplication of being in terms of thought, which yields only the thought of being, merely ensures that the act of thinking shall not be a cobweb of the brain without relation to reality, guaranteeing the validity of thought, that the thing thought actually is, i.e. has validity. No, truth in its very being is the reduplication in me, in thee, in him, so that my, that thy, that his life, approximately, *in the striving to attain it*, expresses the truth, so that my, that thy, that his life, approximately, *in the striving to attain it*, is the very being of truth, is a *life*, …' Søren Kierkegaard, *Training in Christianity* (Princeton, 1967), p. 201 [my emphasis].

Personal Love as 'Hyper-Subjective'

We'll urge that personal love, then, be understood as *hyper-subjective*. With personal love, the beloved is an altogether unique individual, transcending any specifiable collection of attributes and yet foundational of those attributes. Consider a well-known philosophical conundrum. The philosophy instructor asks why a mother should not accept a duplicate for her beloved child or a husband or wife for their beloved spouse. The substituted child or spouse has an identical physical appearance, mental activity, and so on. Yet, the mother or spouse is loath to accept the substitute. However identical the substituted child, the mother loves her one and only little son or daughter, as does the husband or wife love their one and only cherished spouse. If the mother or husband were willing to accept a clone as a substitute for their beloved, doubts would arise that theirs is truly a personal love. Why?

From a logical point of view, a unique individual is designated by a proper name or a, so-called, definite description, that is, a term that picks out one and only one referent. This is not the place to review the centrality of the analysis of proper names and definite descriptions in the history of twentieth-century philosophy. For our purposes, it is enough to observe that philosophical analysts of language emphasize that reference operates through an inter-working of connotation and denotation.[66] The connotation, or the 'sense', of the term, enables a speaker to pick out the denotation, or reference. So, the name, 'Cleopatra', as referring to last Ptolemaic pharaoh, meant many things to many people. (It had a different sense for Mark Anthony than it did for the Roman Senate.) But the name also refers to that one and only one woman that reigned in Egypt from 51 to 30 BC. But even though the definite description, 'the last Ptolemaic pharaoh' refers to only one person, it is a fact, long noted by logicians,[67] that the uniqueness of a person can never be circumscribed by any description, however detailed. There might always be another Cleopatra with just those same features attributed to Cleopatra, the last Ptolemaic pharaoh. Hence the philosophy instructor's conundrum: What does the loving mother or spouse prefer about the genuine beloved when all the attributes of the surrogate are the same?

One may take recourse in *numerical* identity beyond the unique identity presumed by personal names and definite descriptions. But even numerical identity is not comparable to the uniqueness of the beloved. Numerical identity relies on indexical references which themselves ultimately appeal to 'here' and 'now' references. No matter how identical the needles on a pine tree may appear, for example, I may uniquely identify one particular needle, by starting with this needle, 'here', which I touch with my forefinger, and number the rest according to some system of numerical ordering. I can thus indicate the uniqueness of any subject, relying on the orderings based on the unique position-markers of a 'here' and 'now'.

---

66 The distinction, exactingly drawn by Gottlob Frege in 'On Sense and Reference,' Gottlob Frege, (Oxford, 1960), pp. 56–85, has become rudimental in logic textbooks.

67 For example, Aristotle, *Metaphysics*, VII.15, 1039b27–1040a7. Unless otherwise specified, all translations of Aristotle follow the renderings in *The Complete Works of Aristotle* (Princeton, NJ, 1984).

But the uniqueness of the beloved person has a different basis from the uniqueness we assign to subjects numerically through 'here' and 'now' based indexing, as well as through proper names and definite descriptions. Personal love is, as we've called it, 'hyper-subjective'. It outstrips both the uniqueness presumed by proper names and definite descriptions, as well as the uniqueness of numerical identity. Personal love is borne out of an empathetic understanding which 'follows-after-one-another'. It operates on a different ontological level from objects. The concatenation of pre-objective strivings allows us to discern the singular uniqueness of the beloved. To understand this uniqueness, we'll need to contrast ordinary interest-laden valuing of some thing or circumstances with love as a source of value.

Personal Love as a Source of Value

In the late manuscript mentioned before, Husserl states that personal love: 'is not at all hedonic although it establishes joys, "high" joys.'[68] He distinguishes between hedonic values, which have their origin 'finally in sensual feelings', and values that spring from what is loved in a person.[69]

Husserl would seem to be confused in saying that the joys of personal love are not 'hedonic'. Does it make any sense to say that joy does not involve some pleasure, that it is not 'hedonic'? Granted, as ordinary English shows, the word 'pleasure' tends to suggest a more self-centered satisfaction than 'joy'. Someone might say, for example, that a fireman, suffering from smoke inhalation, consoled himself *in the joy* of rescuing a child. But in saying the fireman *took pleasure* in rescuing the child, there is the suggestion that the fireman is, perhaps, a self-centered person, not so pointedly interested in the child's welfare. But even so, the joy a parent feels at seeing their child succeed at university, even though the expense may have involved excessive self-denial and sacrifices, brings with it some pleasure. To say there was no pleasure at all in that joy seems a contradiction in terms.

Husserl's apparent confusion in denying joy is pleasurable (hedonic) has a rather scandalous analogue in the history of Western philosophy. Aristotle, for example, sees no opposition between pleasure (*hēdonē*) and joy (*charā*).[70] Neither does Plotinus.[71] But Stoic philosophers, from Zeno onward, make the opposition between

---

68 Husserl, *Zur Phänomenologie der Intersubjektivität, Dritter Teil*, Husserliana XV, p. 406: [Die Liebe ... ist ganz und gar nicht hedonisch, obwohl sie Freuden, 'hohe' Freuden begründet.] Cited before; see note 52.

69 Husserl, Ibid., p. 406. Cited above; see note 53.

70 Aristotle, in *On the Generation of Animals*, Book I, chapter 18, focusing on the puzzling source of seminal ejaculate, refers to the sexual orgasm as 'the joy' (ἡ χαρά). The passage (723b34–724a2) runs: 'As to the vehemence of pleasure (ἡδονή) in sexual intercourse, it is not because the semen comes from the body, but because there is strong friction (wherefore if this intercourse is often repeated the joy (τὸ χαίρειν) is diminished in the person concerned). Moreover, the pleasure (ἡ χαρά) is at the end of the act, etc. ...' (my trans.).

71 Plotinus combines bodily pleasures and 'joys of the soul' as both unworthy of the primal intellectual principle: 'Certainly, no one would think that bodily pleasure is capable of

pleasure and joy *doctrinaire*.[72] For the Stoic, pleasures are disruptive trouble-makers, but the Stoic sage experiences joy. There is also a patent opposition between 'pleasure' and 'joy' in *New Testament* scripture.[73] Early Church father, Clement of Alexandria, for example, at one point, unequivocally *identifies* pleasure (*hēdonē*) with evil.[74] But Clement also reminds us of the scriptural 'unsurpassable joy' (*charā*) in heaven at the repentance of one sinner.[75] With the development of British empiricist tradition the pendulum has already swung back. British empiricists, such as Hume, make 'pleasure' a necessary condition of 'joy'.[76]

---

blending in with the Intellect, nor yet equally unreasoning joys of the soul.' Plotinus, *Enneads*, VI.7.30, [my trans.].

72 Zeno, considered the founder of Stoicism, sees joy (χαρά) as opposed to pleasure (ἡδονή). Diogenes Laertius, 'Zeno', *Lives of the Eminent Philosophers*, Book II (Cambridge MA, 1929), p. 221. The opposition continues through the middle and late Stoa. Consider Seneca's Letter LIX to Lucilius: 'For we Stoics hold that pleasure is a vice.' Seneca, *Ad Lucilium Epistulae Morales* (Cambridge, MA, 1917), 59.1; p. 409.

73 'Joy' is a mark of Godly behavior. On the other hand, 'worldly pleasures' are obstacles to receiving the word of God. In the 'Parable of the Sower', Luke, 8:4–15, for example, those along a rocky path receive, at first, the Gospel with joy (μετὰ χαρᾶς) but those among the thorns, that is, those choked by life's cares and riches and pleasures of this life (ἡδονῶν τοῦ βίου) do not mature.

The primary term for pleasure among Greek philosophers, be they Academics, Peripatetics, Stoics or Epicureans is *hēdonē*. But, it appears very infrequently in the New Testament. There are just four occurrences: Luke, 8:14:2; Epist. Titus, 3:3:2; Epist. James, 4:1:2; 4:3:2; and Epist. Peter II, 2:13:2. In fact, the New Testament canon all but dispenses with the term for pleasure (ἡδονή) in favor of joy (χαρά). 'Joy,' (χαρά) and its cognates, on the other hand, appear extremely frequently in the New Testament canon. There are over fifty occurrences of 'joy' (χαρά) alone, not counting frequencies of its cognates 'rejoice' (χαίρω), 'grace' (χάρις), and 'free gift' (χάρισμα). The occurrences range from the 'exceeding joy' felt by the wise men seeing the star of Bethlehem (Matt., 2:10), to the great joy of Mary Magdalene and Mary mother of Jesus discovering the empty tomb after the crucifixion (Matt., 28:8), through the acts of Philip in Samaria (Acts, 8:8), causing 'great joy in that city', and then frequently in the epistles of Paul, Peter, and John.

74 'Now consider briefly, if you will, the beneficence of God from the beginning. The first man played in Paradise with childlike freedom, since he was a child of God. For when he fell a victim to pleasure (for the serpent that creeps upon the belly, an earthy evil, reared to return to matter, is an allegory for pleasure), and was led astray by lusts, the child, coming to manhood through disobedience and refusing to listen to the Father, was ashamed to meet God. See how pleasure prevailed!' Clement of Alexandria (Cambridge, MA, 1919), 'Exhortation to the Greeks,' Chapter XI, p. 237.

75 Clement of Alexandria (Cambridge, MA, 1919), 'The Rich Man's Salvation', Chapter 39, p. 351.

76 Hume, for example, bases joy, as well as good and evil on pleasure and pain. Consider Hume in the *Treatise:* ''Tis easy to observe, that the passions, both direct and indirect, are founded on pain and pleasure, and that in order to produce an affection of any kind, 'tis only requisite to produce some good or evil. Upon the removal of pain and pleasure there immediately follows a removal of love and hatred, pride and humility, desire and aversion, and of most of our reflective and secondary impressions.' David Hume, *A Treatise of Human Nature* (Oxford, 1888), Book II, Section ix, 'Of the direct passions', p. 438.

This curious historical turnabout seems to suggest that there are quite different bases for the feeling of 'joy'. In fact Husserl's own investigations indicate a straddling between two different bases for joy.

For the most part, in Husserl's mid-career texts, 'objective' values are based in feelings, and these feelings include pleasure and pain.[77] In *Ideas I* and *II*, for example, Husserl understands that the constitution of values is analogous to the constitution of perceptual truths. Cognition tends towards knowledge and arrives at 'truth' when the representations are 'filled out' in direct intuition. Say, for example, I cannot find my house keys. I look everywhere for them, and finally find them under a newspaper. My representation of the keys is 'fulfilled', or 'filled out', by my seeing them as I look under a newspaper. This is a case of direct perceptual 'intuition'. (The German language especially supports Husserl's doctrine, since the German word for perception, *Wahrnehmung*, parses into 'truth[*Wahr*]-taking[*Nehmung*]'.) Analogously, feelings, and Husserl specifically mentions pleasure and displeasure,[78] are filled out by 'values' through a 'value-taking',[79] that is, through an 'axiological intuition' (value-based intuition), which parallels cognitive intuition.[80] Say, again, I am locked out of my house and I cannot find my keys. I feel annoyed and angry with myself, and resort to dislodging the bolt from the front-door lock by sliding a credit card between the door and the doorjamb. I thereby experience so-called 'axiological intuition'. The credit card is 'filled out' with value since it takes on the value of a tool for breaking into my own house. And it is not just a matter of associating objects with feelings. The break-in value of the credit card is vouchsafed by its factual practical accomplishment. Hence 'axiological intuition', that is, an intuition of value.

But in the very late 1931 manuscript,[81] mentioned above, Husserl insists that a distinction must be drawn between hedonic values that have their origin 'finally in

---

77 In *Ideas II*, Husserl understands feelings of joy, by 'axiological intuition', as objectified in a 'joy-object'. 'Within the joy, we are 'intentionally' (with feeling intentions) turned toward the joy-Object as such in the mode of affective 'interest'.' Husserl, *Ideas, Second Book*, p. 14. [In der Freud sind wir 'meinend' (gemütsmeinend) in der Weise des gemüthaften 'Interesses' dem Freudenobjekt als solchem zugewandt.] Husserl, *Ideen, Zeites Buch*, Husserliana IV, p. 12.

78 '*Gefallens*' and '*Mißfallens*'. Husserl, Ibid., p. 7.

79 Husserl coins the term 'Wertnehmen', that is, 'value-taking', paralleling 'Warhnehmen' [perception]. Husserl, Ibid., pp. 7–11.

80 Husserl, Ibid, p. 9: '*axiologisch Angeschautes*'. Husserl writes similarly in *Ideas I*, 'In the act of valuing, however, we are turned toward the valued, in the act of joy, to the joyful, in the act of loving, to the beloved, in acting, to the action, without apprehending all of this' [my trans.]. [Im Akte des Wertens aber sind wir dem Werte, im Akte der Freude dem Erfeulichen, im Akte der Liebe dem Geliebte, in Handeln der Handlung zugewendet, ohne all das zu erfassen.] Husserl, *Ideen, Erstes Buch*, Husserliana III.1, p. 76. Husserl in *Ideas II* sees the objectification of feelings as part of the constitution of valued objects. 'We observe that the universal-original judgment of value or, generally speaking, each *consciousness which originally constitutes a value-Object as such*, necessarily has in itself a *component* belonging to the *sphere of feelings*.' Husserl, *Ideas, Second Book*, p. 11.

81 In the manuscript dated 13 November 1931 Husserl writes: 'But everything must be newly thought through.' [Aber das alles muss neu durchdacht werden.] Husserl, *Zur Phänomenologie der Intersubjektivität, Dritter Teil*, Husserliana XV, p. 407.

sensual feelings'[82] and values whose source is personal love. 'The valuing of a person is not in that sense, i.e., [the sense] of a mere propensity for enjoyment, but rather its "true value" arises because of what is loved.'[83] As to what 'love in the full sense of the word' might imply, Husserl tells us that it requires a 'loving surrender'[84] and loving abandonment or surrender is 'the opposite of each person who practices it ...'[85]

It is a ubiquitous *aperçue* that love conquers all and that the wise acknowledge love's power.[86] But how is this surrendering aspect of love and affective consciousness so different that it instills a source of value that involves 'high' joys that are not 'hedonic'?

In fact we find a solution if we return to personal love as a lens that opens onto the uniqueness of the other person as based in a history of *Nachverstehen*. Personal love is, as it were, 'micro-cognitive'. It enables a mode of understanding but it operates on a different ontological level from ordinary modes of consciousness, such as perception, recollection, phantasy, desire, as well as value-assessments, which attend to objects. There is a kind of joy in discovering a well-fitting pair of hiking boots, a short-cut through a congested traffic-jam, or an un-crowded secluded beach. These joys fit with Husserl's first sense of establishing value, where value arises from discovering things that are a means for realizing goals. The boots, the short-cut and the beach are imbued with value as they are discovered as furtherances of one's interests. But the joy of personal love, as based in the *Nachverstehen* between lovers, because it is formed upon collations of interactive empathy, cannot be attributed to a relation of the individual lover or friend merely as an individual. We love the 'truth' of the person, in the sense of truth indicated before. That truth is irreducible to the specific objective attributes of the individual, because the truth is based on the conjunction of the pre-objective strivings and struggles of the beloved. But those struggles and strivings are also coupled with our own empathizing with them. Consequently the joy of personal love operates apart from the joys arising from the fulfillment of objective interests. Scheler had rightly observed: '... even when love is unhappy in the sense of unrequited, the act itself is still accompanied by a feeling of great happiness – and equally so when the loved one occasions pain and sorrow.'[87] He enjoyed the agreement in this insight with literary artists, including the likes of Sophocles and Dostoyevsky as noted in the quotes at the head of this chapter.

But how can personal love supervene over the griefs, sorrows, not to mention the mottled collection of everyday annoyances and irritations? The accompaniment of great happiness in personal love, concomitantly with the pains and sorrows, frustrations and irritations that may arise in the course of the love, attests to the two-leveled status of personal love. Regardless of how the loved one occasions pain and sorrow, our personal love concerns the 'truth' of the beloved person that endures

---

82 Husserl, Ibid., p. 406: 'letztlich in sinnlichen Gefühlen ...'

83 Husserl, Ibid., p. 406. See note 53 above.

84 Husserl, Ibid., p. 406: '... eine liebende Hingabe ...'

85 Husserl, Ibid., p. 406: '... die umgekehrt jeder Person, die sie übt ...'

86 So Virgil ends the *Eclogues*: 'Love conquers all, and let us too yield to love.' [Omnia vincit Amor, et nos cedamus Amori.] Virgil, *Eclogues* (New York, 1930), X.69.

87 Max Scheler, *The Nature of Sympathy* (Hamden, CN, 1970), p. 148.

in a world that is separate from our ordinary world of objects and consciousness intentions. This is not to suggest a transcendent world of Platonic essences, or an Augustinian duality of two cities, one mundane and one divine. Rather because a world of persons is founded upon interactive love, there is a special dimension within *this* world, which love, like an additional mode of perception, understands.

Again, we are concerned with a love that extends beyond an interest based in mutual pleasures or utility and which extends to the truth of the other's character. Consequently taking pleasure in a person's sense of humor and good looks, or liking another person because of business advantages, is not simply marginally related to the other person. It is rather a different mode of awareness of the other person. The cognitive contribution of personal love operates according to its own manner of apprehension. In this regard, Scheler was acutely accurate. He understood love in its cognitistic capacities. Scheler writes that love allows us to: 'open our eyes to values higher than those which "interest" would discern ...'[88] Scheler offers the example of reading a beloved's letter: '... it is out of the question to judge it by ordinary standards of grammar or style.'[89] And this is not because love is blind. 'It is usually only the "detached" observer who arrives at this conclusion, because he fails to recognize the particular individual values present in the object, but discernible only to the sharper eyes of love.'[90] Citing Jaspers' agreement with his understanding of love, Scheler quotes: 'In love we do not discover values, we discover that everything is more valuable.'[91]

Bertrand Russell keenly apprehended the cognistic aspect of personal love. Russell describes in his *Autobiography* a 'sort of mystical illumination'[92] that followed upon his witnessing Mr Whitehead's wife, Evelyn Wade, in the throes of 'intense pain owing to heart trouble'.[93] The event took place while Russell and his first wife, Alys, stayed with the Whiteheads in 1901, some fifty years before Russell published his autobiography. Nonetheless, he saw the effects of this experience extending even to his old age.[94] Russell describes the precipitant circumstances. Evelyn Whitehead, in her pain, 'seemed cut off from everyone and everything by walls of agony, and the sense of the solitude of each human soul suddenly overwhelmed me ... Suddenly the ground seemed to give way beneath me ...' Russell continues: 'nothing can penetrate it [the loneliness of the human soul] except the highest intensity of the

---

88 Scheler, Ibid., p. 158.

89 Scheler, Ibid., p. 149.

90 Scheler, Ibid., p. 160.

91 Karl Jaspers, *Psychologie der Weltanschauungen* (Berlin, 1919), in the chapter 'Die Enthusiastische Einstellung in die Liebe'.

92 Bertrand Russell, *The Autobiography of Bertrand Russell, 1872–1914* (Boston, 1951), p. 220.

93 Russell, Ibid., p. 219.

94 Russell writes: 'The mystic insight which I then imagined myself to possess has largely faded, and the habit of analysis has reasserted itself. But something of what I thought I saw in that moment has remained always with me, causing my attitude during the first war, my interest in children, my indifference to minor misfortunes, and a certain emotional tone in all my human relations.' Russell, Ibid., p. 221.

sort of love that religious teachers have preached ...'[95] Curiously we find Russell affirming that this experience promises a solution to the problem of pain. Russell writes: 'A strange excitement possessed me, containing intense pain but also some triumph through the fact that I could dominate the pain, and make it as I thought a gateway to wisdom.'[96]

Russell's remarkable experience was not mystical in the sense of inexplicable. Russell knew the Whiteheads well. He empathetically followed the course of Evelyn Whitehead's illness. Her bodily physiognomy was overlayered with indeterminate previous acts of empathy. Here Wittgenstein's saying, 'The human body is the best picture of the human soul' is altogether apt.[97] If there was a mystical 'moment' associated with Russell's experience, it arose with the conjunction of Russell's empathic responses to a multitude of experiences with Evelyn Whitehead, now overlayered upon the immediate witnessing of her suffering. Russell met this with unguarded empathy. Hence the 'micro-cognition' of personal love. Russell perceived the 'loneliness of the human soul' that, ironically, implies he was *with her* in her isolation.

The apprehension that reaches out to a person is, in a sense, beyond pleasure and pain. Surely not because Russell's love or Mrs Whitehead's person were able to stop her pain. Rather, the focus of his love opened onto an aspect of her identity that all at once is irrevocably dual, interactive and loved. The pain of this true self was thereby no longer isolated but indeed by its nature inter-affective. Consequently pain may be 'dominated' by love to the extent that the truths of the personal world may be put alongside the truths of the objective world, each laying question to other's priority. So, Pascal's *aperçue*, regarding Biblical hermeneutics, applies, at least in part: 'All that tends not to charity [compassionate love] is figurative.'[98]

Husserl's strange remarks in the 1931 manuscript mentioned above then take on a rather keen significance. Husserl wrote that personal love: 'is not at all hedonic although it establishes joys, "high" joys.'[99] Talk of 'high' and 'low' perhaps does not help so much in illuminating this difference. But Husserl's accompanying remarks do better. Husserl tells us that it requires a 'loving surrender'[100] and loving abandonment or surrender is 'the opposite of each person who practices it ...'[101]

What is surrendered in loving surrender? Nothing less than one's self as a conscious willing ego, which phenomenology knows as the 'intentional subject'. In fact the establishing of the identity of the other person through the *Nachverstehen* of lovers requires, from the beginning, such a surrender. From a phenomenological point of view, what is surrendered is the workings of an 'active ego', and with the

---

95 Russell, Ibid., p. 220.

96 Russell, Ibid., p. 221.

97 Ludwig Wittgenstein, *Philosophical Investigations* (New York, 1953), p. 178e.

98 'Tout ce qui ne va point à la charité est figure.' Blaise Pascal, *Pensées* (Paris, 1976), #670, p. 243.

99 Husserl, *Zur Phänomenologie der Intersubjektivität, Dritter Teil*, Husserliana XV, p. 406: 'Die Liebe ... ist ganz und gar nicht hedonisch, obwohl sie Freuden, "hohe" Freuden begründet ...' Cited in full; see note 52.

100   Husserl, Ibid., p. 406: '... eine liebende Hingabe ...'

101   Husserl, Ibid., p. 406: ' ... die umgekehrt jeder Person, die sie übt ...'

surrender goes the truths of 'objective' world, that is, a world populated with fixed, determined objects seemingly existing independently from each other. In the 1931 manuscript, Husserl adds:

> ... and an essential perversion (*Perversion*) lies near, and that consists in treating the loving surrender as a mere means to pleasure ... [102]

The essential perversion, of course, is not about sinful, illicit, or deviant love. Husserl rightly insists that personal love consists in striving 'in the sense' of the beloved's striving.[103] The problem is not about preferring 'higher' over 'lower' values. It is finally nonsense to insist that pleasure plays no part in personal love. The problem lies in understanding how personal love, through inter-affective *Nachverstehen*, can establish identities perceived *in* and *through* love, as Scheler puts it. These identities have uncontestable value since the grounding of their constitution consists, from the beginning, in empathetic acts of care and attentiveness, as determined by interactive *Nachverstehen*.

But if, in personal love, the lover brings together a series of empathies *vis-à-vis* the strivings and endeavors of the beloved, sharing in them, and thus conjoining his or her own feelings, personal love presumes a uniquely logical '*and*' which also is pre-objective. The lover is *with* the beloved in her strivings, hopes and satisfactions, not as a second person added to the first. Nor is the lover identifiable with the beloved. Indeed, all the conjunctions of the lover with the beloved and the summation of empathies that result in the presence of the beloved's history and *truth*, imply a curious logical conjunction that is different from the logical '*and*' strictly speaking, but that nonetheless is analogous to it on an emotional and volitional level. Husserl knew of this '*and*'. In *Ideas I*, Husserl writes: '... there is besides the doxic "and" (the logical "and") an axiological and practical "and".'[104] In the conclusion of this book, we'll focus in more detail on this 'axiological and practical *and*' that is increasingly manifest in the progression of personal love.

---

102   Husserl, Ibid., p. 406: '... und doch liegt hier eine gefährliche Perversion nahe, dass man die liebende Hingabe als blosses Mittel des Genusses behandelt ...'

103   'As one who loves I know, that, whatever I think, feel, strive for, or do, all are necessarily "in the sense" (*im Sinne*) of my beloved, is right for the beloved, and is right for the beloved not only in the sense of not being reprimanded by the beloved, but rather as striven for by me in the sense of the beloved's striving.' [Als Liebender weiss ich, dass, was immer ich denke, fühle, erstrebe, tue, all das notwendig 'im Sinne' meines Geliebten ist, ihm recht ist, von ihm nicht nur nicht getadelt und in diesem Sinne als recht anerkannt ist, sondern als von mir Erstrebtes auch im Sinne seines Strebens ist.] Husserl, *Zur Phänomenologie der Intersubjektivität, Zeiter Teil*, Husserliana XIV, p. 173.

104   Husserl, *Ideas, First Book* (Den Haag, 1982), §121, p. 289.

Chapter 2

Sexual Love

I'd call it love if love
didn't take so many years
but lust too is a jewel. – (Adrienne Rich)[1]

What could be more typical than to find oneself sexually attracted to another, in spite of lack of expectation, and, perhaps, willingness? The Roman poet, Horace, already in middle age, famously rhapsodized:

Venus, you have long suspended your trials, now you would renew them? Be merciful, I beg you, I beg you.[2]

But why the pull of sexual attraction to someone who is unfamiliar, whose allure as Horace marked, portends a war with one's self? As we'll consider, the object of sexual desire has a different constitution from the focus of personal love. With sexual love, there is an emphasis upon touch and kinesthesia that alters the whole/part structure of objects. It brings with it a shift in temporality as well as makes the pleasure of repetitive sexual scenarios curiously new and unique. Husserl's 'On the Theory of Wholes and Parts'[3] will be considered in proposing how sexual love sets askew the ordinary relation between whole and parts in perceptual objects. We'll also consider the contrast between the focus of personal and sexual love. Even with cases of successful long-standing blends of personal and sexual love, is there a tension between sexual and personal love borne out of the varied constitutions of the two kinds of love? Finally, we'll revisit explanations for the incest taboo, considering how this universal proscription against incest, among human societies, depends on an especially violent conflict between the intentionalities of personal and sexual love.

---

1 Adrienne Rich, 'Two Songs', in *Necessities of Life, Poems, 1962–1965* (New York, 1966).

2 Horace, *Odes and Epodes*, Shorey and Laing (eds), (New York, 1910), *Carminum*, Liber Quartus, 1.1–2, p. 94, [my trans.].

3 Husserl, 'Zur Lehre von den Ganzen und Teilen', *Logische Untersuchungen, Zweiter Band*, Husserliana XIX.2 (Den Haag, 1984), pp. 227–300). English translation: Husserl, 'Investigation III: On the Theory of Wholes and Parts', in *Logical Investigations*, vol II (New York, 2001), pp. 1–46.

Sexual Desire, Unlike Personal Love, Objectifies; in so doing, it Modulates the Ordinary Part/Whole Structure of Perceptual Objects

For the lover in the throes of sexual passion, it is not just that so-called 'sexual parts' are emphasized. The lover brings with his or her passion a revision to the ordinary whole/part relation of objects. Like Mandelbrot's fractal geometry, the parts reiterate the whole and *vice versa*. Styles of clothes, muscular development, make-up and jewelry create sexual allure by writing large a genital mapping. Similarly the lover is fascinated with his or her partner's limbs, lips, and so on.

For a long time in English, talk about parts and pieces in uncensored sex-charged conversation has erupted in a curious manner. Two Capulets, spoiling for a fight with equally randy Montagues, banter at the opening of *Romeo and Juliet*:

Sampson:	I will show myself a tyrant: when I have fought with the men, I will be cruel with the maids: I will cut off their heads.
Gregory:	The heads of the maids?
Sampson:	Ay, the heads of the maids, or their maiden-heads; take it in what sense thou wilt.
Gregory:	They must take it in sense that feel it.
Sampson:	Me they shall feel while I am able to stand, and 'tis known I am a pretty piece of flesh.[4]

Shakespeare's play on 'maidenheads' and 'piece of flesh' is not a uniquely Shakespearean verbal play. Slang, playing on the word 'piece', designating both sexual intercourse and a person as the focus of sexual desire, has been in English usage from the Fourteenth century to the present.[5] Some bizarre sounding phrases, such as a 'piece of mutton' and 'piece of muslin', were in currency in the nineteenth century, but have fallen out of usage. But 'piece of flesh, ass, goods, skirt, etc.', have been a part of mildly obscene language use ever since the 1900s and often date from centuries before.

This usage about pieces brings with it a curious emphasis on 'piece' and 'part'. The parts are not merely 'present' in the whole as the core is present in the apple, or the pitch in the musical tone. There is a hidden shift in the relation between part and whole in the Capulet's saying, 'a pretty piece of flesh'. In intense sexual desire, the part would seem to engulf the whole. Like the golden section, which consists in an equivalent ratio between the two parts of the section and the whole, the relation of sexual parts to the rest of the body is reiterated, making the rest of the body and a stand-in for the sexual part.

Cases of the reiteration and transference of sexual parts are abundant from the earliest literary sources. Homer's description of the helmets of Greek and Trojan

---

4   Shakespeare, *Romeo and Juliet* from *The Complete Works of* (London, 1980), I.i:23–31.

5   The references to 'piece' and 'piece of ...' are from Jonathan Green, *The Cassell Dictionary of Slang* (London, 1998), pp. 912–13.

warriors, for example, marks an instance of a transfer and exaggeration of a 'sexual part'. The Homeric military helmet sported a great plume of horsehair. The peak of the helmet from which the horsehair crest sprung was called the *phalos*:

> Then Menelaus, drawing his silver-studded sword,
> Rose up and struck his [Paris's] helmet's horn [*phalos*].[6]

This part/whole relation is captured also in early masterpieces of sculpture. Consider the particularly well-known frieze of Athena Nike fastening her shoe.[7] The sculptor seems to catch the goddess in an awkward moment as she lifts her foot to tie her shoe. The goddess is caught off guard, but as she binds her foot, we become captive to the divinity's power. In fact, no small part of the sculptor's artistry involves the exploiting of a genital mapping through the folds of the goddess's robe. The garment that flows down the goddess's body reiterates the contours of the goddess's sex. The fabric falls in numerous concentric ovals, most tightly near the groin, and then fans out on a larger and larger scale. Of course, the effect requires that we do not notice the reiteration *as* a genital mapping, but merely as the contours of the garment. But it is precisely the suggestion of an unlikely equivalence between parts and wholes that creates a resonance that gives the goddess, even in an untoward moment, a world-shaking centrality. The lover, similarly, relishes this infinite resonance of the beloved partner's limbs and flesh without having to bother with its hidden logic.

With the erotic Biblical book, *The Song of Songs*, parts are followed by similar parts, refusing to submit to an overall holistic ordering. As Julia Kristeva points out, *The Song of Songs* is so ordered that: 'any other change of order would not disturb the value of the whole. Whatever the historical or textual reasons for it, that compositional disorder in fact emphasizes ... that the lyrical meaning is contained in each of the minimal meanings of the text, which thus condense, in microcosmic fashion, the totality of the message.'[8] Structurally, the poem consists in a sequence of perfectly crafted parts, which are followed by other exquisitely crafted parts, but which defy an overriding holistic organization. 'How beautiful you are my love, how beautiful you are! / Your eyes, behind your veil, are doves.' This description of the beloved by Solomon (4:1) could be reshuffled into any other part of the text. Perhaps this conquest of the whole by parts supports lyrically the thought of the poem: 'For love is strong as death, jealousy relentless as Sheol' (8:6). If there are only parts without end, the ultimate completion, death, is overcome.

There are many transfers or borrowings of the forms and shapes of sexual parts in styles of fashion. An almost too obvious instance of transference of sexual parts in fashion was the codpiece of the Middle Ages. Popular during the reign of England's York monarchs, it consisted in a stuffed cloth in the shape of a permanent erection.

---

6   *Iliad*, 3.361–362 [my trans.]. The Homeric term, *phalos* (φάλος), as its Latin cognate, *phalerae*, meaning a metal ornament worn on the breast as a military decoration, unlike the term *phallus* (φαλλός), has a single lambda. Even so, it is homonymic with phallus and can be hardly disconnected from term referring to the male member.

7   The frieze dates from 410 (c), BCE and is now exhibited at the Acropolis Museum, Athens.

8   Julia Kristeva, *Tales of Love* (New York, 1987), p. 92.

Henry VIII wore one of prodigious dimensions, which, according to Beth Marie Kosir, '... often entered the room before he [Henry VIII] did ...'[9] The codpiece clearly had symbolic, and not merely functional, significance. A protective covering of the genitals obviously need not take on the shape of an erect penis. The fashion of the day also included a transfer of the codpiece in women's attire. Women of the period occasionally wore a breast pendant similar in shape to the codpiece.[10]

Fashion presents countless examples of the transfer of sexual parts. When formally attired, the Victorian lady corseted her waist to scarcely tolerable thinness. Her waist became a pedestal upon which rested the cleavage of her breasts, with the décolletage of her bodice exposed and exaggerated, suggesting an offering. Desmond Morris, in *The Naked Ape*, suggests that large breasts are attractive because they reiterate, imagistically, the back view of a woman ready for coitus.[11] If Morris is right about large breasts and their cleavage, then the Victorian lady's bodice would take the matter to extreme, subliminally, suggesting a woman offering sexual readiness on a pedestal.

Men's neckties and the patterning of beards and mustaches, as it has often been noted, suggest an exaggeration and transfer of male sexual genital display. Notorious has been the use of symbolization of sexual parts in advertising. Especially well known is 'Smooth Joe', the cartoon character created for Camel cigarettes. Smooth Joe is often portrayed as smoking a cigarette and driving a sports car, a behavior that young potential smokers might think 'cool'. Not so subtly, Joe Camel's head outlines male genitalia, his nose a flaccid penis and his sagging lips, testicles.

This mapping of sexual parts onto other parts of the body or through clothes, musculature, make-up or jewelry appears even among nonhuman primates. There are many instances among primates, where 'features' of reproductive fitness are expressed by symbolic transference and exaggeration. Further, the symbols may be transferred to the opposite sex, or may involve borrowings from other species of animals and even plants.[12]

---

9 Beth Marie Kosir, 'Fifteenth-Century Life: Modesty to Majesty: The Development of the Codpiece', accessible on-line from ORB: The Online Reference Book for Medieval Studies, http://www.r3.org/life/articles/codpiece.html.

10 The OED, entry 'codpiece', (Oxford, 1971), p. 584, quotes William Harrison in *The Description of England*, II.vii, (1877) I.170: '...their [chaste and sober matrons'] doublets with pendant codpeeses on the brest.' William Harrison, *The Description of England* (Ithaca, NY, 1968), p. 147.

11 Desmond Morris, *The Naked Ape* (New York, 1967), pp. 75–6.

12 The most obvious example of borrowings from other life-forms among human beings are flowers, used ubiquitously to communicate romantic interest: 'In Tahiti, for instance, when groups of young people socialize, a young woman indicates her availability by wearing a cluster of scented frangipani flowers in her hair, over her ear, and a young man by wearing a headband of the same flowers.' John Money, *Gay, Straight, and In-Between: The Sexology of Erotic Orientation* (Oxford, 1988), p. 129. Proust famously has Swann and Odette refer their lovemaking by Odette's favorite orchid, the 'cattleya'. Marcel Proust, *Swann's Way* (New York, 1989), pp. 255–6. The etymology of the word for the flower, as derived from 'orchis', meaning human testicles or ovaries, makes the connection obvious enough.

A species of baboon, *Theropithecus gelada*, for example, has conspicuous red or dark pink markings on its chest. These markings are conspicuous enough that the *geladas* are popularly known as the 'bleeding heart baboons'. In fact, the patches match the pattern of female display for sexual readiness: a brightly distinguished pattern around the clitoris taking the shape of two pink triangles set vertically point to point. But males and females also have the same pattern on their chests. And remarkably, the females' *chest* pattern changes in color and size when the female comes into estrus.[13]

Sexual Parts and Pieces as Objects Organized by Touch

We can better understand the significance of this curious reiteration of sexual parts if we consider the modulation that occurs in elevating touch and kinesthesia to a prominent role in perception. Merleau-Ponty was keenly aware how different senses establish different sensory fields. He returned again and again to the question of how visual, tactile and kinesthetic sensory fields overlap. In his late essay, 'Eye and Mind', he exhorts us to consider the difference between 'mappings' of the visual field and motor projects: 'This extraordinary overlapping [the visual field and the mapping of motor projects], which we never think about sufficiently, forbids us to think of vision as an operation of thought that would set up before the mind a picture or a representation of the world, a world of immanence and of ideality.'[14]

Already in the *Phenomenology of Perception*, Merleau-Ponty characterized how the sense of space becomes altered when a person who is blind from birth gains vision after a cataract operation. The patient has to learn *how* to see. After the operation, 'To distinguish by sight a circle from a rectangle, he has to run his eyes round the outline of the figure, as he might his hand, and he always tends to take hold of objects set before his eyes.'[15] He needs to learn to shift 'his gaze as a gaze and no longer as a hand.'[16] Merleau-Ponty observes that touch brings a different significance to space from sight:

> The fact, for example, that touch cannot simultaneously cover more than a small amount of space – that of the body and its instruments – does not affect merely the presentation of tactile space, but also changes its significance.[17]

Tactile space involves 'a certain "blurring" in the simultaneity of extreme points ...' For the individual whose blindness has been cured by an operation, the breadth of visual perspectives will be a 'true revelation ... because it provides demonstration, for the first time, of remote simultaneity *itself*'.[18]

---

13 Wolfgang Wickler, 'Socio-Sexual Signals and Their Intraspecific Imitation among Primates', in *Primate Ethology*, Desmond Morris (ed.), (Chicago, 1967), pp. 69ff.

14 Maurice Merleau-Ponty, 'Eye and Mind', in *The Primacy of Perception* (Evanston, IL, 1964), p. 162.

15 Merleau-Ponty, Ibid., p. 162.

16 Merleau-Ponty, *Phenomenology of Perception* (London, 1989), p. 223.

17 Merleau-Ponty, Ibid., p. 223.

18 Merleau-Ponty, Ibid., p. 224.

Much of the unique character of the object of sexual attraction may be apprehended if we consider an alteration from a predominantly visually constituted object to one organized predominantly by touch. In sexual attraction, the other's body, increasingly unveiled, pulls in our attention like the vortex of a whirlpool. The unveiling and disrobing of the other's body is a fascination, which would seem to dictate its own rhythm and tempo. Unlike particularly visual phenomena that may be apprehended 'in a single stroke', for example, a letter, a diamond or a star drawn on a blank page, the sexually desired body takes on a different capacity to perceive the objects as a whole. It answers to the rule of tactility that requires proximity and sequential discovery.

A comparison of parts and wholes is surely possible by touch, but not, as with vision, 'at a single stroke'. If you close your eyes and compare by touch the surface of a rectangular tabletop with a square one, the corners feel the same, but the whole shape is felt as square or oblong because of touching the corners at a different rhythm. For touch, the relation of the parts to wholes, the right-angled corners of the square or rectangular tabletop, is a sequence of parts upon parts. So too for the lover, sexual parts involve an alternate relation of parts to wholes from ordinary vision-dominated perception by which we see the object 'at a glance'. With touch, the recognition of the whole object amounts to the promise that parts will be recognizable in themselves, and recurrently so. The result is that the tactile whole is far more like a melody than it is like a shape we can see, all at once, in a single glance. In sexual passion, we do not 'see' a general unity as we see a triangle or a star. Sexual allure involves a heightened reiteration of parts and a sense of the whole that occurs almost as an afterthought. This may compared to the genital mapping, written large, which we have seen occurs in fashion, make-up, advertising, and so on.

Fables that portray erotic love often elevate touch to a prominence above vision. Consider Apuleius' droll masterpiece, *The Golden Ass*. As told in *The Golden Ass*, Eros, alias Cupid, seeing Psyche, immediately falls in love with her. He becomes her lover and houses her in a magnificent palace, visits her only at night, and insists that she never see him. But Psyche knows of him 'only by touch and hearing'.[19] Even so, Psyche thinks him an ideal lover:

> I have no idea who you are, but I love you. I love you desperately, I love you as I love my own soul; I wouldn't exchange your kisses for the kisses of the God Cupid himself.[20]

In this fable of erotic love, it is primarily touch, and not sight, which reigns in sexual enthrallment.[21] Secondarily, Cupid is recognized by his voice. But both touch and audition, do not operate in a 'single glance', but by a repetition of parts. Music,

---

19 Apuleius, *The Transformation of Lucius Otherwise Known as the Golden Ass* (New York, 1951), p. 104.

20 Apuleius, Ibid., p. 106.

21 C.S. Lewis reworks the Psyche/Cupid myth, in *Till We Have Faces*, retelling the myth from the point of view of one of Psyche's sisters. Lewis's version especially supports the thesis offered here, namely that Cupid's invisibility accommodates the touched-ruled world of eros. Lewis has Psyche tell her sister Orual: '..."Yet, you know, it never looked as if the plates or the cup were doing it." And, Orual (her voice grew very low), "when I took the cup,

however else we might consider it, is unimaginable without the repetition of parts, whether as reiterated phrases, motifs, melodies, or rhythms.

The shift away from a vision-dominated organization to a tactile one is commonplace erotic poetry. Consider the erotic love poem that is perhaps as celebrated as any in Latin literature: 'Let us live, my Lesbia, and let us love.'[22]

> ... Suns may set and rise again. For us, when the short light has once set, remains to be slept the sleep of one unbroken night.
>
> Give me a thousand kisses, then a hundred, then another thousand, then a yet a thousand, then a hundred. Then, when we have made up many thousands, we will confuse our counting, that we may not know the reckoning, nor any malicious person blight them with evil eye, when he knows that our kisses are so many.

By pluralizing 'sun' (*soles*), Catullus removes us from the primary unifying source of the visual world, the sun. In saying 'For us, when the short light has set' (*nobis, cum semel occidit brevis lux*), he presumes the Greek and Roman physiological doctrine whereby vision arises from a commingling of the external light, say from a lamp or the sun, with the internal light emitted from the transparent medium in the eyes.[23] Thus in a second sense, the possibility of vision is put to rest. In Catullus' threefold bidding for a thousand then a hundred kisses, he plays upon the fundamental categories of enumeration: 'hundreds', 'thousands'. These categories will be set aside by the countlessness of kisses. But counting also, for its enactment is vision-dependent and only remotely possible in the touch-based world of lovemaking. For as we have considered touch is ruled by parts, and the counting of whole objects, and as well, whole events and times, become remote when the constitution of objects is part-determined from the beginning.

Nudity and the Temporality of Sexual Love

Once we allow that sexual love promotes a world where tactility reigns over vision, aspects of sexual love unravel. Consider for example the allure of nudity.

The nudity of the sexually attractive body, as opposed to its nakedness, promises a kind of erotic geomancy. We long to discover the heightened sensitivities of the other's body, as the geomancer sets out to divine hieratic marks upon the land. Tactility, unlike vision, requires shifts in a texture and an arrival at boundaries for noticing differences. The voyeur, who merely gazes at a woman undressing, allows his eyes to function as hands. He thereby 'feels' the texture of the skirt as the woman disrobes. His gaze lights upon whatever is exciting, on what is, in fact, invisible, but what is nonetheless satisfying, since his gaze functions as touch.

Since, with the sexually desired body, touch reigns over the intersensorial unity of the other person's flesh, the sexual 'part', is no longer 'present' in an object

---

I – I – *felt* the other hands, touching my own.'" C.S. Lewis, *Till We Have Faces* (New York, 1956), p. 114.

22 Catullus, 'The Poems of Gaius Valerius Catullus', in *Catullus, Tibullus and Pervigilium Veneris* (Cambridge, MA, 1962), Carmina #5, pp. 7–8.

23 Aristotle, *Sense and Sensibilia*, Chapter 2, 438a25–438b17.

in the manner in which it is in a perceptual object whose unity is predominantly organized by vision. The very 'objectivity' of the body of a sexually desired person has undergone a modulation. The hiddenness as revealed in nudity is unlike the hiddenness of perceptual objects whose hidden sides are 'there' but merely, as yet, indeterminate. In nudity the other's body is not wholly disclosed. It remains a sequence of uncoverings.

Consider how this is different from our ordinary perception of a vision-dominated perceptual object. An apple, for example, is seen as imbued with parts that correspond to the different sensory faculties. The apple, even as seen, does present intersensory aspects. It *looks* tasty. Perhaps there is even anticipated a 'crack' that would splinter the air in taking the first bite. This intersensoriality of the object's sensory 'parts', which is dominated by vision, brings with it a paradigmatic temporality. As indicated, the whole of the object is seen 'at one stroke'. So Aristotle had already acknowledged that vision, unlike hearing and touch, involves simultaneity of the 'seeing' of 'having seen'.[24] But, as Merleau-Ponty well understood, the intersensoriality of an object enables the elevating of one sensory aspect over another. 'I hear the hardness and unevenness of cobbles in the rattle of the carriage, and we speak appropriately of a "soft", "dull" or "sharp" sound.'[25]

The lover in sexual passion experiences a synesthetic realignment. As we have proposed, the lover sees in his or her partner an alluring physiognomy that, synesthetically, incorporates a heightened sense of tactility into the visage of the lover. A different temporal paradigm follows. The increased desire to touch incorporates temporal conditions of touching, that is, sequential uncoverings of texture. The 'temporal thickness' manifests itself as the allure of the lover's nudity, as opposed to their nakedness.

That sexual attractiveness is touch-dominant alters the sense of repetition even in terms of the novelty of the sexual act. Again there are well-known literary descriptions. Proust in *Swann in Love* has Charles Swann and Odette de Crécy famously initiate a sexual ritual that begins with Swann's straightening the orchids, the cattleyas, on Odette's bodice. Later, 'Do a cattleya' becomes Swann's and Odette's locution for making love. But in spite of the repetition of the ritualistic love scenario, Proust explains that Swann in love-making feels 'a pleasure which had never before existed, which he was striving now to create, a pleasure – as the special name he gave it was to certify – entirely individual and new.'[26] Although the sexual scenario is repeated, the pleasures are curiously new and unique. Swann's lovemaking with Odette, in spite of the repetition seems '... as it might have seemed to the first man when he enjoyed it amid the flowers of the earthly paradise ...'[27]

This should come as no surprise. Touch draws out the recognition of the object. It is not a matter of simply seeing a glass of water, but of anticipating a sequence of swallows, each with their own quelling of thirst to different degrees. The recognition

---

24 Aristotle, *Nicomachean Ethics*, X.4, 1174a14; *Sophistical Elenchi*, 178a9; *Metaphysics*, IX.6, 1048b29.

25 Merleau-Ponty, *Phenomenology of Perception*, p. 229.

26 Proust, Ibid., p. 256.

27 Proust, Ibid., p. 256.

of objects trails behind the richness of sensory experience. The blind man feels the curb through his cane. But he feels the curb, not the rectangular strip of concrete pavement. The recognition of parts allows for comparisons, but comparisons between *objects* become a more remote possibility. With touch recognition, the Principle of Identity of course holds, but it extends to parts of objects, and only derivatively to the objects themselves. As applied to the sexual act, there is a different criterion of similarity. Variations, which appear minimal from the point of view of a visual whole, become drawn out. The passing from the present into the past is no longer the destiny of a whole moment. For as we shall consider, the temporal moment for touch becomes whole through ongoing repeated tactile stimulation which dilates the temporal moment, making little sense of a present moment fading into the past. Rather, there is an intensely saturated sense of promise. So, in the throes of sexual passion we are at a loss to make comparisons of the lovemaking of last week, yesterday or today. As Proust states, its pleasures are 'entirely individual and new'.[28]

Husserl on Wholes and Parts

New York University philosophy professor, Kit Fine, ranks Husserl's 'On the Theory of Wholes and Parts' especially highly as: '... perhaps the most significant treatise on the concept of part to be found in the philosophical literature.'[29] In fact, the problem of the relation of parts to wholes is an old one in the history of philosophy. Already, Aristotle had analyzed how 'wholes' (ὅλα) differed from 'totals' (πάντα).[30]

In his investigation 'On the Theory of Wholes and Parts' Husserl is especially concerned with framing a 'glueless' account of how an object is whole. Husserl was aware that proposing an encompassing form that would bind the unity together results in an endless regress.[31]

Husserl's approach is perhaps better understood by considering an ordinary way of thinking about the relation of parts to wholes. Suppose wholes and parts are conceived in terms of form and matter. The *wholeness* of an apple then, for example, is due to a combination of form and matter, say, a certain spheroid shape containing matter consisting of apple pulp, some seeds, and an outer skin. But this form/matter approach has minimal application for by simply adjusting the context, and considering apples as they appear in desserts, as candied apples or brandy-braised apples, for example, we conceive the apples are whole regardless if they are peeled, cored, without seeds, and so on. Further the form/matter approach breaks down altogether when we consider amorphous sensuous substances, such as whole milk or whole blood. Also, there is little use of the notion in explaining non-sensuous

28 Proust, Ibid., p. 256.

29 Kit Fine, 'Part-whole', p. 463.

30 Aristotle, *Metaphysics*, V.26, 1024a1–3.

31 Husserl's statement runs: 'Our conception avoids these endless regresses of parts which are always splitting into further series. Nothing *really* exists – in the sense of being a possible object of sense-perception – beyond the aggregate of a whole's "pieces", together with the sensuous forms of unity, which rest on these pieces conjointly.' Husserl, 'Investigation III: On the Theory of Wholes and Parts', in *Logical Investigations*, vol II, §22, p. 37.

wholes, such as, the whole of Hume's *Treatise*, or of times, as when we say 'I kept silent the whole time'.

Husserl's analysis of wholes and parts, unlike the one based in form and matter, is based in a relation of *parts to parts*. What is required is that there is a single *Foundation*, which may involve one or more parts, but which necessarily ranges over the full content of the rest of the parts. In the precise language of the treatise, these parts, which are necessarily 'non-independent' relative to the Whole, are called 'moments'. Contrastingly, those capable of being independent from the Whole are called 'pieces'.[32] Husserl can then define the relation of Wholes to Parts, through the notion of *Foundation*. 'By a Whole we understand a range of contents which are all covered *by a single foundation* without the help of further contents. The contents of such a range we call its parts.'[33] 'A single foundation' then is a collection of one or more non-independent parts that range over all the collection of parts.[34] The comprehensiveness of this definition allows Husserl to define the relation of wholes and parts not only for sensuous perceptual objects, but for coherent bodies of matter, such as whole milk or blood, and even for non-sensuous wholes and 'whole times'.

A star drawn in pencil on paper is whole, for example, if one of its parts, not the graphite, nor the paper pulp, but the characteristic shape, is a *moment*, that is, a non-independent part, ranging over the full extent of its parts. The moments that make up the *Foundation* may be multiple.[35] What is required is that at least one *Foundation* ranges over the total contents. The apple that falls off the tree is whole because of multiple non-independent parts: the spheroid shape, the pulp, the seeds and the skin. If the apple fell off the tree without any one of these parts, it would not be a whole apple. But the candied and braised apples are also whole. We simply need to restrict the Foundation to the non-independent parts that range over the full extent of the parts, namely a spheroid shape and apple pulp. These two parts are enough to make the apple dessert whole. Whole milk and whole blood will include, necessarily, certain non-independent parts: for milk, the cream; for blood, the platelets and clotting factors.

Husserl's theory of Wholes and Part applies to temporality, as well. Husserl uses it to explain the 'specious present', as a 'whole moment' of time. William James had described the 'specious present' in the *Principles of Psychology*:

---

32 'Each part that is independent relatively to a whole *W* we call a piece (Portion), each part that is non-independent relatively to *W* we call a Moment (an abstract part) of this same whole *W*.' Husserl, Ibid., §17, p. 29.

33 Husserl, Ibid., §21, p. 34.

34 Husserl's explicit definition follows: '*A content of the species A is founded upon a content of the species B*, if *A* can by its essence (i.e. legally, in virtue of its specific nature) not exist, unless a *B* also exists: this leaves open whether the coexistence of a *C*, a *D* etc., is needed or not.' Because Husserl includes in the definition, 'this leaves open whether the coexistence of a *C*, a *D* etc., is needed or not,' he implies that non-independent parts which make up the Foundation may be multiple. Husserl, Ibid., §21, p. 34.

35 As indicated in the footnote above, Husserl adds in the definition of Foundation, 'this leaves open whether the coexistence of a *C*, a *D* etc., is needed or not.'

In short, the practically cognized present is no knife edge, but a saddle-back, with a certain breadth of its own on which we sit perched, and from which we look in two directions into time. The unit of composition of our perception of time is a *duration*, with a bow and a stern, as it were – a rearward- and a forward- looking end. It is only as parts of this *duration-block* that the relation of succession of one end to the other is perceived.[36]

We obtain the non-independent part that is needed to make the specious present 'whole' if, in Husserl's language, we 'conceive of any time-lapse, however small, as filled with a rigidly unchanging content ...'[37] In fact the specious present amounts to noticing a 'non-independent' part of the perceptual field which is, seemingly, unchanging. That non-independent part, for example, may be an auditory stillness, a stalling of any perceived locomotion, or a quieting of one's own bodily movement and kinesthetic stimuli. In each case, a part of the perceptual field is made into a 'moment', which ranges over its contents and yields a temporary stasis or 'specious present'. It also explains how we speak of 'the whole time' in general. So the Shakespearean drama, *King Henry the Eighth*, opens with the Duke of Buckingham regretting his confinement to his room because of sickness: 'All the whole time / I was my chamber's prisoner.'[38] The non-independent part that makes Buckingham's time is his chamber a 'whole time,' is his having, all the while, the 'ague'.

Returning then to temporality associated with touch, we find that wholeness cannot be established by a shape, all at once, as is the case with the figure of the star, or the sphericity of the apple, for touch has no access to shape in the sense of a co-present boundary given all at once. We may sense the wholeness of a wineglass, say, by rubbing our fingers over its surfaces, noting its smoothness and lack of sharp edges, as our hand expands and contracts with the contours of the glass. By touch, then, we sense the wineglass is whole. But we do so by feeling its boundaries, realizing that the glass terminates below as I bring my hand beneath it and terminates above as I bring my hand over it. Without sensing the boundaries of the touched object we cannot discern that we have it whole.

The notion of boundaries plays an important role in 'On the Theory of Wholes and Parts'. Husserl writes:

> The division of a whole into a plurality of mutually exclusive pieces we call a *piecing* or *fragmentation* of the same. Two such pieces may still have an identical 'moment': their common boundary, e.g., is an identical moment of the adjoining pieces of a divided continuum.[39]

---

36 William James, *The Principles of Psychology* (Chicago, 1952), p. 399.

37 Husserl's whole statement runs: 'If we conceive of any time-lapse, however small, as filled with a rigidly unchanging content (if indeed the Idea of Nature permits such a conceptual possibility) and if we conceive of the whole of reality as reduced, during this period to such a changeless being, then the causal principle certainly demands that such being should persist unchanged *a parte post* for all eternity (though *a parte ante*, it may have arisen out of eternal rest or law-governed change).' Husserl, Ibid., §25, p. 44.

38 Attributed to Shakespeare, *King Henry the Eighth* from *The Complete Works of* (London, 1980), I.i:13–14.

39 Husserl, Ibid., §17, p. 29. [Die Einteilung eines Ganzen in eine Mehrheit sich ausschließender Stücke nennen wir *Zerstückung* desselben. Zwei solche Stücke können noch

Archeologists work to map exactly where ancient fragments of pottery are found. They do so to better enable the piecing together of fragments whose edges match. They can more easily find pottery shards that have, in Husserl's language, a 'common boundary'. It is precisely this common boundary that also is a non-independent part and that establishes the *whole* amphora or krater. But this translates to tactile-kinesthetic perception and has altogether obvious application in regard to sexual behavior.

How might common boundaries be established by touch? Through touch, it would be possible to feel how two pieces of the wine glass fit together. Say the base of the glass has broken off from the stem. I might simply run my fingers over the detached base, feel that the contour of the broken base matches the contour of the broken stem, and thereby sense how the pieces make up the whole wineglass. But this is a special case of an almost absurdly obvious way in which a whole can be established by touch through a common boundary. The ongoing and repeated tactile-kinesthetic stimulation that occurs in the friction of penile/vaginal copulation, as well as with whatever sexual activity that involves friction between sexual organs and bodily orifices, also establishes a tactile-kinesthetic 'common boundary'. Indeed, it is difficult to imagine any interactive tactile-kinesthetic sensorium that could do so more completely than the tactile sensing of 'common boundary' in sexual intercourse. On the level of tactile and kinesthetic sensation, this amounts to the constructing of a tactile-kinesthetic Whole. Further it is a Whole complemented by intense pleasure and satisfaction. And, since sexual love concerns not a strong delineation of a specious present – in James's words, a 'duration block' in face of a future and past – but rather a wholeness in time structured by tactile-kinesthetic friction, this extremely pleasant and satisfying tactile-kinesthetic Whole has an amorphous extension bounded roughly by the 'moment' that ranges over the requisite tactile-kinesthetic intimacy and that makes 'whole' the act of love.

Husserl's 'On the Theory of Wholes and Parts', then, as applied to the topic of the constitution of the sexual object, illumines several of its peculiarities. If we accept that sexual desire promotes tactility, then the theory of whole and parts explains how sexual parts usurp their ordinary relation with the configuration of the human body. There is an alteration in the anatomical relation of sexual parts to the whole of the human body, which like the ancient *hermae* would confute the bodily form of the god Hermes with the phallus, the lingam with the god Shiva, or the yoni with the goddess Shakti. This curious exaggeration and reiteration of parts makes sense if we realize that the *Foundation*, for the sexual part is not the anatomical body made evident through vision, but a bodily whole whose *Foundation* is based in tactility and kinesthesia. In sexual love, ensconced not in nakedness, but in nudity, the male and female sexual parts become sovereign in a tactile-kinesthetic unity, because it is precisely these parts alone that presage the possibility of the tactile kinesthetic whole. And insofar as sexual love involves the anticipation of sexual expression, writing sexual parts large in make-up, fashion, coiffure, and so on, amounts to an

---

ein identisches Moment gemeinsam haben. So ist die gemeinsame Grenze ein identisches Moment für die angrenzenden Stücke eines eingeteilten Kontinuums.] Husserl, 'Zur Lehre von den Ganzen und Teilen,' Husserliana XIX.2, p. 273.

accurate superimposition of the tactile-kinesthetic *Foundation* back onto the visual field.

Cautionary remarks are in order, given the introduction of the notion 'tactile-kinesthetic Wholes'. The notion is problematic. How might we conceptualize it? Very likely conceptualizing this odd notion will introduce a visual imagistic complement of some sort. Perhaps the graphic image of sexual penetration or copulation is adduced. Perhaps it is complemented by the more abstract notion of interlocking geometric shapes. In any case, likely a *visual* image is summoned up as a rule of thumb to even entertain the notion of a 'tactile-kinesthetic Whole'. But, of course, a visually-dominant object, and this would include a visually dominant image, is precisely what needs to be discounted if the notion of a 'tactile-kinesthetic Whole' is to be given its due. We are in a quandary because we are easily misled in apprehending the sense of a 'tactile-kinesthetic Whole'. Our very conceiving of it is vision-dominant.

How, then, are we to apprehend, even for argument's sake, a 'tactile-kinesthetic Whole' without the complement of vision-dominated imagery? Perhaps taking the matter to a more complex level of abstraction will help. Consider a digression into an age-old 'perfection' of the relation of parts and wholes. As is well known, the relation of parts and wholes known as the 'divine' or 'golden' section was incorporated often into ancient architecture.[40] The ratio is easily stated: part A is to part B as part B is to parts A and B together. Now let us imagine that such a perfection of parts and wholes operates in the constitution of the sexual loved person. It would mean that the sexual part, say the penis or vagina, fits with the body of the sexually loved in such a way that the sexually loved's body, at the same time, also expresses the unity of the lover and the sexual loved. The act of union of different conjoining parts, at the same time, coincides with the unity itself, through the middle term, if you will, of the sexually loved person's body. Admittedly whimsical, this application of the divine ratio to 'sexual parts' nonetheless is complex and possibly intriguing enough to suspend attaching a simple visual image to the notion of 'tactile-kinesthetic Whole'. Further it is in keeping with the sense in which a sexual part overpowers the merely visual organization of the sexually loved's body. The sexually loved's body is both the complement of one's own sex, which unlocks or embraces it, while at the same time, so it would seem by some mysterious coincidence, promises *by itself* the union of the lover and the sexually loved. The sense of the 'tactile-kinesthetic Whole' is further conveyed inasmuch as, to judge from the tradition of architectural and artistic uses of the divine ratio, this mysterious union would seem divinely inspired. In any case, we surely come closer to the manner in which the 'tactile-kinesthetic Whole'

---

40 It can be found exactingly in the so-called Great Pyramid, the pyramid of Cheops. If the apothegm, that is, the straight line extending from the middle of any one of the pyramid's bases to the pyramid's top, is put into ratio with the straight line extending from the middle of any one of its bases to the base's center, one arrives, to a remarkably exact degree, at the golden or divine ratio. It expresses a ratio of 89/55 or 1.618. That matches the decimal equivalent of the divine ratio to three decimal points. Peter Thompkins, *Secrets of the Great Pyramid* (New York, 1978), p. 190.

is experienced, that is, by imagining or by embracing the sexually loved's body, the attractive body itself promises the bestowal of a non-visually conceivable union.

An Explication of a Notorious Depth Psychological Doctrine

Acknowledging that the constitution of the sexual object promotes touch to a level that alters its temporality and spatiality helps put into perspective various notorious claims made by depth psychologists. In particular, consider the long-standing psychoanalysts' insistence that so-called 'castration fear' plays heavily into sexual, and even personality, development.

Aristotle had already understood mutilation as a peculiar privation of Wholes. According to the Aristotelian analysis, mutilation requires that wholes: 1) retain their identity as a species – a mutilated cup is still a cup; 2) have parts whose position makes a difference – water and fire cannot be mutilated; and, 3) are deprived of parts which are neither determinative nor accidental conditions of the species – missing a heart or liver is not a mutilation of the human body, nor is baldness, but a missing extremity is.[41] Male genitalia *and* female genitalia, then, *both* fit the criteria for the possibility of mutilation. Psychoanalysts could have avoided defining the fear gender-centrically in terms of male genitalia as the notion of 'castration' implies. Moreover, the recourse to paleo-anthropological fables was unnecessary. Freud was grasping when he explained that castration fear was a 'real occurrence in the primaeval times of the human family'.[42] On the other side of the fence, those who explain castration fear as based in an existential condition could have avoided the error of overgeneralization. In Jacques Lacan's neo-Freudian account, for example, castration fear derives from the horrifying recognition of our human fragmentation, the very fragmentation that the infant has to 'cover up' through its identifications with the world as it builds up a coherent personality.[43] Whereas Freud narrowly based castration fear on a primal fear of literal castration, having to later include girls insofar as their own psychosexual development involved a recognition that they were absent a penis,[44] Lacan's account made it curious why we were speaking of 'castration' at all. The source of the fear had little to do with male *or* female genitalia.

In quite different ways, both these approaches miss that the Whole at issue is one composed through the interlocking of sexual parts, as tactile-kinesthetically organized. The classic Freudian explanation could have avoided basing the fear on male genitalia, too anatomically conceived. The neo-Freudian Lacanian explanation could have avoided basing the fear too much on suppressed existential *Angst*. Further,

---

41 Aristotle, *Metaphysics*, V.27, 1024a10–28.

42 Sigmund Freud, *Introductory Lectures on Psychoanalysis*, Volume XVI in the *Standard Edition of the Complete Works of Sigmund Freud* (London, 1953–74), pp. 370–71.

43 Jacques Lacan, 'The mirror stage as formative of the function of the I', in *Écrits: A selection* (New York, 1977), pp. 1–7; and, 'The subversion of the subject and the dialectic of desire in the Freudian unconscious', in *Écrits*, pp. 292–325.

44 Sigmund Freud, 'New Introductory Lectures on Psycho-Analysis,' in *The Major Works of Sigmund Freud* (Chicago, 1952), p. 859.

the *genuine* Freudian discovery that symbols recurrently appearing in anxiety dreams, which are analogues of genital mutilation, would have been given its due.

The issue is placed on its proper footing once it is acknowledged that the specific sexual Wholes in question need not be conceived in narrow anatomical terms. The Whole in question is a tactile-kinesthetic Whole established by touch through common boundaries. As such, it spans the range of what psychoanalysts called 'psycho-sexual development'. Children may experience an interlocking tactile-kinetic Whole from oral/breast contact. They may as well experience it through non-gender-specific hand/genital manipulation. The tactile kinesthetic sexual Whole arises regardless whether the hand touching and the sexual organ touched is a case of childhood manual/penile masturbation or manual/clitoral masturbation. In either case, a co-stimulation takes place between flesh, touching and touched, that involves a maximizing of a tactile-kinesthetic sensibilia. There is an arrival at parts that fit. The hand and fingers are shaped to maximize genital stimulation. Consequently, by flesh on flesh, touching on touched, a Whole becomes constituted.

Further, because it is founded on tactile-kinesthetic sensations, it is based in the sense that is most necessary for animal life: touch. Consequently, the threat of the loss of this keenly pleasurable tactile-kinesthetic Whole would not necessarily require psychodynamic violence to spur it on. The cause of the fearfulness might lie in a tyrannous paterfamilias, an unsatisfiable virago mother, or in a threatening sibling. But in fact any manner of insult to the body-projects, connected with the blissful arrival at tactile-kinesthetic Wholeness, practically-speaking, would create the threat to one's sexual well-being. If, as we have argued, sexual desire leads touch to prevail over vision, a sexual part is from the beginning given its significance by two-party tactile co-stimulation, even if those two parties are oneself touching and oneself being touched. The abrogation of that co-stimulation would amount to an annihilation of the sexual part itself.

The Contrast Between Personal and Sexual Love

As these reflections on the tactile foundation of sexual love suggest, personal love and sexual love have quite different manners of constitution. In personal love, the devoted man or woman cherishes his or her beloved, who is unique, and a source of value. The beloved becomes unique through interactive *Nachverstehen*. The beloved is, then, as we've considered, 'hyper-subjective'. By contrast, in the throes of sexual passion, lovers are occupied with a world where sexual parts would seem to assimilate anatomical bodies. The contrast between the two types of love is put fairly by contemporary cult novelist Chuck Palahniuk, author of *Fight Club* and *Choke*:

> Sex is the immediate symbol for romantic love in books and songs and movies. Love, L-O-V-E, love is what my grandparents have after 60 years of being together, supporting and serving each other.[45]

---

45 Monica Drake so quotes Chuck Palahniuk in an article she published in *The Portland Mercury*, 2, 20, (2001): 18 Oct–24 Oct, 'Sex: Fiction's Hamburger Helper: How Authors Wrestle with Sex on the Page'.

The differences between the constitution of the personal and sexually loved leads us to approach the longstanding issue of whether or not there is an inherent tension, or perhaps even opposition, between personal devotion for the beloved and the fascination with the sexually attractive. There is a long history on the topic. Ovid thought that the availability of the marriage partner cools and quells sexual attraction, and could be remedied by making the spouse 'hard-to-get', or at least 'hard-to-get-to'.[46]

The Cupid and Psyche of Apuleius' fable[47] got along fine erotically until Psyche shone a lamp upon Cupid. She investigated Cupid's weapons, and pierced her thumb with one of his arrows: '... and thereby of her own accord she fell in love with Love.'[48] And suitably as far as the claim here of the tactile-dominance of sexual love goes, Cupid flew away, while poor Psyche desperately tried to cling to him, finally losing strength, and tumbling back to earth.[49]

Montaigne addresses especially the question of whether the personally loved and the sexually loved conflict in their constitution. As he sees it, a good marriage: 'rejects the company and conditions of [erotic] love, and tries to represent those of friendship.'[50] 'Men do not marry for themselves, let them say what they will; they

---

46   '... 'tis this which prevents wives from being loved: to them their husbands come whenever they will; add but a door, and let a doorkeeper say to you with stubborn mouth, "You cannot;" once shut out, you too, sir, will be touched by love.' [Hoc est, uxores quod non patiatur amari:/ Conveniunt illas, cum voluere, viri;/ Adde forem, et duro dicat tibi inanitor ore 'Non potes,' exclusum te quoque tanget amor.] Ovid (Publius Ovidius Naso), *The Art of Love, and Other Poems*, (Cambridge, MA, 1929), III, 585–8.

47   Carol Gilligan has offered recently an insightful feminist reading of the Apuleian fable in *The Birth of Pleasure: A New Map of Love*. Gilligan explains that this tale marks 'the radical nature of love between a woman and a man, caught behind the lines of patriarchy, and the high adventure of their efforts to escape into a new psychological territory'. Carol Gilligan, *The Birth of Pleasure: A New Map of Love* (New York, 2002), p. 33. The reading offered here of the Apuleian fable does not conflict but, if anything, complements Gilligan's reading. A patriarchic culture that inculcates unequal gender roles would contribute to the conflict between personal and sexual love. Personal love, if it is to be *inter*personal, requires a relation between social equals, as Husserl indicates personal love implies respect. (See note 53 below.) Sexual love, on the other hand, does not. Sexual love easily becomes an opportunity for institutionalized gender inequality putting it into conflict with personal love. Thus, Cupid's and Psyche's final arrival at marriage does amount to an overcoming of the conditions perpetuating gender inequalities.

48   [sic ignara Psyche sponte in Amoris incidit amorem.] Apuleius, *The Golden Ass, Being the Metamorphoses of Lucius Apuleius* (London, 1915), V.23.5–6, p. 232.

49   In Apuleius' tale, Jupiter resolves the conflict between sexual and personal love. Cupid must give up his boyish devotion to infidelities. '... by fastening the fetters of marriage securely upon him ...' And, Jupiter commands that Psyche drink a cup of nectar, elevating Psyche to immortal status and promoting a marriage 'between social equals.' Apuleius, *The Transformation of Lucius Otherwise Known as the Golden Ass* (New York, 1951), p. 142.

50   Michel de Montaigne, 'Upon Some Verses of Virgil', *The Essays* (Chicago, 1952), p. 411.

marry as much or more for their posterity and family ...'[51] He contrasts erotic love: 'Love [erotic] hates that people should hold of any but itself, and goes but faintly to work in familiarities derived from any other title ...'[52] Montaigne's understanding of marriage is not in keeping with a romantic ideal, to which lip service is paid in the US, whereby good marriages are founded upon on partners in love for life. Montaigne, in saying that erotic love 'hates that people should hold of any but itself', does suggest an essential tension between sexual and personal love. Indeed he touches upon a conflict between sexual and personal love as we've understood it. Personal love, as founded in inter-empathetic strivings, builds an enduring partnership. But if sexual love is self-concerned, as Montaigne suggests, a tension between the two kinds of love arises. Husserl, we may recall, declares that personal love involves *respect* (*Verehrung*).[53] There is a striving in personal love towards overcoming differences in social status that need hardly be the case with sexual love. The man in the throes of lust, by contrast, may make a woman into a goddess. But lust, alas, may also be less adoring. Sexual attraction may culminate in the partner's humiliation or degradation. Consider the extreme cases as attested to in 'Slave Diaries'. White landowners fathered children by black slaves. This did not prevent some at least from selling their partners and not recognizing the offspring of these unions.[54] Obviously, such histories egregiously exemplify how sexual love may not induce social parity.

As is well know, Margaret Mead in *Coming of Age in Samoa* proposed there was no conflict between personal and sexual love among young Samoans. The story of felicitous young islanders who mature free of conflicts between personal and sexual love has turned out to be a myth that Mead herself engendered.[55] Derek Freeman has argued in detail how Mead's conclusions were unjustified. Her portrayal of Samoans was idealized. Her conclusions are methodologically flawed.

Personal love leads to 'pair bonding'. But current anthropological research[56] finds little, if any, tie between sexual behavior and 'pair bonding'. Professors of psychology and psychiatry, Paul R. Abramson and Steven D. Pinkerton, summing up behavior drawn from sources as varied as primate behavior and Hell's Angels practices, write: 'Strictly speaking, pair-bonding cannot be a primary function of

---

51 Montaigne, Ibid., p. 410.

52 'L'amour hait qu'on se tienne par ailleurs que par luy, et se mesle láchement aux accointances qui sont dressées et entretenues soubs autre titre ...' Montaigne, 'Sur des vers de Virgile', *Œvres completes* (Paris, 1962), III.v, p. 827.

53 This appears in a manuscript dated November 1931, published in Husserl, *Zur Phänomenologie der Intersubjektivität, Dritter Teil*, Husserliana XV, p. 406. Husserl's full statement runs: 'In all [personal] love lies respect, in all respect, bliss as an essential gift.' [In aller Liebe liegt Verehrung, in aller Verehrung Seligkeit als wesensmässige Mitgabe.]

54 For example, Frederick Douglas, *Narrative of the Life of Frederick Douglas* (New York, 1977), pp. 1–4.

55 Margaret Mead, *Coming of Age in Samoa: A Psychological Study of Primitive Youth for Western Civilisation* (New York: 1928).

56 As mentioned in the introduction, we need not exclude anthropological studies, nor need we exclude literary illustrations from a phenomenology of love and hate. In attempting to discern the constitution of an object, whatever may broaden the array of possibilities by which we can discern the inherent 'logic' by which a type is constituted can serve the investigation.

sexuality; in fact, in many instances evolution would favor promiscuity, at least for males.'[57] Sexual pleasure functions in a multitude of ways. Sexual pleasure can reinforce pair-bonded reproduction, but there is abundant evidence that sexual pleasure also functions to prevent hostility, the easing of social tensions,[58] as well as increasing the likelihood of insemination of the female by habituating *promiscuous* sexual relations.[59] It would seem questionable that the focus of personal and sexual love is functionally in agreement.

We may capture the contrast between the constitution of the personally and the sexually loved through distinctions we have drawn. That personal love is 'hyper-subjective' and that sexual love is fascinated with 'sexual parts' does not give us reason to doubt *tout court* that personal and sexual love conflict. We'd expect, however, that a fair model of how personal and sexual love interrelate would be analogous to the way that the mappings of sensory fields and motor projects interrelate. Recall Merleau-Ponty declared that we never think enough about how the mappings of the visual field and motor project interrelate.[60] The same follows for the relation between the personally and sexually loved.

Consider the famous Aristotelian puzzle: 'Why is it that an object which is held between two crossed fingers appears to be two?'[61] Try closing your eyes, then crossing your right and left index fingers and placing them on a table surface. After a moment of shifting to tactile apprehension, it will seem as if there are two different surfaces under your fingertips. But with the eyes open again and the gaze upon table's surface or with the surface touched by the two fingers, now uncrossed, it is difficult, if not impossible, to imagine that one is touching two different objects. Why? As Merleau-Ponty well understood, the habitual motor projects of the two crossed fingers make the two objects plausible. With the eyes closed, the field of motor projects overturns the visual field. But once the eyes are open, vision again dominates the 'sense' of the perceptual given, returning us to the apprehension of a single table surface.

In the case of the co-alignment of the personally and sexually loved, it would seem the situation is analogous. Just as our everyday use of objects conspires to unify the several sensory fields, our activities with the person loved conspire to unify the differences between the constitution of the individual who is personally and sexually loved. Obviously, there are very good reasons to enjoy in one person the two manners of loving. If the beloved is a spouse, and parent of one's children, one saves the partner from jealousy, distrust and resentment. One likely preserves

---

57 Paul R. Abramson and Steven D. Pinkerton, *With Pleasure; Thoughts on the Nature of Human Sexuality* (Oxford: 2002), p. 42.

58 Abramson and Pinkerton, Ibid., p. 44.

59 S.B. Hrdy, 'The primate origins of human sexuality', in R. Belling and G. Stevens (eds), *The Evolution of Sex* (San Francisco, 1988).

60 'This extraordinary overlapping [the visual field and the mapping of motor projects], which we never think about sufficiently, forbids us to think of vision as an operation of thought that would set up before the mind a picture or a representation of the world, a world of immanence and of ideality.' Cited above. Maurice Merleau-Ponty, 'Eye and Mind', in *The Primacy of Perception* (Evanston, IL, 1964), p. 162.

61 Aristotle, *Problems*, Book XXXV, 'Problems Connected with the Effects of Touch', #10, 965a36.

the integrity of family life. The happy co-alignment of sexual love and personal love in one person, even apart from the felicity of the union, is complemented as well by social, economic and legal constraints.

Nonetheless, as we have considered, personal love and sexual love entail an alteration in the way in which the person loved is conceived and, so typically, the move from personal love to sexual love involves, at least, an ephemeral shift in perspective of the loved person. In the figurative language of the Apuleian fable, sexual love, as contrasted with personal love, involves a mask. The symbol of the mask is apt, not just because it is the mask of the stubborn pack-animal,[62] but simply because it is a mask. The mask may become a permanent acquisition. But as the sexual interests increase in adolescence or decrease with senescence, lovers easily find that the mask fits imperfectly. As such the mask of sexual love may be contrasted with the capacity of personal love to discern, as we discussed in the previous part, the 'truth' of the beloved. The happy soul who has a requited profound personal *and* sexual love with his or her spouse or partner knows that he or she has the incomparable felicity of having a lover *and* a best friend in one person, which is all the more gratifying, as they adduce different lovable aspects of the beloved person. Nonetheless, the constitution of the sexually and personally loved differ in spatial and temporal aspects as well as in manners of self-revealing and self-concealment.

An Extreme Conflict Between Personal and Sexual Love: The Incest Taboo

Once we open the door to understanding the differences in amorous projects, we also usher in how sexual love and parent/child love, as a very special type of personal love, conflict violently.

Anthropologists may agree on few features of cross-societal practices, but the incest taboo is an exception. By precept if not by practice, parent/child incest, and

---

62 The donkey is a fitting comic mask for lust and crazed eros for many reasons. Perhaps most well known is Shakespeare's use of it, *A Midsummer-Night's Dream* from *The Complete Works of* (London, 1980), IV.1.77–78. In the thrall of sexual passion, the envelopment by sexual parts, is in a sense, 'asinine'. The pack animal is known for its thick-headedness and stubborn repetitiveness. Like sexual passion, it stubbornly becomes enthralled with vaginas, penises, breasts, lips, and limbs, which seem made for lovemaking. But as Robert Graves remarks in his introduction to the *The Golden Ass*, the jackass, as a matter of fact, is really far more sagacious than the horse. Apuleius, *The Transformation of Lucius Otherwise Known as the Golden Ass* (New York, 1951), p. xv. And indeed, sexual love may be far more sagacious than we would acknowledge. Consider Johnston's and Franklin's study which would indicate that, judging from the women's faces that men find the most attractive, the ages of maximal sexual attraction matches the age of maximal female fertility. V.S. Johnston and M. Franklin, 'Is beauty in the eye of the beholder?' *Ethology and Sociobiology*, 14 (1993): 183–99.

in particular mother/son incest, is a universal human taboo.[63] Durkheim,[64] Morgan,[65] Frazer,[66] Tyler,[67] Freud,[68] Lévi-Strauss,[69] and Karl Marx,[70] to cite some particularly influential thinkers, all offer accounts for the proscription. Generally, explanations for the taboo sort out into three types of functional explanations. One account focuses on the deleterious genetic effects upon children of incestuous unions. The taboo inhibits negative recessive genes from accumulating in successive generations. An accumulation of the results of studies by Adams and Neel,[71] Carter,[72] Baird and McGillivray,[73] and Seemanová[74] indicates that a very high mean rate (31.4 percent) of children of incestuous unions, in excess of a reference group, have severe physical and mental abnormalities. According to the second functional explanation, the incest

---

63   It is generally accepted among anthropologists that the incest taboo is universal in human societies. See William Arens, 'incest taboos', in *The Dictionary of Anthropology* (Oxford, 1997), pp. 257–9. There is, however, a curious exception among divinities. In Greek mythology, for example, Hera is Zeus' sister as well as his wife. P.B. Adamson, in 'Consanguineous Marriages in the Ancient World', details the status of consanguineous marriages in ancient Egyptian, ancient Near Eastern, ancient Middle Eastern and ancient Greek societies: 'The concept of divine incest most probably originated in southern Mesopotamia not later than the beginning of the third millennium BC and probably considerably earlier. Sumerian traders then brought it to Egypt in predynastic times. It was accepted by the rulers of Upper and Lower Egypt and finally by the majority of the indigenous population.' (P.B. Adamson, 'Consanguineous Marriages in the Ancient World', *Folklore*, 93, I (1982): 89. Incest was normalized among Egyptian pharaohs from the IVth dynasty until Roman power overthrew the dynasty of the Ptolemies at the end of the 1st century BC. But as Adamson observes, in all such ancient societies incest was not permitted among the ordinary people, but tolerated, and often found suitable, among rulers, *provided that they were conceived of as divine*. If a necessary condition of the taboo is that parent/child love and sexual love are 'alien' pleasures in the Aristotelian sense, as proposed here, not surprisingly, the deification of rulers would count as an exception inasmuch as the parenting of divinities, given their supernatural status, in the minds of their credulous followers, does not require ordinary human nurturance.

64   Emile Durkheim, *Incest: the Nature and Origin of the Taboo* (New York, 1962); [La Prohibition de l'incest et ses origines, *l'Année Sociologique*, 1897].

65   Lewis Henry Morgan, *Ancient Society* (New York, 1877).

66   James Frazer, *Totemism and Exogamy* (London, 1910).

67   Edward Burnett Tyler, 'On a method of investigating the development of institutions', *Journal of the Royal Anthropological Institute*, 18 (1889): 245–69.

68   Sigmund Freud, *Totem and Taboo: resemblances between the psychic lives of savages and neurotics* (New York, 1918) [Totem and Tabu, Leipzig, 1913].

69   Claude Lévi-Strauss, *The elementary structures of kinship* (Boston, MA, 1969); [Les structures élémentaires de la parenté, Paris, 1949].

70   Friedrich Engels, *The Origin of the Family, Private Property and the State* (Chicago, IL, 1920); [Ursprung der Familie, des Privateigentums und des Staats, Zurich, 1884].

71   M.S. Adams and J.V. Neel, 'Children of Incest', *Pediatrics*, 40, (1967): 55–62.

72   C.O. Carter, 'Risk to offspring of incest', *Lancet*, 1 (1967): 436.

73   P.A. Baird and B. McGillivray, 'Children of Incest', *Journal of Pediatrics*, 101 (1982): 854–7.

74   E. Seemanová, 'A study of children of incestuous marriages', *Human Heredity*, 21 (1971): 108–28.

taboo minimizes sexual competition within the nuclear family. According to a third account, the taboo produces links with social groups outside the nuclear family and thereby creates social networks bonded by family ties.

There is little question that some or all of these functions are promoted by the incest taboo. But a problem, long recognized by anthropologists, lies in the fact that family-bonds, if established in childhood, make erotic feelings towards close kin repugnant since family ties seem to cancel out or nullify the emotional life of erotic passion, regardless of whether or not there are *de facto* blood ties. There is considerable evidence in support of the view that family ties, among children outside the same natal group, nullify erotic feelings after the children have become sexually mature.

Wolf and Huang,[75] for example, found in their study of *sim pua*, a traditional form of Chinese marriage, that non-blood related children who grow up in the same family have less sexual interest in each other when reaching maturity. In *sim pua*, a family adopts a non-kinship infant female into a household to be raised, ultimately, for marriage with an infant son. Wolf and Huang found that these children, upon reaching sexual maturity, are reticent to marry. If they do marry, *sim pua* marriages result in a higher divorce and lower fertility rate as compared to arranged marriages between strangers. Studies of non-blood related children, in other parts of the globe, seem to confirm the same result. Joseph Shepher,[76] for example, documented the absence of marriage and sexual liaisons between children who lived together in the same *kibbutz*, despite the fact that they were encouraged to marry. Studies of McCabe[77] and Walter[78] demonstrated, respectively, in a study of 93 marriages in Lebanon and 275 marriages in Morocco, that early childhood association inhibits sexual attraction. It would seem that among Arabs, as among Israelis and Chinese, that children when reaching adulthood resist mating with those with whom they have grown up as members of their families. In fact, an exclusion between early family bonding and sexual attraction appears also in nonhuman primates. Many studies of nonhuman primates support the thesis that animals of various primate species prefer to find sexual partners outside their natal group.[79]

How then can such an exclusion between family-like bonds established in childhood and sexuality be explained?[80]

---

75 A. Wolf and C.S. Huang, *Marriage and Adoption in China, 1845-1945* (Stanford, CA, 1980).

76 J. Shepher, *Incest* (New York, 1983).

77 J. McCabe, 'FBD marriage: Further support for the Westermarck hypothesis of incest taboo?' *American Anthropologist*, 85 (1983): 50–69.

78 A. Walter, 'The evolutionary psychology of mate selection in Morocco', *Human Nature*, 8 (1997): 113–37.

79 A. Maryanski and J. Turner, *The Social Cage* (Stanford, CA, 1992).

80 I have argued elsewhere that an explanation of the incest taboo requires the inclusion of a condition that accounts for why the taboo is particularly human, or at least human and primatial. Peter Hadreas, 'Phenomenology and the Incest Taboo', *Journal of Phenomenological Psychology*, 33, 2 (2002): 203–22. The argument offered here in its essential points is the same as the argument offered before, except here I rely on Aristotle's principle: 'alien pleasures amount to virtual pains.' *Nicomachean Ethics*, X.5, 1175b16–17. In the earlier article, I relied

An adequate specification of the *sufficient conditions* for the universality of the incest taboo requires a causal condition that would address why the taboo is peculiarly *human*, or perhaps, peculiarly human and *primatial*.[81] A phenomenological understanding of the two 'thematic interests'[82] that are necessary conditions of biological survival, that is, reproduction and the nurturance of infants through childhood, reveals how the taboo is peculiarly *human*, provided both conditions are conceived as thematic interests in the phenomenological sense, and as such subject to a 'canceling out' of opposing 'meanings'.[83]

Literary works that depend on *the belief* that an incestuous union occurred regardless of whether or not incest occurred, *as a matter of fact*, underscore that the taboo relies on an intentive conflict. For example, in John Dryden's and Nathaniel Lee's 1769 adaptation of *Oedipus Tyrannos*, Oedipus sleepwalks and then returns to bed with Jocasta where he admits to incestuous dreams. But the incestuous dreams Oedipus confesses are not with his actual mother, Jocasta, with whom he, as a matter of fact, is having sexual relations, but with Merope, the woman who raised him and whom he believes to be his mother. For such a twist in the classic Sophoclean version of the Oedipus story to evoke horror, the audience is called on to recognize that the *belief*, and not the *fact*, of a parent/child incest evokes the taboo. Even the Sophoclean version of *Oedipus Tyrannos* relies on the presumption that Oedipus,

---

on Husserl's principle that the stronger intentive meaning, if duly inconsistent with a weaker intentive meaning, will 'cancel out' or 'explode' the weaker significance.

81 Maryanski and Turner, Ibid.

82 I am using the terms 'theme' and 'thematic' in keeping with the later usage Husserl assigns to the terms. In earlier writings, 'themes' are sequences of acts of consciousness, in which the Ego 'seizes upon' or 'takes hold of' an intentional object. In Husserl's language, it [the Ego] '"*still keeps*" in grip what it just had in its grip: seizing upon the new thematic Object, or rather seizing upon the new member of the total theme as primary theme ...' Husserl, *Ideas, First Book*, §122, p. 291.

In later writings, Husserl broadens the usage of 'theme' and 'thematic' to indicate an ongoing focal theoretical, axiological, or practical interest. Cf. Husserl, *Phenomenological Psychology*, p. 112. Husserl, in fact, specifies the later use of 'theme' in the marginal note to the section of *Ideas I*, §122, where he discusses, the *theme*: 'Here I do not use the headings of theme and thematic consciousness in the particular use of my other investigations. Likewise the term "thematic" can be understood in still other ways. Theme can also be interpreted in relation to "theoretical interest".' Husserl, *Ideas*, First Book, p. 291.

83 Husserl variously returns to such terms as 'annulment', 'nullification' or 'canceling out' to describe how the misperception becomes corrected. For Husserl's description of the 'cancellation' (*Durchstreichung*) and 'exploding' (*Explodieren*) of one intentive meaning by another see, for example, *Ideas I*, §§106, 138, 151. Husserl further indicates that this 'canceling out' of a misperception has an analogue in the case of values and plans of action. In fact, as he states, it applies to every object of 'positional consciousness'. This would apply then as well to the practical and affective intentionalities which make up the 'thematic interests' of sexual and parent/child love. Cf. Husserl, *Experience and Judgment*, p. 90: 'What holds in the analysis of the example of external perception holds in analogous manner for every other intending, object-positioning consciousness (positional consciousness) and for its objectivities.'

as a riddle-solver, is destined to unravel the inconsistencies of his childhood, and finally to confront, and come to believe, the circumstances of his birth.

Comedic presentations of the incest taboo, as for example between Figaro and Marcellina in *The Marriage of Figaro*, also rely on *the belief* that incest exists, or might exist, for its proscription. Since the repugnance of incest arises from intentional relations that conflict with one other, the taboo appears even in imagination. Phaedra, after all, never actually has sexual relations with her stepson, Hippolytus. The tragedy is propelled by the mere prospect of their incest as well as Theseus' false belief that incestuous relations occurred.

The incest taboo is a peculiar feature of *human* conduct, since, as human beings, we are particularly intentive animals. Personal love and sexual love become intensely at cross-purposes in the special case of personal love that is between parents and children. First, consider the personal love for children versus sexual love from the point of view of a child's development. Parenting is occupied with the infant's and child's long-term development. The father and mother, as father and mother, and the same would apply to the single parent, are expected to support the development and maturation of the child. Their 'project' is ongoing and its temporal horizons extend across the child's development. Further, the parental commitment need not spring solely from parent/child love. If parents tend to be derelict in their parental duties, the force of law and public opinion urges them on. Parenting, then, entails numberless desires, plans, deliberations as well as perceptions and judgments, clustering about the child's maturation. Contrast this ongoing interest in a child's development with the immediate looks, sensuous appearance, manners, and gestures, which are the focus of sexual attraction. Sexual attraction focuses upon sexual parts as integrated through tactile-kinesthetic Wholes. It is, in a sense, 'hyper-partial'. The fascination of sexual love detaches, if not opposes, sexual love from developmental concerns.

There are other powerful conflicts that arise from the collision of parent-child personal love and sexual love. By popular opinion and force of law, if not by natural disposition, family roles are 'obligation-laden'. As Husserl writes in a manuscript dating from 1921, family roles are a main source of moral obligation: 'Every family member is a responsible subject, a subject which, in accordance with the circumscribed and special case, has an "I should" born out of this generality.'[84] Sexual passion, by contrast, detaches one from the obligations of social roles. As we considered in describing the shift in the object of sexual passion, the time-honored way of depicting the contrast between the personal and sexual love is the assuming of a mask, which removes the lover's person, even from her or his self. Coming out of a love trance, Titania confides: 'My Oberon! What visions have I seen! Methought I was enamoured of an ass!'[85] Sexual behavior, at least in the act, frees lovers from the mundane social approval or obloquy that they otherwise confront.

There is another way in which personal love between parents and children and sexual love collide. The contrast between *public* and *private* realms of experience

---

84 Husserl, *Zur Phänomenologie der Intersubjektivität, Zeiter Teil*, Husserliana XIV, p. 180.

85 Shakespeare, *A Midsummer Night's Dream* from *The Complete Works of* (London, 1980), IV.1.77–8.

is done special violence. Parent/child relations are openly, often proudly, discussed, both inside and outside of family circles. This is further enforced by legal constraints. In the US, for example, parents are enjoined to make parent/child relations a matter of public record. But sexual passion recoils from the public world. We have argued that sexual attraction privileges the desire to touch. This is incorporated into the physiognomy of the object of sexual desire. Nudity elicits the desire to touch. As illustrated by Apuleius' tale of Psyche and Cupid, sexual passion is dispelled by the light of day. Sexuality is a private affair,[86] not only because, as is often observed, mating and nesting animals are vulnerable to predators. The sense of touch requires proximity and does not accommodate the sociality that the distant senses provide. Parent/child personal love as a source of social pride, then, further opposes the intimacy of sexual love.

If we assume that sexual love and parent/child love incite 'thematic interests' that are opposed, as these contrasts would suggest, then one interest would 'cancel out' the other in the phenomenological sense. In fact the canceling out of pleasures that arises from lesser conflicting interests has long been noted in the history of philosophy. Aristotle was astute on this issue. He offered the following principle: 'alien' *pleasures*, that is, pleasures that conflict with predominating pleasures, function as virtual *pains*.[87] Students who long for music are *pained* by having to do their geometry instead. Accordingly, parents devoted to the upbringing of their child take pleasure in the child's development, its first steps, its first words, and its progress in school. But these pleasures of parent/child love conflict with sexual pleasures. For the parent, the pleasure of parent-child sexual attraction then, as an 'alien' pleasure, is 'a virtual *pain*', even to the extent that the mere prospect of incest is barely imaginable and horrifying.

The incest taboo counts a special and extreme case in which sexual and personal love conflict. This is not to deny the relevance of the three functional accounts of the incest taboo mentioned at the beginning of this section. It is not contested that the incest prohibition has various *functions: viz.* 1) the prevention of the accumulation of recessive genes; 2) the sustaining of a more peaceful upbringing; and, 3) the fostering of extra-familial social ties. Harmful effects arising from incest have been confirmed statistically. Even so, these functions do not explain why a behavioral avoidance of incest does not appear in species *other than* human beings and, possibly, some primates. After all, the prevention of the accumulation of recessive genes, the securing of maturation and the establishing of non-kinship bonds are useful to other species besides human beings and primates. But, the incest taboo is especially an aspect of *human* behavior. The intentionality of consciousness, by which we may reflect on the objects of our desires, and come face-to-face with their discord, in this special case of personal and sexual love, supplies that condition.

---

86 Anthropologist, Barrington Moore, states: 'it seems safe to posit at least a desire for privacy as a panhuman trait.' Moore details the cross-cultural insistence upon privacy in sexual activities in *Privacy: Studies in Social and Cultural History* (Armonk, NY, 1984).

87 Aristotle, *Nicomachean Ethics*, X.5, 1175b16–17: 'For alien pleasures do pretty much what proper pains do, since activities are destroyed by their proper pains.'

Summary

The logical underpinning of sexual love relies on the relation of wholes to parts. But parts play into sexual love in a way that cannot be fathomed if we make vision the paradigm of perception. Sexual desire obeys the ordering of touch, whereby parts are given *seriatim*, and not, as with vision, all in one glance. With tactility-driven perception, there is a shift in the ordinary relation of parts to wholes. The shift appears in many ways: A genital mapping is reiterated in fashions, make-up and grooming. Nudity, as contrasted with nakedness, appears as a relation of parts where some remain hidden, but promise delight through uncovering. There is also a temporality associated with sexual allure that obeys the inter-sensoriality organized by touch. It makes the repetition of the sexual act unlike the repeated seeing of a vista, however delightful. The sexual act is articulated through a touch-driven 'give and take', that forestalls identifications between repeated sexual acts, however similar the two acts might be from an abstract point of view.

Husserl's treatise in *Logical Investigations* titled 'On the Theory of Wholes and Parts' illumines how there can be tactile-kinesthetic wholes that are unified by pervasive 'moments', such as the very 'boundaries' of the sexual parts. In tactile terms, this means that the sexual act is made whole by the repeated inter-tactility of copulation, or indeed by any repeated inter-active sensing generated by touching and touched. And, given the pleasure that arises from such an act, sexual love opens onto a world of tactile-kinesthetic unions. The conviction that such a union will be denied can only result in a powerful severance from the prospect of intense pleasure and union that is poorly expressed symbolically as 'castration fear'. In fact the dreaded severance applies to any sexual part, male or female, so long as the coupling of sexual parts in a touching/touched interaction is at issue.

Sexual love contrasts with personal love. Even with cases of felicitous coexistence, for example, a spouse or partner who is both a lover and a best friend, they draw out different aspects of the beloved person. Further, with parent-child personal love, the conflict between the personal and the sexual becomes violent enough, that the merely imagined coincidence of the two is intolerable. This conflict of different amorous projects shows that incest taboo has, among its various causes, one that is *intentive*. As such, it supplies the cause for why the incest taboo is both a universal and a peculiarly *human* phenomenon.

Chapter 3

Hatred

and Hatred ceaselessly raging,
sister and comrade of murderous Ares,
at first she rears her head only a little, but then,
planting her crest in heaven, she strides upon the earth.

(Homer, *The Iliad*, IV, 440–44)

After such knowledge, what forgiveness? Think now
History has many cunning passages, contrived corridors
And issues, deceives with whispering ambitions,
Guides us by vanities. Think now
She gives when our attention is distracted
And what she gives, gives with such supple confusions
That the giving famishes the craving. Gives too late
What's not believed in, or is still believed,
In memory only, reconsidered passion. Gives too soon
Into weak hands, what's thought can be dispensed with
Till the refusal propagates a fear.

(T.S. Eliot, *Gerontion*, from *The Complete Poems and Plays*)

Several types of hatred are identified in this part. As we'll consider, with all types of hatred two conditions prevail. First the hater has ill-will for the hated. We'll refer to this condition of hatred as a 'principle of harm or ill-will.' Second, in all types of hatred there is a wholesale shifting of blame to the hated individual or group. We'll call this second principle the 'principle of blame' or 'the extra-vituperative principle'.

But although these two features of hatred, ill-will and blame, are well known, what is less recognized is that the different types of hatred, in a multitude of ways, manifest the logical properties of generality and logical exclusivity.

The especially virulent and destructive form of hatred we'll consider in this section takes generalization and logical exclusivity to a limit, and as such, arrives at a kind of perfection of hatred. When teenagers Eric Harris and Dylan Klebold opened fire at Columbine High School on 20 April 1999, killing thirteen people, their action may have appeared to be unfocused. But their violence expressed a limiting case of hatred. Klebold says on one of the video-tapes that he and Harris left as explanation of their motivation: 'N---rs, spics, Jews, gays, f---ing whites…I hope we kill two hundred and fifty of you.'[1] In fact Harris and Klebold had taken the generalization of the hated to the level of a necessary and essential generality.

---

1 Nancy Gibbs and Timothy Roche, 'The Columbine Tapes', *Time* (20 December 1999): 42.

Further, their hatred unfolded to maximal volitional expression of an 'exclusive *or*'. The 'us-them' opposition had progressed to the degree that the co-existence of Harris and Klebold and their classmates was impossible. These claims, of course, require considerable explanation, which will be the goal of this chapter.

Hatred in General is a 'Passion'

Philosophers, biologists and psychologists from Kant[2] and Darwin[3] to Gordon Allport,[4] have separated states such as hatred, envy, and revenge from emotions, such as shame, fear and anger. The former are habitual and may proceed impassively with little, if any, physiognomic expression and the latter come and go and are readily apparent in bodily expression.

---

2   Kant drew the distinction in the *Critique of Judgment*: 'There is a specific distinction between emotions (*Affekten*) and passions (*Leidenschaften*) … Emotions are impetuous and irresponsible; passions are abiding and deliberate. Thus resentment (*Unwille*), in the form of anger, is an emotion: but in the form of hatred (vindictiveness) it is a passion.' Kant offers this distinction in a footnote to 'General Remark upon the Exposition of Aesthetic Reflective Judgments'. Kant, *The Critique of Judgement* (Chicago, 1952), p. 508, [my trans.] The German text without ellipsis: [Affekten sind von Leidenschaften spezifisch unterschieden. Jene beziehen sich bloß auf das Gefühl; diese gehören dem Begehrungsvermögen an, und sind Neigungen, welche alle Bestimmbarkeit der Willkür durch Grundsätze erschweren oder unmöglich machen. Jene sind stürmisch und unvorsätzlich, diese anhaltend und überlegt: so ist der Unwille, als Zorn, ein Affekt; aber als Haß (Rachgier) eine Leidenschaft.] Kant also elaborates the distinction in *Anthropologie in pragmatischer Hinsicht*. There he states: 'Emotion is a surprise through sensation, whereby the composure of mind (*animus sui compos*) is suspended.' By contrast, he says of passions: 'Since the passions can be coupled with the calmest reflection, one can easily see that they must neither be rash like the emotions, nor stormy and transitory; instead they must take roots gradually and even be able to coexist with reason.' Kant, *Anthropology from a Pragmatic Point of View* (Carbondale, IL, 1978), §74, p. 156. Kant stresses that the passions do the greater damage to clarity of mind, and to rationality. With emotions Kant writes, the freedom of the mind is merely 'impeded,' [*gehemmt*]. But in the case of passions, the freedom of the mind is 'annulled' [*aufgehoben wird*]. Kant, *The Critique of Judgment*, p. 508.

3   'A man may have his heart filled with the blackest hatred or suspicion, or be corroded with envy or jealousy; but as these feelings do not at once lead to action, and as they commonly last for some time, there are not shown by any outward sign, excepting that a man in this state assuredly does not appear cheerful or good-tempered.' Charles Darwin, *The Expression of the Emotions in Man and Animals* (Oxford, 1998), p. 83.

4   Gordon Allport in *The Nature of Prejudice* distinguishes between hatred as a passion, and emotions such as anger and fear. 'Since it [hatred] is composed of habitual bitter feeling and accusatory thought, it constitutes a stubborn structure in the mental-emotional life of the individual.' Gordon W. Allport, *The Nature of Prejudice* (Garden City, NY, 1958), p. 341. Willard Gaylin in his recent study of hatred, *Hatred: The Psychological Descent into Violence*, also stresses the distinction. 'Hatred is more than an emotion. It is also a psychological condition; a disorder of perception; a form of quasi-delusional thinking.' Willard Gaylin, *Hatred: The Psychological Descent into Violence* (New York, 2003), p. 29.

Saying that hatred is a passion, and thereby 'abiding and deliberate', as Kant understood, of course does not mean that it cannot flair up into violent emotional expression that targets the killing of individuals because they are a member of a hated group.

A particularly horrific stage in the Serbian program of ethnic cleansing took place in the Muslim UN established 'safe zone' village of Srebrenica in the summer of 1995. Serb forces shelled, then overran the town, which had been an enclave for Muslim Bosnians. Non-local Serbian army forces, along with local troops and militias, separated the civilian men from the women and children and, according to Red Cross files, executed 6,546 unarmed civilians, nearly all men.[5] The manner of execution indicates that the killings were well organized and proceeded, so it would seem, coolly without rage. The captives were, for example, methodically told to remove their shoes. Their executioners understood from four years of war that stripping bodies of any personal items of clothing made the bodies less identifiable.[6] Further, this largest European atrocity since World War II was surely abetted by non-enlisted Serbian civilians. Honig and Both in their study of the Srebrenica massacre pose the question: 'Why did the Bosnian Serbs kill the [Muslim] men of Srebrenica in cold blood?' They offer the response that non-civilian Serbs had come to share in the project of 'ethnic cleansing' promulgated by Slobodan Milosevic. As Honig and Both bluntly state: 'Muslim men posed a pointed threat to the Serbs, who were educated in the traditions of a people's war and who aimed to create an ethnically pure Serb territory.'[7]

As the history of such atrocities attests, the expression of hatred can be anything but nonviolent. But such extreme expressions of ethnic violence also show that hatred is different from anger. Aristotle already had contrasted anger with hatred. The angry person wishes that the subject of his ire should suffer; the hateful person wishes that the hated person should perish. And indeed the perpetrators of the Srebrenica massacre endeavored to annihilate the hated group. Aristotle had also noted that angry people can feel compassion for the subjects of their ire, those who hate do not.[8] Accordingly, the civilian Serbian population that abetted the massacre, apparently, proceeded with impunity. Clearly, hatred may explode into violence. Still it counts as a form of passion, in that it is abiding and deliberate. And as we shall see, especially in these most unbounded collective expressions of hatred, it manifests distinct logical structures.

---

5   Jan Willem Honig and Norbert Both, *Srebrenica: Record of a War Crime* (New York, 1997), p. 65.

6   Honig and Both, Ibid., 178.

7   Honig and Both, Ibid., 177.

8   The passage in question is from the *Rhetoric* and runs: 'Anger is always concerned with particular cases, for example, with Callias or Socrates, but hatred is concerned with classes; for instance, every one hates a thief or slanderer. Anger is curable in time, but hatred is not; the aim of anger is pain, but the aim of hatred is evil; ... And anger is accompanied with pain, but hatred is not accompanied with pain; for he who is angry suffers pain, but he who hates does not. And, many of those who become angry feel compassion, but none of those who hate, for the former wishes that the focus of his anger should suffer, the latter, that he should perish.' Aristotle, *Rhetoric*, II.4, 1382a5–15, [my trans].

Marginal Types of Hatred

Let us set aside two marginal types of hatred. First, *trivial dislike*. Children, for example, may say they hate broccoli or persons may drop conversationally that they hate macramé or the motets of Josquin Després. This feigned type of hatred may function rhetorically as hyperbole. It underscores personal preferences. But it is not a matter of passionate involvement. With trivial dislike, neither the principle of ill-will nor extra-vituperation apply. It is often a mere pose of hatred.

Another marginal, but clearly more intense, guise of hatred is *phobic hatred*. Hating snakes, toads, heights, water, or the number '13' may be long-standing and focused upon a class of objects. People are remarkably diverse in how they focus their irrational antipathies. But phobic antipathy is different from hatred proper. The person who hates snakes or toads may assume a hateful attitude toward the fearful object to distance the irrational fear. As such, it qualifies as an assimilation of hatred proper. But, it remains largely a matter of fear and not hatred. And there is only a partial transfer of the more central circumstances of hatred. Unlike hatred proper, there need not be ill-will for its object. The arachnophobe may have ill-will for spiders. But the claustrophobe can hardly have ill-will for closed spaces, nor the acrophobe for heights. The claustrophobe or acrophobe is happy to avoid enclosed spaces or heights. Eliminating them is out of the question.

Individual-Focused Hatred – A Classic Illustration

Individual-focused hatred introduces the domain of hatred proper.[9] Here appear the two principles common to all types of genuine hatred. So the classical exemplar of unrestrained hate is Euripides' Medea, whose nurse says, 'with love for Jason had been thrilled throughout her soul,'[10] then exclaims, 'now everything is hatred'.[11] She declares that Jason is 'most hateful to the gods, to me and to all of mankind'.[12] As the tragedy unfolds, we find Medea, betrayed by Jason, about to marry a Corinthian princess. Medea, who saved Jason from various mythical monsters, killing some of her kinspeople in the process, will be banned from Corinth. She has one day to pack up. There is little question that the 'principle of ill-will' is relevant. Medea has abounding ill-will for Jason: 'May I see him at last, him and his bride, in these halls, shattered in ruin!'[13] Medea engineers as painful and destructive state of affairs for Jason as she can muster. There is also in abundance the principle of extra-

---

9 Hume, for example, immediately rules out what we have called here 'marginal' instances, of hatred, that is, trivial dislike and phobic hatred, declaring, 'Our love and hatred are always directed to some sensible being external to us ...' David Hume, *A Treatise of Human Nature* (Oxford, 1888), Part II, § i, p. 329.

10 Euripides, 'Medea', *Euripides in four volumes* (Cambridge, MA, 1912), 8. [my trans.].

11 Euripides, Ibid., 16.

12 Euripides, Ibid., 467–8.

13 Euripides, Ibid., 163–4.

vituperation. Medea blames Jason for her infanticide. As she states: 'Children, you are destroyed by your own father's lust.'[14]

As the case of Medea illustrates, scorn, betrayal, and injustice at the hands of another person are typical sources of individual-focused hatred. There also may follow intense violence. Statistical evidence indicates that police, responding to violent or potentially violent domestic disputes, will more likely be injured or killed by an enraged husband, wife or family relative, than by armed criminals.[15] But even so, individual-focused hatred is significantly different from group-focused, violent hatred. As recognized even by such ancient writers as Plutarch,[16] individual hatred may be remedied, even eliminated, if the betrayal is disproved or the injustice adequately repaired. If Jason abandoned his plans to opportunistically marry the daughter of the king of Corinth, if he declared his undying love for Medea, and if he then backed it up by leaving with her for some place friendly to Colchian princesses, perhaps Medea would have abandoned some of her hatred. She even might have changed her plans to kill their children and to flay alive his bride-to-be. It is hard to say, of course. But, for our purposes it makes no matter. The point is that, in the case of violent individual-focused hatred, the *de facto* circumstances that prompt the hatred may be addressed. And if they are significantly altered, the hatred may end. Whether the causes involve jealousy, scorn, betrayal or injustice, the circumstances may be shown to be misrepresented, fabricated, altered, sincerely regretted and atoned for by a suitable redress. It is quite different with group hatred, as targeting, for example, racial, ethnic or religious groups. Such targeted types elude the disproof of their allegedly odious attributes.

The Development of Group-Focused Hatred from Individual-Focused Hatred

Max Scheler, in *Ressentiment*, charts the development of hatred from an individual person to a group. As Scheler describes the progression, first there is consciousness of an act, real or imagined, which, allegedly, is a slight, insult or outrage. There is also the focusing upon a physical or moral trait of the hated person that incites the outrage. So, Medea rails against the trait she finds hateful in Jason, his 'shamelessness'.[17] She also generalizes, declaring shamelessness to be the worst of human failings. For Scheler, in order for this individual-focused hatred to progress to group hatred, the expression of revenge must be held in check. And, the insult or outrage cannot altogether disappear from consciousness.[18]

---

14 Euripides, Ibid., 1364.

15 Rush W. Dozier Jr., *Why We Hate* (Chicago, 2002), p. 193.

16 Plutarch, 'Of Envy and Hate', *Moralia* (Cambridge, MA, 1959), 538C, p. 105.

17 Euripides, Ibid., 469–72.

18 Scheler writes in *Ressentiment*: 'First of all there is the repression of the original object of emotion. I hate a certain person or want to take vengeance on him, and I am fully conscious of my reasons – of the act by which he harmed me, of the moral or physical trait which makes him distasteful to me. If I overcome my impulse by active moral energy it does not disappear from consciousness, only its expression is checked by a clear moral judgment.' Max Scheler, *Ressentiment* (Milwaukee, WI, 1998), p. 50.

For a paradigmatic illustration of the development of individual to group hatred, let us continue with classical illustrations. In fact we may turn to the work lodged at the beginning of European literary tradition for a paradigmatic case. Homer's description of Achilles' shift from the specific hatred of Agamemnon to Hector and the Trojan host in general illustrates the pattern.

As readers of the epic poem know, the first word of the *Iliad*, marks its theme, *rage*. But, in fact, Achilles' rage travels. In the journey, Achilles' rage shifts from individual hatred to group-hatred.

The reasons for Achilles' individually-focused hatred of Agamemnon are multiple. They are also typical. There is the dwelling upon unjust treatment,[19] and the shame and humiliation caused by the individual held in odium.[20] There is also the focusing on a character trait that is especially hateful. Achilles, like Medea, identifies Agamemnon's abiding hateful character trait as 'shamelessness'.[21] Already we see the principle of ill-will and extra-vituperation expressed. Achilles hopes for Agamemnon's ruin[22] and heaps the blame for what the Greeks and Trojan's have suffered upon the head of Agamemnon.[23]

As hatred progresses from the individual to group it 'radiates', as Scheler puts it, in all directions to 'any person, relation, object, or situation' connected with the hated individual.[24] So, Achilles' hatred 'radiates' to Agamemnon's extensive bribes.[25] Accordingly, Achilles tells his old family-friend, Phoenix, that he will become hateful if he respects Agamemnon's wishes.[26]

But still individual-focused hatred has not yet settled upon a group. This involves the extension of a logical underpinning that is inchoate in simpler forms of hatred, that is, generalization. The odious trait of an individual shifts to a class that embodies those traits. As Scheler states: '... it turns into a negative attitude toward certain apparent traits and qualities, no matter where or in whom they are found.'[27] And to

---

19 Abiding by Agamemnon's commands, Achilles thinks he has borne the brunt of the fighting, while Agamemnon remains protected behind the lines of battle. Homer, *The Iliad* (Cambridge MA, 1924), IX, 331–4.

20 Agamemnon has abducted Achilles' concubine Briseïs, saying 'so that you [Achilles] will know how better I [Agamemnon] am than you.' Homer, Ibid., I, 185–6 [my trans.].

21 Homer, Ibid., I, 149; IX, 372.

22 Achilles rages against Agamemnon desiring his destruction. 'May he go to ruin without impediment. His wits taken away by Zeus the counselor,' and so on. Homer, Ibid., IX, 376–7.

23 Homer, Ibid., I, 148–60.

24 Scheler writes: 'But if, on the contrary, the impulse is "repressed," it becomes more and more detached from any particular reason and at length even from any particular individual. First it may come to bear on any of my enemy's qualities, activities, or judgments and on any person, relation, object, or situation which is connected with him in any way at all. The impulse "radiates" in all directions.' Scheler, Ibid., p. 50.

25 'Hateful to me are his [Agamemnon's] gifts. They are worthless to me.' Homer, Ibid., IX, 378 [my trans.].

26 Homer, Ibid., IX, 607–15.

27 Scheler's full statement: 'At last it [hatred] may detach itself even from the man who has injured or oppressed me. Then it turns into a negative attitude toward certain apparent

be sure, Achilles generalizes what he finds odious about Agamemnon: 'Hateful to me, even as the gates of Hades, is a man that hides one thing in his mind and says another.'[28]

Scheler's account is doubtless relevant as far as he takes the topic, that is, to the point at which the hater loathes a certain class of persons. The child who's raised by an overbearing father or humiliating mother may grow to hate authoritarian men or blameful women. Scheler rightly charts how hatred generalizes. But Scheler does not take the matter to full-blown monolithic group hatred. And, he leaves out how hatred also takes advantage of opposition. As it progress to group-hatred, in particular, it exploits readily available 'us-them' social antagonisms.

Achilles' hatred for Agamemnon shifts accordingly. Previous to the shift, Achilles had spoken with ample respect and admiration of Hector.[29] The killing of Patroclus provides the occasion for Achilles to overcome the sorry circumstances of his personal hatred of Agamemnon. Hector's outrage, as a matter of fact, involves no personal insult, humiliation, or special injustice. Hector dutifully wages war. He did not know that the man he killed was Patroclus. But Achilles trains his fury towards the bloody destruction of Hector. The 'extra-vituperative' aspect of hatred increases. The litany of emotions and injustices that had been plaguing Achilles disappears as he focuses on Hector. It relieves him of his humiliation.[30] He dispenses with the injustices he has received from Agamemnon. He puts aside his personal hatred for Agamemnon altogether, and seizes upon the opportunity of the ready at hand 'us-them' opposition. Achilles now represents the 'home' folk at large, the Achaean host, which is opposed to the 'alien' folk at large, the Trojans, who are defined in their opposition as 'those who bear ill-will towards us'.[31] Achilles' rage has seized the opportunity of generalized 'us-them' opposition.

Achilles' treatment of Hector's corpse is especially relevant in that it expresses a denial of Hector's individuality. As every reader of the *Iliad* knows, Achilles drags Hector's corpse around the tomb of Patroclus, triumphing in his victory over him.[32] Later, unable to sleep, Achilles drags Hector's corpse around the tomb of Patroclus

---

traits and qualities, no matter where or in whom they are found. Here lies the origin of the well-known modern phenomenon of class hatred.' Scheler, Ibid., pp. 50–1.

28 Homer, Ibid., IX, 312–13.

29 Homer, Ibid., IX, 356. There, for example, Achilles refers to Hector, with whom he then chooses not to fight, as δῖος, variously translated as 'divine', 'worthy', and 'trusty'.

30 Achilles no longer pines over the concubine, Briseïs, whom Agamemnon had denied him. Now Achilles says it would have been better if Briseïs had been slain by Artemis when she was captured. Homer, Ibid., XIX, 56–60.

31 'Until Patroclus met his fatal day, even till then, it pleased me in my heart to spare the Trojans, and many I took alive and sold. But now, there is not one who shall escape death ...' Homer, Ibid., XXI, 100–105 [my trans.]. In so saying, Achilles arrives at a state that we shall later describe as finding in the hated group an identity that is defined in terms of a dedication to destroy the 'home' culture or 'home folk'.

32 Homer, Ibid., XXII, 395–404.

many more times,[33] again face down. Achilles' brutality provokes even the god, Apollo's, reproach.[34]

Aristotle offered an exegesis of Achilles' treatment of Hector's corpse. Aristotle explained that Achilles, legendarily from Thessaly, reenacted the Thessalian custom of dragging the corpses of murderers around the tombs of their victims.[35] So, Achilles, in taking his horrifying revenge, assigns the person, Hector, to a hateful class, that is, the class of murderers. But, he does more. By dragging Hector face down, *he enacts* the defacement, striving to remove the features of Hector's person, his face.

The progression of Achilles' individual-focused hatred to group hatred, although clearly charting the stages of development, falls short of the last stages of fully unfurled violent group-focused hatred. And, here we must dispense with classical illustrations and draw upon a factual case.

The murder of James Byrd Jr. by John William King and two other white men has an awful similarity to the brutal defilement of Hector. But the comparison stops short of the degree of generalization of the hated group and the intractability of 'us-them' enmity. The real hate-crime, in its extreme brutality, received much publicity. On 7 June 1998, John William King and two other white men stopped the forty-nine year old African American, James Byrd Jr., and offered him a ride. Byrd got into their truck. King and his companions beat him senseless. Then King and the two others chained Byrd's ankles together and left him behind their pick-up truck. King dragged Byrd at high speed about three miles. The hate-crime was an expression of fully unfurled group-focused hatred. It represents a further extension of the two principles of hatred mentioned above. The victim, unlike Hector, was not dead upon his defacement. He was not involved in *mano a mano* deadly armed contest. Byrd had no quarrel with his murderers. In the real case of the murder of Byrd, the principle of harm is extended inexorably and monolithically to members of a group. The three perpetrators had ties to the Ku Klux Klan and the Aryan Nation.[36] Their 'home-group' (white Aryan) made the 'alien-group', (blacks, Jews, and so on) *necessarily* party to an 'us-them' opposition. To understand the fully unfolded development of hatred from individual- to group-focused hatred, we'll need to consider more specifically the logic of its progression.

---

33 Homer, Ibid., XXIV, 12–17.

34 Homer, Ibid., XXIV, 46–54; Homer, Ibid., XXIII, 25; XXIV, 18.

35 The fragment, F 166 R, is collected in Aristotle, *The Complete Works of Aristotle* (Princeton, NJ, 1984), p. 2432: 'Why did Achilles go on dragging Hector around the tomb of Patroclus treating the corpse contrary to established custom? There is a solution, Aristotle says, referring to the customs of the time – they were like that, since even today in Thessaly men drag [corpses] around the tombs.' This fragment is filled out by another from Callimachus, #588: 'In old times as now, a Thessalian man drags a murderer around the tomb of his victim' [my trans.]. Callimachus, *Fragmenta*, vol. 1, (*Fragmenta incertae sedis*) (Oxford, 1949).

36 Dozier, *Why We Hate*, p. 29.

An Intimation of the Strange Logic of Group-Focused Hatred

The progress of hatred to violent group-focused hatred involves the development of an increased intension of generality and of an exclusive 'either-or'[37] opposition. The basis for the 'either-or' opposition emerges if we consider the recent, seemingly ludicrous, opposition to a toy for children.

As most every child in the US knows, Pokémon is a game whose characters appear in cartoons, toys, trading cards, comic books, clothing and video games. Introduced by Japan's Nintendo corporation in 1995, Pokémon games and paraphernalia have become a multi-billion dollar industry. In Arab countries, Pokémon became popular among children around 2000, roughly at the same time as the escalation of the Israel-Palestinian *second intifada*. Soon, Japanese embassies in the Middle-East received queries from Middle-Eastern parents and government officials. Does the most popular of Pokémon's characters, 'Pikachu,' mean, 'I am a Jew?' Some questioned whether the word, Pokémon, means: 'There is no God in the universe.' Although admitting that he was personally unfamiliar with the game's fantastical world, Sheik Abdel Monem abu Zent, a former member of the Jordanian parliament, and leading anti-Pokémon activist was quoted as saying:

> It has been proven that this toy is part of a Jewish plan to corrupt the minds of our young generation because it alludes to blasphemous thinking, it mocks our God and our moral values and therefore is extremely dangerous for our youth.[38]

Of course, many in the Arab world found the Pokémon conspiracy theory ludicrous. Nonetheless, *fatwas*, or edicts, were issued in Saudi Arabia, Oman, Qatar, Dubai, Jordan and Egypt declaring that Pokémon was unacceptable to Islam. And, the alleged moral infection spawned by Pokémon did not only spring up in the Middle East. Complaints from US Jewish parents and the Anti-Defamation League led Nintendo to withdraw a card containing an image that vaguely resembled a swastika.[39] Further, a Christian church in Mexico determined the game was unacceptable for Christian children. It insinuated symbols of the demonic.[40]

In fact, the preposterous claim that Pokémon is anti-Islamic, anti-Semitic or anti-Christian reveals one side of the hidden logic of group-targeted hatred. Pokémon, after all, is toy *for children*. In fact, the logic of group-focused, hatred begins to show some of its hidden structure if we consider that 'generational' relations are presumed to be at issue. No less than the transmitting of a tradition that sustains the rationale for the sequence of generations, so it is imagined, is threatened.

---

37 Logicians distinguish between the inclusive 'or' and the exclusive 'or'. The first, for example, is expressed in saying: 'Either you increase your exercise through running or swimming.' With the inclusive '*or*', both of the alternatives may be realized. In the exclusive 'or', however, one alternative precludes the other, for example: 'Either you are in your 20s or you are in your 30s.'

38 Michael Slackman, 'Arabs See Jewish Conspiracy in Pokémon', *Los Angeles Times*, 24 April 2001, pp. A1ff.

39 Dozier, *Why We Hate*, p. 223.

40 Dozier, Ibid., p. 223.

Husserl on the Opposition between 'Homeworlds' and 'Alienworlds' and the Emergence of the Logical Exclusive 'Either-Or' in Group Hatred

As discussed in late manuscripts, Husserl's distinction between home and alien worlds illuminates one side of the foundation of violent group hatred. These doctrines, dating from the last decade of Husserl's life, only recently entered into the mainstay of phenomenological scholarship. Their introduction has been accomplished largely through the groundbreaking work of Husserlian scholar, Anthony J. Steinbock.[41]

Husserl expands the breadth of human subjectivity to include a correlative involvement with a 'home' and an 'alien' world. These worlds follow necessarily upon the acquisition of historical consciousness. What is particularly key in this doctrine is that one cannot acquire a home tradition except in relation to a 'foreign' world. The home tradition delimits the foreign tradition and *vice versa*. The presence of an alien tradition arises with even a minimal or superficial or connection to a 'home' tradition. In the US, celebrating, say, Fourth of July or Thanksgiving, however passingly or superficially, juxtaposes a 'home' world and a 'foreign' world. The fourth of July, as a US tradition, with the playing of anthems, flying of flags, and passing reflection on current US international politics, calls forth some appropriation of US political traditions and introduces some degree of historical consciousness. But, it does so in contrast to an alien tradition. Husserl does not suggest that there need be an 'us' and 'them' opposition between the home and alien world. There is no necessary implication of enmity. (Consider the kind of memorial nod paid at Thanksgiving to the cooperation between early Mayflower colonists and the local indigenous American Indians.) Nonetheless the 'home' and 'alien-world' dichotomy may be exploited by group-focused hatred.

Key to Husserl's notion of a 'home-world' is that it involves a tradition and this in turn requires a manner of 'generativity'. Husserl accordingly, refers to the phenomenology that deals with these matters as 'generative'.[42] In order for a tradition to be maintained it must be renewed, or regenerated. There must be a return to memorials, holidays, formulaic allegiances, perhaps, recitations of prayers, and the traditional teaching of fairy tales, myths, and legends associated with cultural forebears. This does not mean that the 'generativity' of the tradition must be fixed. It is constantly revised, but it cannot proceed without repetition. A core of stories, commemorations, holidays, recited political and religious creeds, and so on, need to be in place. They amount to a generative matrix that sustains and renews a tradition.

---

41 As especially conveyed in Anthony J. Steinbock, *Home and Beyond, Generative Phenomenology after Husserl* (Evanston, IL, 1995).

42 'Generative problems' are distinguished from genetic problems in *Cartesian Meditations*, for example: 'But with that, to be sure, the above-indicated *generative problems* [*generativen Probleme*] of birth and death and the generative nexus of psychophysical being have not been touched.' Husserl, *Cartesian Meditations, An Introduction to Phenomenology* (Den Haag, 1973), p. 142. [My revision of Cairn's translation. Cairns translates 'generativen Probleme' above as 'genetic problems'. It should be 'generative problems'.]

The generativity of a tradition produces a sense of familiarity.[43] It also places people in a history that extends before and after their individual lives. In so doing it makes alien traditions 'copresent'. Since all traditions, 'home' and 'alien', are necessarily woven into the broad expanse of historical time, there is a positive sense of the copresence of people in an alien or foreign world. Husserl sometimes describes the copresence of those in alien worlds as 'mythical',[44] meaning not fictitious, but fantastical. Their history is given as 'there' but not filled out concretely. Husserl underscores that this dichotomy is unavoidable, given the assumption of historical consciousness. Even so, the dichotomy implies no inherent xenophobic hostility, nor even opposition to the foreign world. In fact, the copresence of the 'foreign world' easily sees the 'alien' world as an alluring greener pasture, a utopian realm. The distinction is at the root of cultural distinctions that have a multitude of manners of peaceful and cooperative alliance. But among its worst manifestations, are the distortions brought to it by particularly violent and destructive group hatred.

The 'home' and 'alien-world' distinction, which Husserl uncovered, may be (mis)appropriated and supply the ammunition for the extreme 'either-or' opposition in violent group-focused hatred, as expressed for example in the James Byrd Jr. hate crime. As mentioned, the three perpetrators had ties to the Ku Klux Klan and the Aryan Nation.[45] Their 'home-group' (white Aryan) made the 'alien-groups' (blacks, Jews, and so on) *necessarily* party to an 'us-them' opposition.

An inchoate 'either-or' opposition is already implicit in the relatively less destructive individual-focused hatred. Medea's nurse says that her mistress, 'with

---

43 The formative influence of generative phenomenology surely extends to Dilthey. The two thinkers established a lively relationship in the first decade of the twentieth century that continued up to Dilthey's death in 1911. '... We find similar themes occurring in a generative phenomenology that are peculiar to Dilthey, especially the question of historicity and the historico-spiritual movement of intersubjective accomplishments evaluated in terms of the temporal space [*Zeitraum*] of generations.' Steinbock, *Home and Beyond*, p. 259. There are also comparable notions in *Being and Time*. Heidegger, in *Being and Time*, §§74–6, sees Dasein's capacity for self-historization as based in the repetition of a heritage. On one occasion, Heidegger emphasizes the term 'generation' in explaining Dasein's historicizing. 'Dasein's fateful destiny in and with its "generation" goes to make up the full authentic historizing of Dasein.' Martin Heidegger, *Being and Time* (New York, 1962), p. 436. [Das schicksalhafte Geschick des Daseins in und mit seiner »Generation« macht das volle, eigentliche Geschehen des Daseins aus.] Heidegger, *Sein und Zeit* (Tübingen, 1973), pp. 384–5. But we must note, upon introducing the key term, 'generation', Heidegger also footnotes a work by Dilthey, namely, 'Über das Studium der Geschichte der Wissenschaften vom Menschen, der Gesellschaft und dem Staat' (1875). Even so, however Dilthey's work may have informed both Husserl's and Heidegger's historiology, Dilthey hardly can be made into the source of generative phenomenology. The key Husserlian distinction between homeworld and alienworld emerges from Husserl's own research. As Steinbock observes, 'To the best of my knowledge, neither Dilthey nor Heidegger ever use the expressions "*generativ*" or "*Generativität*", and the theory of constitution as the reconstitution of normatively significant *homeworlds and alienworlds* appear quite unique to Husserl's theory of intersubjectivity.' Steinbock, Ibid., p. 260.

44 Husserl, *Zur Phänomenologie der Intersubjektivität, Dritter Teil*, Husserliana XV, p. 432, n. #2.

45 As recounted in Dozier, *Why We Hate*, p. 29, cited above.

love for Jason had been thrilled throughout her soul.'[46] But given Jason's infidelities, Medea exclaims, 'now all is hatred'.[47] This is an 'either-or' opposition embedded in individual-focused hatred; the hatred is perhaps *post hoc* love, perhaps *propter hoc* love.

Psychiatrist Willard Gaylin offers a point-by-point similarity between love and hatred attachment.[48] Gaylin's comparison is worth quoting in full:

1. Both [hatred and love] are supported by powerful feelings, but both encompass more than feelings in their definitions. They are not simply emotions like rage, fear, guilt, or shame.

2. Both require a passionate attachment that must endure over a significant time.

3. Both require an object of their attachments. In a love relationship, the attachment is generally to an individual and the object is invariably idealized; in hatred the object of fixation is usually to a group and the object population is demonized.

4. Those who love or hate are obsessed with the objects of their emotional states and insist on sharing their lives with them.

Of course love, unlike hate, follows neither the principle of harm nor of extra-vituperation. But Gaylin's comparison does show that, with individually-focused hatred, such as is exemplified by both Medea and Achilles,[49] there is a ground of comparison that makes turning toward hate, at the same time, an implicit falsification of love. The similarities between love and hate, enduring passionate involvement, attachment to the loved or hated, and a pairing with the loved or hated, for better or worse, set up the grounds for making the hatred of an individual, at the same time, a deception or betrayal of possible love. And this implicit opposition between love and hate introduces an affective 'exclusive-*or*' even amid the passionate hatred of an individual.

But if the exclusive '*or*' enters inchoately into the simpler individually-focused hatred, it definitively and explicitly enters into group-focused hatred. Husserl's discovery of the primacy of homeworlds and alienworlds explains how hatred has, readily available, an 'us-them' opposition that it might exploit. In the group-

---

46 Euripides, *Medea*, 8.

47 Euripides, *Medea*, 16.

48 Willard Gaylin, *Hatred: The Psychological Descent into Violence* (New York, 2003), p. 241.

49 As mentioned, Achilles refers to Hector, with whom he then chooses not to fight, as δῖος, Homer, Ibid., IX, 356. There is also perhaps a love/hate ambivalence expressed in Achilles' pursuit of Hector. Achilles chases Hector three times around the citadel of Troy before they come face to face for battle. In the chase, Homer compares Achilles to a hawk and Hector to a trembling dove. In the Greek text the hawk [Achilles] is referred to by a masculine relative pronoun, the dove [Hector] by a feminine relative pronoun. *He* pursues *her*, and she trembles under him while his spirit leaps in excitement at the possibility of catching her. There is a suggestion of erotic love but there is also the sense of a predator about to seize its prey. Homer, Ibid., XXII, 139–42.

hatred that makes the hated group monolithically odious, it is precisely issues of 'generativity' in the Husserlian sense, that unlock the sense of the violent 'us-them' opposition. The anti-Semite, for example, may decry that the Jew propagates Jewish mentality, not through the Jewish home, but rather through some spidery conspiracy promulgated by a Jewish controlled media. The anti-Semites' 'homeland' and traditions, they declare, are endangered.[50] Similarly, white US racists' historical obsession is with their 'whiteness', mistakenly believed to be preserved as 'pure' over generations. Historically, the white racist imagined that 'black blood', in the smallest mixture undermines the purity of the white race. Consider the legislation against miscegenation, statutory in thirty US states until the 1960s Civil Rights Movement. It presumed that 'white' blood is made 'black' through miscegenation. Any child of white and black intermarriage becomes black.[51] The black 'race' becomes the enemy by its threat to undermine the genetics of the home folk. Similarly, the homophobe believes the homosexual desires to convert 'straight' children to homosexuality through 'queering' the young. Again, the reasoning shows its basis in generational issues. For the homophobe, the homosexual threatens to lead the young to cross over to a biological status that precludes generating further generations.

Misogyny, which stereotypes women as prone to evil influence, reveals a similar logic. As Julia Kristeva details in *About Chinese Women*, cultures that violently inferiorize women make the father the symbolic source of family lineage:

> ... this symbolic (and not genetic) paternal authority is considered to be something that distinguishes humans from other animals, and is praised as proof of civilization. Then again, the father embodies at once the function of symbolic authority and the qualities of woman: he is 'the father and the mother', gentle and severe, authoritarian, but not punitive. In the imagination of the culture, the symbolic father dispossesses the mother of her maternity, and thus, her role in the social balance.[52]

Symbolically, the mother is made marginal to family lineage. However she might carry, nurse and rear her children, the father is *the* progenitor. Consequently, the

---

50 This manner of paranoia is rampant in anti-Semitic hate literature. For example, William Pierce writes in *The Turner Diaries*, the book which the Federal Bureau of Investigation saw as providing Timothy McVeigh with a blueprint for the 1995 Oklahoma City bombing: 'If the White nations of the world had not allowed them to become subject to the Jew, to Jewish ideas, to the Jewish spirit, this war [in which Whites kill all non-Whites] would not have been necessary.' Andrew MacDonald, pseudonym for William L. Pierce, *The Turner Diaries* (Fort Lee, NJ, 1996), p. 195.

51 Of the thirty US states that had anti-miscegenation laws that stayed on the books until the civil rights movement, sixteen kept their laws until the Supreme Court overturned them in 1967. For example, Virginia's Racial Integrity Act of 1924 made it 'unlawful for any white person in this state to marry any save a white person, or a person with no other admixture of blood than white and American Indian.' The Virginia statute continued: 'every person in whom there is ascertainable any Negro blood shall be deemed and taken to be a colored person.'

52 Julia Kristeva, *About Chinese Women* (New York, 1986), pp. 73–4. Kristeva is referring here specifically to traditional Chinese Confucianistic patriarchy. But she finds that the father in patriarchal societies becomes *the progenitor* of his family line in Greek, Judaic and Christian traditions as well.

maternal woman's challenging the patriarchal male amounts to making parentless the generational lineage of the home folk.

Because of whatever vestigial traditions the Jew retains, the home tradition of the Anti-Semite is threatened. By whatever color, behavior or mannerisms, or role of leadership, the black, homosexual or woman retains, the perpetuation of the home tradition of the racist, homophobe or misogynist is threatened. It should not be surprising that the individuality of the member of the group is left out of the equation. It is assumed that Jewish traditions, however vestigial, generically will undermine the home folk, that color genetically will sully, that homosexuality as a shadowy mass movement will corrupt, and that femininity, as an historical devolution, will betray. From the point of view of malevolent hatred, it is this inexorable undermining of the home tradition that counts. It is precisely the conviction that one's home culture is being usurped and overrun that marks the shift to group hatred in the sorry hater riddled by recurrent rage, fear, shame, and rejection. Violent group-focused hatred presumes the exclusive 'either-or' as an issue of life and death. The exclusive 'either-or' becomes not only a matter of belief and evaluation, but also of decision-making. Only one of the two disjuncts may be realized. In the mind of the hater, upon the fulcrum of this 'either-or', totters the life and death of the home group. If the hater, who descends into malevolent hatred, has a signature horror film, it would surely be *The Invasion of the Body Snatchers*, in which fearful, but decidedly 'normal', white, English-speaking people, by surreptitious inoculation, become the reproductive 'pods' of aliens.

The Logic of Generalization in Monolithic Group-Focused Hatred

There is a second logical complement to monolithic group-focused hatred. There's also a progressive intensity of generalization. In our introductory classical illustrations we mentioned that Medea and Achilles generalize from hateful traits of Jason and Agamemnon to what they deem the man's most hateful trait in general, 'shamelessness'. But monolithic group hate takes the manner of generalization further.

Husserl's discovery regarding homeworlds and alienworlds, as fundamentally *co-constituted* and *co-dependent*, relates to the manner in which violent group-hatred maximizes the principles of harm and extra-vituperation and thereby, intensifies generalizations. The principles of hatred are maximized by three developments: First, a 'home-type' and an 'alien-type' are drawn from some components of the generational histories of a homeworld/alienworld duality. Second, the home-type and an alien-type are elevated to the status 'home-ideals' and 'alien-counter-ideals', which are supposed to have certain *necessary* attributes. In this second development the generalities shift from *empirical* to *essential*, or in phenomenological terms, to *eidetic*, generalities. And, third, the alien counter-ideal is refashioned to be necessarily occupied with the undermining and destruction of the home-ideal. In effect, conceptual machinery is fabricated, which provides maximal opportunity for the expression of both the principle of harm and the principle of blame or extra-vituperation. Henceforth, if people from the home culture find credible the contrivance of 'home-ideal' and its anti-pode, an alien 'counter-ideal', the conceptual machinery is available to justify the bloody destruction of the alien group.

We may invert Plato's celebrated 'Analogy of the Divided Line', to illustrate the forging of this conceptual machinery. All students of philosophy know that Plato in the *Republic* proposes how people progress towards true knowledge. Along with a line drawn between perceptual and intellectual objects, Plato asks us to draw a second line between imperfect intellectual objects, such as the triangles and squares drawn in the geometer's diagrams, and the intellectual essences themselves, that is, the Forms.

Malevolent group hatred takes on its us-them opposition in this way. First, there are ordinary empirical generalizations, as determined by whatever ethnic, racial or religious distinctions prevail in a culture. And, as Husserl demonstrates *there will be* necessarily home-alien distinctions. Such dichotomies are unavoidable given historical position-taking. The dichotomy so far is innocuous and innocent of any evaluative claims. One's own tradition is simply better known, more familiar, while the alien tradition is not filled out and thereby 'mythical'. But the home/alien distinction is grist for the mill of hatred, especially since hatred is driven by the so-called principle of ill-will or harm. As applied communally, hatred comes to drive an inversion of the development Plato's describes.

As Plato declared, to attain truly compelling knowledge, empirical generalities will not be enough. Far more compelling are objects of knowledge that have *necessary* relations to each other. So one needs to shift from *empirical* generalities to *essential* generalities. In phenomenological terms, we must shift from an empirical generality to a pure *eidos*.[53]

Inverting Plato's celebrated ascent to 'the principle of the good', monolithic group-focused hatred, driven by the principle of harm, descends to an extreme of harmfulness, indeed to a 'perfection' of hatred. The home-group must make its features *necessary* attributes. To be white, male, Christian, Muslim, and so on, must involve features that are *necessarily* superior. And, the idealized 'home folk' must

---

53 Husserl devotes a large part of *Ideas I*, as well as several sections of *Experience and Judgment*, *Analyses Concerning Active and Passive Synthesis*, *Phenomenological Psychology* and *Cartesian Meditations* to essential generalization for which he coins the term, *eidos*. In capsulated form, Husserl explains the necessary and *a priori* nature of the attributes of an *eidos* inasmuch as an *eidos* depends upon a consideration of particular cases, not as actual existing things, nor even on likely existing things, but on particulars as 'mere possibilities'. It is this feature of an essential generality, or *eidos*, which gives the *eidos* 'a necessary structure ... and therewith *necessary laws* which determine what must necessarily belong to an object in order that it be an object of this kind.' Husserl, *Experience and Judgment* (Evanston, 1973), p. 352. In saying any color whatsoever *must* be delimited by a shape, it is not claimed that shape applies to an arbitrary collection of cases. Rather, the *mere possibility* of color is at issue, and, as such, the inference is true of the infinite field of colors; it is therefore necessary. Hence the method of 'seeing' an *eidos* (the central methodological strategy of the eidetic reduction, or *Wesenschau*) as it is discussed throughout the post-transcendental works mentioned above. The method is expressed particularly clearly in *Experience and Judgment*: '... where a pure *eidos* is to be seen as an *a priori*, this seeing has its special methodological form ... namely that indifference with regard to actuality which is generated in variation, whereby what presents itself as actual acquires the character of an arbitrary example, an indifferent point of departure of a series of variations.' Husserl, Ibid., §88, pp. 348–9.

discover an antipode, an alien group, also with *necessarily* inferior features, which are inexorably set upon undermining the home group. Sartre's famous remark, 'If the Jew did not exist, the anti-Semite would invent him,'[54] is right on the mark. The invention involves a hellish ingenuity, perhaps hammered out over centuries, which finally construes various accommodatingly ideal hate targets. Historically, on the short list, at least in the West, have been Jews, Blacks, effeminate homosexuals, and anti-patriarchal women.

Of course this hate list is sketchy and necessarily incomplete. Not only does it leave out targets with less ubiquity, such as the Bosnian Serbs hatred of Bosnian Muslims and *vice versa* in the recent Bosnian War, and so on, but new targets are continually forged. US Americans are recently a hate target to many Middle Eastern peoples. Yet, the long-standing position of Jews, blacks, effeminate homosexuals and competitive, male-challenging women, high on the list of hate targets, reveals how these groups serve four different peculiar, yet chronic, constellations of fears, resentments, and self-doubts of their haters. Indeed, Sartre's dictum might be expanded across the four groups. Not only would the anti-Semite invent the Jew if he didn't exist; but, that impossibility, the pure White, would create a world infiltrated by Blacks; the patriarchal male, who conceives himself as author of the family line, would invent witches and sirens; and the heterosexual, who insists that only male/female sex is legitimate, would invent the sodomite as a categorial outcast.

But why this insidious and especially destructive twist of history that targets groups for convenient hatred? As quoted at the beginning of this chapter, T.S. Eliot writes in *Gerontion*:

History has many cunning passages, contrived corridors
And issues, deceives with whispering ambitions,
Guides us by vanities.

Hatred, we should recall, as a passion, is quite different from emotions. It is abiding and deliberate. As Allport states: 'By its very nature hatred is extra-punitive, which means that the hater is sure that the fault lies in the object of his hate.'[55] The extra-vituperative principle or principle of blame makes hatred useful. Hatred overrides the sorry status of a litany of personal suffering and failures. Hatred overcomes personal mediocrity, fears, shame, and anger. It eclipses these rueful states by obsessively focusing on a cause outside of ourselves. Communal participations seeking targets of group hatred, insidiously, do a manner of social service.

It has often been argued that violent hatred is finally self-destructive, both on a personal and social level. Pumla Gobodo-Madikizela in her recent book, *A Human Being Died that Night*, comments on the testimony and interviews of Apartheid's perpetrators of racial violence. She writes:

---

54 Jean-Paul Sartre, *Anti-Semite and Jew* (New York, 1948), p. 13.
55 Gordon W. Allport, *The Nature of Prejudice* (Garden City, NY, 1958), p. 341.

... violence does not confer what it promises; that is, what seemed at first a moment of honor reclaimed may draw itself out into a life of bondage to aggression as the person moves from one short-lived sense of honor regained to another.[56]

On a personal level, the criminal racist becomes bound in time to his or her violent solution. The habit dulls the racists' 'mission'. The specter of suffering and death it causes so evidently has nothing to do with the 'evil' the racist imagines is at his door. Written large, in terms of people's ethnic and religious hatred, long-term conflict is also self-destructive. Franklin Delano Roosevelt, to mention one leader among many who notes the political truism remarked: 'The value of love will always be stronger than the value of hate ... Any nation or group of nations which employs hatred eventually is torn to pieces by hatred ...'[57]

But Gobodo-Madikizela's and FDR's statements do not address the convenience that such hate targets offer in the short-term. Such targets offer an opportunity for many to temporarily circumvent their fears, self-doubts, and resentments.

Perhaps worse, it would seem to be human foible that the hated assimilate the traits projected upon them by their haters. Members of the targeted group may put on the masks of those stereotypes to become more familiar and acceptable to their oppressors. Sartre in *Anti-Semite and Jew* describes the tragedy of the 'inauthentic Jew': 'He is so afraid of the discoveries the Christians are going to make that he hastens to give them warning, he becomes himself an anti-Semite by impatience and for the sake of others.'[58] Hatred or rejection that US African-American and American-Indians experience may be internalized to self-hatred. This is likely reflected by increases in suicide rates. Especially in urban areas, the suicide rate among black women has increased 80 per cent over the last twenty years. Among American Indians the rate has also risen. In some tribes it is five times the national average.[59]

The Generalization in Violent Group-Focused Hatred is 'Pseudo-Eidetic'

The demonizing of the hated group is '*pseudo-eidetic*'. In maximizing the principles of harm and extra-vituperation, it presents a limiting case of hated. The principle

---

56 Pumla Gobodo-Madikizela, *A Human Being Died That Night* (Boston, 2003), p. 56.

57 Franklin D. Roosevelt, campaign address, Worcester, Mass., 21 October 1936.

58 Sartre, Ibid., p. 103. Perhaps Sartre's remarks appear outdated in that the more than half century history of the state of Israel has enabled at least Israelis to detach themselves from being under the thumb of their oppressors. But stereotypes can be impediments not only by assimilation but also by defiance. Jeffrey Goldberg's recent (2004) article in *The New Yorker*, 'Among the Settlers', provides sorry examples. Goldberg interviews a man born in the Lower East Side of Manhattan who came to Israel 'thirty-six years ago with his wife ...' The man is an Israeli patriot. He fought in the 1973 Yom Kippur War and lost part of an arm and part of his vision in an Egyptian rocket attack. Goldberg suggests that the man imagine himself in the place of a Palestinian. The man interrupts him: '*Stop being Jewish!* Only a Jew could say, "Imagine yourself a Palestinian". Could you imagine a Palestinian imagining himself to be a Jew?' Jeffrey Goldberg, 'Among the Settlers', *The New Yorker*, 31 May 2004, p. 55.

59 (The) *Merck Manual of Diagnosis and Therapy*, 17th edn, (Whitehouse Station, NJ, 1999), §190, 'Suicidal Behavior', p. 1545.

of harm, as we've emphasized, is common to all types of hatred, but it increasingly gains fuller expression by making its target necessarily evil. The phenomenological notion of essence or *eidos* applies to generalizations that extend across the infinity of all *possible* instances of the type. So, color has a pure *eidos*, in that the mere possibility of color entails, in all instances, that whatever has color also has shape. And so White racists hold that Blacks *necessarily* are evolutionary throwbacks and Black racists hold that Whites are necessarily social predators. But the contrived groups are *pseudo*-eidetic since necessary properties cannot be ascribed to a folk or tradition whether 'home' or 'alien'.

The conceptual machinery requisite for demonizing Jews, inferiorizing blacks, discounting homosexuals, and vilifying male-threatening women is not the creation of a single anti-Semite, racist, homophobe or misogynist. Countless, long since dead, now anonymous bearers of ill-will, contributed to the collage of insidious motives, historical fabrications and pseudo-science which frame the alien-group's, alleged, inherent enmity. The supposed evils of the counter-group are hammered out, perhaps over centuries. A destructive social rationale, thereafter lies dormant, to be resuscitated as the will to hate requires. Finally, it succors the personal failures of the home-group, and justifies their plunder, exploitation and marginalization.

D.W. Griffith, in *Birth of a Nation*, portrays a heroic Ku Klux Klan; and Leni Riefenstahl, in *Triumph of the Will*, depicts an ideally heroic Teutonic race. Both cultivate the notion that such ideal 'home' types exist. One may point to the precipitating historical conditions: the humiliations and privations of Southern US White gentry during the US Reconstruction Era, and the humiliations and impoverishment of the German working class following the reparation conditions of 1919 Treaty of Versailles. Nonetheless, the idealization of both the home-group and the alien-group into *eidē* must involve fallacious generalizations. A leading 'racial scientist,' Ludwig Gumplowicz, honestly summed up the state of anthropological research at the end of the nineteenth century:

> The sorry role played by all anthropological measuring of skulls and the like can be appreciated by anyone who has ever tried to gain enlightenment through these studies of mankind's different types. Everything is higgledy-piggledy, and the 'mean' figures and measurements offer no palpable result. What one anthropologist describes as the Germanic type, another deems apposite to the slave type. We find Mongolian types among 'Aryans', and we constantly land in the position of taking 'Aryans' for Semites and vice versa if we abide by anthropological categories.[60]

The idealized 'white race', as contrived in US racism is, of course, a ludicrous fantasy. In the US, ancestry has been the principal criterion of the racial assignment, 'white' and 'black'.[61] The criterion that determines 'blackness' is the mix of European and African descent. But with breath-taking irrationality, it is also maintained that any contribution of African ancestry determines a person to be black. Consequently, what anthropologists refer to as 'the phenotypic range' of a race, that is, the range of

---

60 Cited in G. Lukacs, *The Destruction of Reason* (London, 1980/1962), p. 693.

61 Faye Harrison, 'race', in *The Dictionary of Anthropology* (Oxford, Blackwell, 1998), p. 394.

facial and anatomical features associated with a race, makes any features associated with blacks, however mitigated by an interracial mix, evidence for being wholly black. So American blacks span the complete black-white continuum, making some so-called 'blacks' indistinguishable from so-called 'whites'.

Making the distinction even more irrational is the presumption that European and African descents are mutually exclusive. A presumption so patently false to anyone who has traveled in Southern Mediterranean countries, among other places, that it is barely worth restating.

As for the second 'eidetic' component of malevolent hatred, that the home-type has a necessary relation to a counter-type, we again have a false contrivance, a '*pseudo*-eidetic' relation. Both the home-ideal and the foreign counter-type are concocted so that the Arab, Jew, or US American *can only* undermine the core beliefs of the ideal home-type. Describing the Nazi hatred of Jews, Robert S. Wistrich in 'The Devil, the Jews and Hatred of the 'Other'' states the relation exactingly:

> Nazi racism sought to annihilate Jews not for what they did, for their faith, their customs, or political opinions, but for what they were alleged to be, for their very *being*. The fatality of birth condemned Jews to death, every Jew and all Jews, everywhere and always. They were the counter-type, the paradigmatic 'other' race inassimilable, inclassable [sic], outside the natural hierarchy of races, beyond the human pale.[62]

As Wistrich states, the hatred applied to Jews 'everywhere and always'. Anti-Semitic Nazis had the intellectual stupidity of making a pure *eidetic* (essentialist) claim. The remaining top of the list of hate-group targets is similarly based on necessary and essential opposition. For the White racist, the Black *can only* taint the White's blood; the homosexual *can only* insinuate homosexuality in heterosexual youth; and the aggressive, competitive woman *can only* betray male leadership. The 'home ideal' *is defined* in relation to the 'foreign counter-ideal', and so devised to be *necessarily* devoted to the undermining of the 'home folk'.

But, by the very nature of 'home' and 'foreign' traditions, such necessary relations must be false. Generations are kinds of continuities, typically linked by the emigrations, the migrations, and the pioneering of ancestors and forebears. There is no possibility of obtaining an *eidos* here. Husserl marks the limits placed on determining an *eidos*: 'But the genus can become seen as pure *eidos* only if we do not ask about something real and thus not about actualities, but raise all actuality to pure possibility, to the realm of free optionalness.'[63] As we have considered, for a tradition to be ongoing it must be subject to renewal, and, as such, it must be unfinished. Only in this way can one take one's position in historical time. Contrastingly, an eidetic determination ranges over the whole of the infinity of possible instances of the type. Such an extension can never be obtained from a tradition in progress. Consequently, an eidetic judgment brought to a home or foreign tradition must be '*pseudo*-eidetic.'

---

62 Robert S. Wistrich, 'The Devil, the Jews, and Hatred on the "Other"', in *Demonizing the Other* (Jerusalem, 1999), p. 4.

63 Husserl, *Phenomenological Psychology: Lectures, Summer Semester, 1925* (Den Haag, 1977), §9b, 'Seeing Essences as Genuine Method for Grasping the *A Priori*', p. 56.

A Further Indication of the Two Logical Underpinnings of Hatred:
Removal from the Ladder of Abstraction

The class targeted by violent group hatred embraces an essential generalization, but unlike other generalizations it, strangely, is not subject to the usual subsumption under increasing degrees abstraction, that is, species under genus and lower genera under higher genera.

Husserl, along with philosophers and logicians from Aristotle to Kant, recognized that any particularly unique thing also brings with it an apprehension of its type or kind. Husserl also presumes the traditional view that generalities admit a hierarchical ordering according to increasingly inclusive 'higher' generalities.[64] Husserl, and the phenomenological tradition, in fact, made their own contribution to explicating how concepts apply to individuals.[65]

According to current textbook accounts, the ladder of abstraction may be conceived by the connotation of terms (intensions) or the denotation of terms (extensions).[66] The distinction follows the basic *sense* versus *reference* dichotomy, elemental to theories of meaning since Frege. The connotation of the term, 'animal,' for example,

---

64 In various texts, Husserl explains the on-going production of universals according various levels of generality by degrees of similarity, 'complete', as opposed, to 'partial' and 'mere similarity' and further by 'higher levels' apprehension of similarities built upon lower levels of generalities. *Experience and Judgment* (Evanston, 1973), §84, pp. 334–7.

65 As students of the history of philosophy know, such general types are known as 'universals', a Latin import of καθ᾽ ὅλον, meaning literally, 'according to the whole'.

From as early as his investigations into the constitution of an object in internal time-consciousness, Husserl brought a unique perspective to the connection of particulars to universals. As explained in the *Phenomenology of Internal Time-Consciousness*, Husserl saw the presence of a perceived object, say an apple tree, as resulting from 'retentions', overlayered upon each other. The different perspectives I see of the apple tree, as I walk around it, are seen as *of the same apple tree* because of the structuring of internal time-consciousness. The intense degree of similarity of the tree's 'adumbrations' or perspectives, allows one adumbration to be overlayered upon the next and perceived as coincidental. But if one adumbration should be dissimilar enough, the whole concatenation 'explodes' or is 'canceled', as Husserl puts it. Say, seeing the tree from the back, I notice that it is an empty painted shell, the whole series immediately collapses, retroactively and is 'canceled' in favor of my 'seeing' a discarded piece of theater scenery. In short, Husserl uncovered that, from the beginning, the perception of a particular object is a unity within a multiplicity. The arrival at a universal from particulars in fact simply continues the process of finding unity in multiplicity by various manners of coincidence, uniformity, similarity and pairing. Thus, the universal is not a self-contained ideal object, but the result of an *ongoing process* that arises even in the perception of the particular object. Husserl, *Experience and Judgment*, p. 330: 'Despite all the Platonic turns of phrase by which we have described its relation to the particular, the ideality of the universal must not be understood as if it were a question here of a being-in-itself devoid of reference to any subject. On the contrary, like *all* objectivities of understanding, it refers essentially *to the processes of productive spontaneity* which belong to it correlatively and in which it comes to original givenness. The *being of the universal* in its different levels is essentially a *being-constituted* in these processes.'

66 See for example, Patrick J. Hurley, *A Concise Introduction to Logic*, 5th (ed.), (Belmont, CA, 1994), pp. 81–5.

is made increasingly more specific, in the series, 'mammals', 'equines', 'zebras'. Denotation is about the *de facto* entities named by the term. Consequently, increased denotation involves more and more instances. So the line of terms is reversed. As a matter of fact, zebras *are* equines, equines *are* mammals, and mammals *are* animals. In some cases there are connotations, or intensions, which have no denotations, as with terms that have specific meaning but no existing instances. So, the terms 'fantastical creature', 'flying horse' and 'Pegasus' involve an increasing intension but there is no question of extension, since flying horses do not exist. But whether one is concerned with connotation or denotation, terms, like Chinese boxes, may be organized according to inclusion within more general terms. Finally the denotation of terms may name a single thing, say, this year's Kentucky Derby winner.

But, the classes or types that are targets of malevolent hatred, oddly enough, neither apply to particular individuals *as individuals*, nor do they allow inclusion under broader generalities.

Who is the father or mother of the hated Jew, Arab, American, Black, Chechen, Tutsi, and so on? The question is oddly off point. And it is not simply for lack of interest. The violently hateful individual may seek out the hated person's mother or father to find another member of the class to harm or destroy. The Jew, Arab, Chechen, Hutu, Tutsi, US American, and so on, as targets of class hatred, are also not European, African, Chinese, Indian, or Australian, nor are they human beings. Women, for the rabid misogynist, are not Americans, nor for that matter, Europeans, Christians, Jews, Muslims, or Buddhists, and so on, but viragos or witches whose identity transgresses ethnic and national boundaries. The hated Palestinians, for example, at least to the bigot in the throes of anti-Palestinian odium, are not Israeli. Further, recent expressions of intense Israeli hatred of Palestinians, as is typically true of such hatred, see Palestinians as not even animals. Consider for example, the statement of Effie Eitam, leader of Israel's National Religious Party:[67]

> I [Eitam] don't call these people [Palestinian rebels] animals. These are creatures who came out of the depth of darkness. It is not by chance that the State of Israel got the mission to pave the way for the rest of the world, to militarily get rid of these dark forces ...

How do classes such as Israelis, Palestinians, US Americans, and so on, irrationally depart from the ladder of abstraction, requisite of the sensibility of general terms? Extreme group hatred maximizes the principles of harm and blame. By exploiting not only the logical underpinning of essential generalization, as well as taking advantage of the exclusive '*or*', it removes the class of hated individuals from degrees of generalization. It thrusts the exclusive logical '*or*' onto the linkage between increasingly general terms. Terminology is no longer held in place through the web of increasing generality. No surprise that the hated Jew or Tutsi can only be connoted metaphorically, as 'vermin', or a 'cockroach', and so on. The exclusive '*or*' piques

---

67 As related by Jeffrey Goldberg, Eitam continues: 'We will have to kill them all,' he [Eitam] said. 'I know it's not very diplomatic. I don't mean all the Palestinians, but the ones with evil in their heads. Not only blood on their hands but evil in their heads. They are contaminating the hearts and minds of the next generation of Palestinians.' Jeffrey Goldberg, 'Among the Settlers,' *The New Yorker*, 31 May 2004, p. 59.

the 'us-them' division. Even the logical train of increased intentions is excluded by the logical '*or*'. With intense hatred, the hated figure is either a Palestinian *or* a human being. They cannot be both. And since we must have connotation before we can specify denotation, a removal from a ladder of extension follows in its wake of the severance from the ladder of intension. This reveals the degree to which logical distinctions are exploited and aid in the development of extreme degrees of hatred.

A Paradigm Case of the Logical Underpinnings of Group-Hatred: The 1995 Oklahoma Federal Building Bombing and *The Turner Diaries*

Timothy McVeigh's 1995 bombing of the Federal Building in Oklahoma City, which resulted in the killing of 168 people and the injuring of more than 500, was the worst terrorist act committed in the US before 11 September 2001. It exemplifies extreme group-focused hatred. Obviously McVeigh perpetrated the principle of harm by the blatant disregard of whether his victims were men, women or children. McVeigh's behavior also fits with the extra-vituperative principle or principle of blame. McVeigh never expressed the slightest remorse for his actions.[68]

McVeigh blamed the FBI and the US federal government for his actions. He saw the bombing of the Oklahoma City Federal Building as a retaliation for the 1992 FBI standoff at Ruby Ridge, Idaho, ending in the death of the wife and son of white separatist, Randy Weaver; and, the 1993 fire explosion of Branch Davidian building near Waco, Texas ending in the death of seventy-five members of the religious group. But, in fact, such motives for revenge could have scarcely resulted in the fully unfurled group-hatred of the Oklahoma City Federal Building bombing. Revenge for these acts presumably could be directed at the agents of the Ruby Ridge and Branch Davidian tragedies. With years to plan his revenge, McVeigh could have stalked the FBI personnel who were responsible for the 1992 and 1993 stand-offs. Even if his revenge 'radiated' to US government personnel in general, why the killing of the nineteen children and non-employees, whom McVeigh later characterized as 'collateral damage'?

McVeigh's own testimony was riddled with extreme 'us-them' ideology. McVeigh's account of the development of his plan for the bombing,[69] along with the sorts of explosives, indicate McVeigh was influenced by notorious 'hate literature', in particular *The Turner Diaries*, which he was carrying when captured.

The Turner Diaries convey a paradigmatic expression of fully developed group-hatred. First published in 1978 by the now deceased William L. Pierce, *The Turner Diaries* was published under the pseudonym Andrew Macdonald. In the 1960s Pierce was assistant to George Lincoln Rockwell, founder and head of the American Nazi Party. *The Turner Diaries* is in the form of a journal kept by Earl Turner, described

---

68 Dozier, *Why We Hate*, p. 266.

69 McVeigh said that it was the passage of gun control legislation that led him to begin actively plotting the Oklahoma City bombing. Lou Michel and Dan Herbeck, *American Terrorist: Timothy McVeigh and the Oklahoma City Bombing* (New York, 2001).

Similarly, it is the confiscation of firearms from 'White' households by the Jewish/Black US power coalition that sets off the race war in *The Turner Diaries.*

as a trained electrical engineer growing up in the Los Angeles area. Pierce casts the journal as written in the Old Era, and published on the 100th anniversary of the Great Revolution, during which all non-Whites in the US, and later in Europe and Asia, were killed.[70]

The journal begins by recounting the days in November 1989, when the Zionists and their Black henchmen went door-to-door, confiscating guns. This sets off a race war of Whites against non-Whites. As obsessively detailed, the ensuing guerrilla warfare begins by centering on the bombing of the Washington FBI headquarters. The explosives used in the bombing of the FBI headquarters are elaborately detailed. Pierce specifies 'ammonium nitrate fertilizer[71] ... sensitized with oil and tightly confined'[72] lodged in a truck at the main entrance of the FBI building.[73] This matches the explosives McVeigh used in the Oklahoma City bombing. (Pierce knew explosives. He himself held a PhD in physics, a sad coincidence of rabid hatred and an advanced university degree.)

The 'Revolution' culminates, as far as the US goes, with the detonation of numerous nuclear bombs by the Organization, and in counter-attack by the Soviet Union and the Zionist/Black run US government, in which some 60 million are killed. Along the way, Turner can take pride in the Organization's accomplishment, for example, as he gazes upon field farm workers:

> My most profound impression comes from the fact that every face I saw in the field was White: no Chicanos, no Orientals, no Blacks, no mongrels. The air seems cleaner, the sun brighter, life more joyous. What a wonderful difference this single accomplishment of our revolution has made![74]

This novel exemplifies the extreme manifestation of the logical complements expressed in monolithic group-hatred. First, there is forfeiture of individual identity in favor of identification with a monolithic-group, 'the Organization'. This culminates with the rite of Union. 'These were *real men*, *White* men, men who were now *one* with me in spirit and consciousness as well as in blood.'[75] [Pierce's emphasis.] Second, the home group or 'home folk' is idealized: 'These men are the best my race has produced in this generation – and they are as good as have been produced in any generation. In them are combined fiery passion and icy discipline, deep intelligence and an instant readiness for action, a strong sense of self-worth and a total commitment to our common cause.'[76] We've referred to this as the false essential or pseudo-eidetic generalization in this extreme hatred. Third, the home ideal is linked with a counter-type dedicated to the undermining of the home tradition: 'Now it was either the Jews or the White race, and everyone knew the game

---

70 MacDonald, pseudonym for William L. Pierce. William L. Pierce, *The Turner Diaries*, 2nd edn (Fort Lee, NJ, 1996), 'Foreword'.

71 Pierce, Ibid., p. 35.

72 Pierce, Ibid., p. 36.

73 Pierce, Ibid., p. 37.

74 Pierce, Ibid., p. 171.

75 Pierce, Ibid., p. 203, Pierce's emphasis.

76 Pierce, Ibid., p. 203.

was for keeps.'[77] And again, 'The Enemy we are fighting fully intends to destroy the racial basis of our existence.'[78] We discussed this as the development of hatred according to an exclusive '*or*'. Fourth, the (mis)application of the exclusive logical '*or*' by excluding the group in question from its connection to individuals and higher genera. The alien-group is removed from the class of human beings and animals. 'We must understand that our race [White race] is like a cancer patient undergoing drastic surgery in order to save its life. There is no sense in asking whether the tissue being cut out now is innocent or not.'[79] It becomes clear that McVeigh had arrived at the most deadly form of hatred.

Of course, some may even arrive at the sickening hatred expressed in the *Turner Diaries*, believe its propaganda, and, thankfully, never take action. That requires a shift from beliefs and evaluation to volition. But, we'll leave to the conclusion of this book how the belief-based and the emotional exclusive '*or*' becomes a volitional '*or*'. There, we'll consider the added conditions, which when put in place, enable the maximally hateful individual to take action.

Monolithic Group-Hatred, sadly, does not imply Psychopathology

Cases of violent, group-focused, hatred cannot adequately be assigned to clinical psychopathology. There is little question that there are psychotic killers. Perhaps the most famous individual in recent years is Theodore Kaczynski, known as the Unabomber. The bombings of Kaczynski were clearly hate crimes but there is a difference between such individuals and the class of people who perpetrate violent hate crimes, especially those leaders who promulgate hate crimes. Psychotics, according to current psycho-pathological characterization, have 'a tenuous hold on reality'.[80] They are necessarily lone wolves. Their distorted sense of reality makes them less capable of summoning cohorts and mobilizing racial and ethnic prejudice.

So-called psychopaths are another matter. There is little question that psychopathy, that is, the condition whereby an individual has no sense of conscience, shame or guilt, exists. The classic description of psychopathic behavior dates from the 1940s. Hervey M. Cleckly studied individuals who had violated social norms and harmed others, yet were not typical criminals. Cleckley's description of psychopathy involves sixteen criteria. The list includes an absence of nervousness, and a lack of remorse and shame.[81] David T. Lykken in the 1950s was the first person to obtain laboratory evidence of a fear deficit among psychopaths.[82] Recent work indicates that the psychopath is unable to process emotion-relevant and emotion-eliciting circumstances. This has been linked to the 'emotion-deficit' features of

---

77 Pierce, Ibid., p. 182.

78 Pierce, Ibid., p. 34.

79 Pierce, Ibid., p. 197.

80 Gaylin, *Hatred: The Psychological Descent into Violence*, p. 139.

81 Hervey M. Cleckley, *The Mask of Sanity* (St. Louis, 1941).

82 David T. Lykken, 'A Study of Anxiety in the Sociopathic Personality', pp. 6–10.

psychopathy.[83] It is no surprise that psychopaths, with their lack of shame, remorse and fear, who assume leadership roles, especially amidst a discontent population, become a medium for the mobilization of malevolent hatred among others. Some of the most destructive despots of modern history, such as Idi Amin and Pol Pot, were likely psychopaths.[84]

But psychopathology, in the form of psychosis or psychopathy, will not explain the phenomenon of violent group hatred in general.

First, not surprisingly, there are degrees of psychopathy so that a distinction from so-called 'normal' behavior is not so easily made. Franz Fanon documents the case of a European police inspector whose job was to torture Algerian patriots. Fanon's account of the police inspector's conduct fits, in part, the diagnostic criteria of psychopathy. Fanon's patient, generally, expressed no remorse from his daily torturing of Algerian rebels. Rather, he complained about the long hours: 'Sometimes I torture people for ten hours at a stretch ... You may not realize it but it is very tiring.'[85] Nonetheless, the man still expressed some remorse. He consulted Fanon in his professional capacity as a psychiatrist to help him with his vestigial pangs of conscience. As Fanon writes with biting irony: 'to help him to go on torturing Algerian patriots without any pricking of conscience, without any behavior problems and with complete equanimity.'[86] The police inspector also expressed regrets that his unfeeling capacity to cause others horrible suffering was 'radiating' into his family life.

But, apart from degrees of psychopathy, unabated violent group hatred extends to atrocities committed by 'normals', or at least by those with no history of psychosis or psychopathic behavior. Members of the Polish Reserve Police Battalion 101 massacred Jewish mothers and children at Jozefow, Poland on 12 July 1942. The reaction of these men was not in keeping with the psychopath's inability to feel remorse or shame. One member of the battalion says: 'I thought I'd go crazy if I had to do that again.' But as psychiatrist Gaylin records: 'With time and conditioning, the men continued their massacres, and remarkably, they did not go crazy.'[87]

In the *Rape of Nanking*, Iris Chang describes the 'normal' Japanese young men, who often, at first, agonized over their deeds, but who, in time, lost their remorse becoming 'killing machines'.[88] A veteran officer, named Tominaga Shozo, recalled his transformation. Day after day, the commanding officers taught the recruits how to bayonet and cut off the heads of living prisoners. At first, Shozo was overwhelmed by the horror: 'The scene was so appalling I felt I couldn't breathe.'[89] Another recruit, named Tajima, states his reaction when ordered to kill a bound Chinese prisoner. 'In

---

83 R. Day and S. Wong, 'Anomalous Perceptual Asymmetries for Negative Emotional Stimuli in the Psychopath', pp. 648–52; C.J. Patrick, M.B. Bradley, and P.J. Lang, 'Emotion in the Criminal Psychopath: Startle Reflex Modulation', pp. 82–92.

84 Gaylin, Ibid., p. 146.

85 Franz Fanon, *The Wretched of the Earth* (New York, 1963), 'Case No. 5', p. 268.

86 Fanon, Ibid., pp. 269–70.

87 Gaylin, Ibid., pp. 146–7.

88 Iris Chang, *The Rape of Nanking: The Forgotten Holocaust of World War II* (New York, 1997), pp. 54–9.

89 Chang, Ibid., p. 58.

my heart, I begged his pardon, and – with my eyes shut and the lieutenant's curses in my eyes – I plunged the bayonet into the petrified Chinese. When I opened my eyes again he had slumped down into the pit. 'Murderer! Criminal!' I called myself.'[90] But as Tominaga Shozo recalls, later committing atrocities became routine, even banal. He states: 'Good sons, good daddies, good elder brothers at home were brought to the front to kill each other. Human beings turned into murdering demons. Everyone became a demon within three months.'[91]

These transformations of 'normals' into cold-blooded killers, cited above, took place in wartime. But that is not enough to make it a matter of psychopathology. Ever since Thucydides, writers describing wartime behavior have argued that war provides the opportunity for violence from otherwise nonviolent people because it allows people to feel free from the constraints of law. As Thucydides explained, war provides the opportunity for: 'human nature to triumph over laws, to become accustomed to do wrong in spite of laws, to delight in showing that its passions are ungovernable, to be stronger than justice, and to be hostile to anyone showing superiority.'[92] The members of the Polish Reserve Police Battalion and the Japanese infantry 'killing machines' may not have been so transformed outside of war. But that is not enough to make their behavior 'abnormal', since, tragically, wars are not abnormal. On the contrary, such behavior is the normal wartime behavior of many men and women.

A home folk pitting itself against an alien group, whom it believes is necessarily a source of racial, ethnic or religious 'contamination', alas, also cannot be dismissed as psychopathological. In fact such oppositions recurrently become a matter of popular belief.

Consider the sorry career of the early twentieth century political thinker, Lothrop Stoddard. Stoddard graduated *magna cum laude* from Harvard, received a law degree from Boston University and later returned to Harvard to earn a PhD. Besides being a highly respected and sought-after lecturer in his day, he published numerous books. Most successful was *The Rising Tide of Color Against White World Supremacy*. Published in 1920, it became a best seller, running through fourteen editions. Stoddard's thesis was 'nativist'. He presumed the ultimate superiority of Anglo-Saxon culture, and argued that it was destined to be corrupted by the genetic and political mingling of non-Nordic races. The impending rise of nonwhite political forces spelled imminent chaos on a worldwide scale. For example, in discussing the pernicious effect of the 'brown race's' intermingling, Stoddard writes:

... west-central Asia, which in the dawn of history was predominantly white man's country, is to-day racially brown man's land in which white blood survives only as vestigial traces of vanishing significance. If this portion of Asia, the former seat of mighty white empires and possibly the very homeland of the white race itself, should have so entirely changed

---

90 Chang, Ibid., p. 57.

91 Chang, Ibid., p. 58.

92 Thucydides, *History of the Peloponnesian War* (Cambridge, MA, 1920), Book III, Chapter 84.2 [my trans.].

its ethnic character, what assurance can the most impressive political panorama give us that the present world-order may not swiftly and utterly pass away?[93]

It will not do to toss the work of Stoddard onto the ash-heap of books written by pathological cranks. Indeed, in their day, these views had currency even among US presidents. About a decade earlier, President Theodore Roosevelt wrote that we must appreciate 'race importance'. He wrote that we need to face the struggle between whites and the 'scattered savage tribes whose life was but a few degrees less meaningless, squalid and ferocious than that of wild beasts'. Theodore Roosevelt believed that the elimination of the inferior races would be 'for the benefit of civilisation and in the interest of mankind'.[94]

Perhaps it's some consolation that he did not implement his racism. Unlike Nazi politicians, Teddy Roosevelt had not fully ascended the ladder of group-hatred to active policy-making. Hitler's minister of propaganda, Joseph Goebbels, wrote in his diary for 27 March 1942: 'The Jews will destroy us if we do not defend ourselves against them. This is a war of life or death between the Aryan race and the Jewish virus.'[95] But Goebbels embraced the actions taken by Nazi politicians. Teddy Roosevelt, in this regard, was not so malignant.

No matter who was the worse racist, Teddy Roosevelt, Stoddard, or Goebbels, the sad fact that the 'home group' and 'alien group' distinction, which Husserl has demonstrated is unavoidable, easily becomes misappropriated as an 'us-them' conflict. Further, the 'us-them' conflict, especially with the help of hate-mongering cultural and political leaders, often escalates into the deadly pitting of an ideal home folk against an, allegedly, essentially evil alien group. And, clinical psychopathology, such as understood today, would not include among the mentally ill the majority of such cultural and political leaders, nor the majority of their followers.

Violent Hatred's Shadow: Prejudicial Discrimination

Does racial, sexual, ethnic and religious prejudicial discrimination deserve to be included with violent group-hatred? Some theorists draw a thick line between prejudicial discrimination and hatred. In prejudicial discrimination, the black, Asian, or American is made 'invisible', not hated, but overlooked.[96] Others argue that prejudicial discrimination is similar enough to destructive monolithic hatred that its harmful effects cannot easily be distinguished from violent hatred. It relies

---

93 Lothrop Stoddard, *The Rising Tide of Color against White World-Supremacy* (New York, 1920), Chapter I: The World of Color.

94 Theodore Roosevelt, 'The Winning of the West', in *The Works of Theodore Roosevelt*, vol. 9 (New York, 1926), pp. 56–7.

95 As quoted by Yisrael Gutman, 'On the Character of Nazi Antisemitism', in Shmuel Almog, *Antisemitism Through the Ages* (Oxford, 1988), p. 369.

96 Gaylin, Ibid., pp. 25–6.

on stereotypical, 'essentialist' generalizations and presumes 'us-them' differences, providing, at least in effect, a social armamentarium for doing harm.[97]

Consider the first position. It's argued that prejudicial discrimination involves an incapacity to perceive the sufferings of the discriminated group because of the group's alien or foreign status. But there need be no ill-will.[98]

In *The Adventures of Huckleberry Finn*, Mark Twain, with deadly irony, conveyed how racial prejudice endures without manifest hatred. In explaining to Aunt Sally why he was late, Huck made up a story about an explosion in a steamboat:

> 'We blowed out a cylinder head.'
> 'Good gracious! Anybody get hurt?'
> 'No'm. Killed a Nigger.'
> 'Well it's lucky; because sometimes people do get hurt.'[99]

Ralph Ellison, in *The Invisible Man*, depicted the majority of a racist community not as hating blacks, but as making blacks *invisible*, and thereby becoming empathetically 'blind'. Arguably, those who inferiorize a group of people, but bear them no ill-will differ profoundly from those who stereotype a group, have ill-will for the group, and perpetrate their harm. Probably the worst blight in US history since the Civil War involves the treatment of Southern post-bellum African-Americans. Between 1882 and 1919, more than three thousand African-Americans were lynched.[100] Mustn't a distinction be drawn between the vicious odium of the comparatively small number of active perpetrators of lynchings and the nonviolent racial, ethnic and gender inferiorizing accepted by vast numbers of US citizens in the nineteenth and twentieth century? As psychiatrist Willard Gaylin states: '... even among members of the Ku Klux Klan, only a minority could participate in burning black children or lynching black men.'[101]

Gaylin is likely correct that passivity in the face of evil is due, perhaps, to cowardice, or, perhaps, to sequestering feelings or hatred. Still, it is different from *violent* active hatred since the hater has not stepped over the line into *action*. But culpability for actions, unfortunately, is not so easily assignable.

Pumla Gobodo-Madikizela, in *A Human Being Died that Night*, discusses her interviews with renowned Apartheid death squad chief, Eugene de Kock. She raises the issue: Is violent hatred worse than passive, non-committal, and conspiratorial injustice? She writes: 'South African leaders tried to distance themselves from the

---

97 Daniel Moynihan, for example, in 'The Negro Family: The Case for National Action', adopts the stance that prejudicial discrimination against US blacks is not merely a question of making Blacks 'invisible' but very patently implies ill-will, often violently so. 'The very essence of the male animal, from the bantam rooster to the four-star general is to strut. Indeed in 19th century America a particular style of exaggerated male boastfulness became almost a national style. Not for the Negro male. The "sassy nigger" was lynched ...' Daniel Moynihan, 'The Negro Family: The Case for National Action', in L. Rainwater and W.L. Yancey (eds), *The Moynihan Report and the Politics of Controversy* (Cambridge, MA, 1967), p. 62.

98 Gaylin, Ibid., so argues, pp. 23–9.

99 Mark Twain, *The Adventures of Huckleberry Finn* (New York, 1952), p. 216.

100 As quoted in Dozier, Ibid., p. 29.

101 Gaylin, Ibid., p. 22.

ugliness of Apartheid violence by denying that it existed at all: the policy was to see no evil, hear no evil, speak no evil – and therefore admit no evil.'[102] Germany's Nazi party leaders, on the other hand, saw neither moral nor legal wrong in their genocidal killings. Gobodo-Madikizela writes:

> The Nazi conscience was so warped that it had become a clear conscience. One might say without too much exaggeration that the apartheid conscience, by contrast, was so ridden with guilt that it had to be circumvented.[103]

Were Apartheid's politicians better or worse than Nazi party leaders? The point is not to balance a scale with Eugene de Kock's evil on one side and Goebbels' or Himmler's on the other. Gobodo-Madikizela's question is more probing. Is denied malice the worse evil? As Gobodo-Madikizela points out, on the one hand you have Nazi politicians and leaders such as Slobodan Milosevic and Augusto Pinochet, who explicitly connected themselves to the actions of their foot soldiers. On the other hand, you have the Apartheid politicians who left few paper trails to their crimes. The evidence was sparse just because the consciences of Apartheid politicians 'had to be circumvented'. Apartheid politicians hid their operations in ambiguous phrases that, as Gobodo-Madikizela points out, 'later enabled politicians to deny the real intent behind the words'.[104] As a result, their crimes continued without notice.

In truth, prejudicial discrimination, bigotry and active violent hatred do not fit into a neat continuum of increasing evil. This becomes apparent by sketching some criteria by which the degree of active violent hatred might be rated. The following criteria are relevant:

1. Time: Are the violent acts passing, sporadic, continuous, or long-standing?

2. Degree of conscious intention: Is the violent act set off by an unthinking, 'knee-jerk' attitude? Is the ill-will unconscious? Or, is the violent act decided upon with deliberate and self-reflection?

3. Direct or indirect action: Do the violent acts involve middle men/women or are they enacted face-to-face?

4. Denial: Do the perpetrators of violent acts deny responsibility, or do they openly admit their deeds?

Such criteria demonstrate the difficulty in assigning culpability for active violent hatred. Criterion one concerns the time-horizon of the action. Surely recurrent hate crimes are worse than single eruptions. But what about cases where the perpetrator has genuine remorse and a commitment to restitution? Would that make the long-standing perpetrator less culpable than the one-time offender who has no remorse? Criterion two concerns the degree of conscious deliberation. What of cases where the careful deliberation is removed from the enactment of the hate crimes? Nakajima Kesago was the chief of secret police for Emperor Hirohito in the 1930s. He strategized the

---

102 Gobodo-Madikizela, *A Human Being Died That Night*, p. 64.

103 Gobodo-Madikizela, Ibid., pp. 68–9.

104 Gobodo-Madikizela, Ibid., p. 64.

invasion and destruction of Nanking and supervised the atrocities. But he did not enact the killings. The foot soldiers did. The mere *enactment* of the killings cannot be, then, a necessary condition of culpability.[105] Consider criterion three. Pinochet's lieutenants were links to the chain of orders that resulted in tortures and killings. They neither made the plans, nor enacted the executions. Presumably they were less culpable? But, those close to Pinochet were in a better position to oppose him. Are they then more culpable than the henchmen who directly enacted the crimes? And what of criterion four, the degree of denial? Consider a complicitous trial judge in a racist regime. He continues to implement racially biased laws. Suppose also that he has covert ill-will for his defendants. He compartmentalizes his feelings. Making excuses, he remains on the bench for decades. Because of their unimpeded longevity, his actions may harm more people than Timothy McVeigh's or John William King's horrific brutality.

The motives for prejudicial discrimination and bigotry doubtless arise from many sources: economic exploitation, non-reflective scapegoating and also likely, alas, unconscious sadistic impulses. The manners of expressing ill-will consequently appear with different styles of ratiocination, emotionality, and discourse. Economic exploitation hides behind religious and historical tradition, as sadism hides behind punitive justice. Attempting to determine degrees of ill-will oversimplifies the matter, since there are qualitative differences arising from manners of deployment. It becomes clear that judging whether prejudicial discrimination and bigotry involves malevolent hatred, at the very least, requires reflection on particular cases. Prejudicial discrimination may well be hatred, 'in the dark'. Bringing it to the light of day requires an examination of motives, manners, as well as socio-political doctrines that, in effect, serve to keep the ill-will hidden. Shining a spotlight on one monstrous outcropping of violent hatred tends to leave in the shadows many complicitous persons and background conditions. Given the immense difficulty in suitably illumining prejudicial discrimination, it is likely better to err on the side of attempting to improve *future* circumstances, rather than err on the side of attempting to extract the degree of complicity from the *past*, in the name of justice.

In this book's conclusion, we'll return to the logical underpinnings of hatred, and consider how strategies may be developed for its abatement.

Two Benign Forms of Group Hatred: *Civil Hatred* and '*Philosophic Misanthropy*'

We cannot end this description of the development and logical underpinnings of hatred without considering two relatively benign forms of hatred. They may be distinguished by the unusual development of the 'oppositional *or*' aspect of hatred. They also, arguably, serve socially constructive purposes.

In *civil hatred*, the targets of hatred are malfeasances clearly harmful to civil society. Aristotle boldly declared that thieves and slanderers are generally hated.[106] Today, serial killers and child pornographers are popularly hateful. Civil hatred

---

105 Chang, Ibid., pp. 35–9.
106 Aristotle, *Rhetoric*, 1382a6–7.

differs from monolithic group-focused hatred in that the individuals are hated, as a member of a type, but their status as individuals is not altogether left out.

The term 'stereotype' is commonly used to distinguish the way in which hatred generalizes people. It's sometimes pointed out that stereotypical features may be favorable or pejorative. Well-worn complimentary stereotypes include, for example, that overweight people are good-humored, good-looking people are sociable, blacks are athletic, the English are well spoken, and so on. Examples of pejorative stereotyping are that blondes are dumb, that Germans lack a sense of humor, and so on. But regardless of whether the stereotyping is flattering or deprecatory there is an extreme variety of generalization involved. The apprehension of the person is simplified to the extent that generality is given as complete.

The origin of the term 'stereotyping' tells much of the story. The term arises from the history of typography. Printing involved movable type well into the eighteenth century. But, by the late eighteenth century a process conceived by an Edinburgh goldsmith, William Ged, was brought into general use. Ged's idea was to make a mold from movable type out of plaster or *papier mâché*. Through pouring molten metal into the mold, a stereotype was created, that is, a single solid typeface.

The typographic analogy is well taken. With a single solid typeface, any type-letter was fused with the complete page. Similarly, stereotypical generalizations are a special case of essential generalizations. They presume the completeness of the type. Stereotyping the Scandinavian as morose is more than an empirical generalization or an essential generalization of them. It is a rule of thumb simplification that presumes to tell the whole story of the Scandinavians' emotional disposition leaving *them* out of it. Accidental traits are irrelevant. In the case of violent group-hatred, the name-calling not only evokes loathsome creatures, it evokes creatures for whom individual differences count for little. In preparation for the 1994 Tutsi genocide, Hutu propagandists labeled Tutsis as *inyenzi*, that is, cockroaches, and scum,[107] as Nazis referred to Jews as vermin. Cockroaches, scum, vermin, and so on, have neither positive traits nor significant differences.

A comparison may be drawn between the 'hyper-subjective' uniqueness that emerges in personal love and the completeness presumed by monolithic group-focused hatred. As personal love discovers more than species or numerical identity, monolithic group-focused hatred proposes more than an essential type. Shape is an essential trait of every swatch of color. But, nonetheless, it is not supposed that a particular swatch of color lacks its own individual shape. But with stereotypes, one instance is as good as the next. Stereotyping the overweight as jolly, or the Jew as intelligent, discards token aspects of the type, enough so to make them irrelevant. It involves a 'hyper-generalization', if you will.

The whole-cloth attribution of loathsome traits and denial of individuality presumed by monolithic group hatred marks its difference from civil hatred. In the case of civil hatred, the history of the individuals who become serial killers is relevant. Social psychologist Roy Baumeister argues that an increase in serial killers coincides

107 Philip Gourevitch, *We wish to inform you that tomorrow we will be killed with our families: Stories from Rwanda* (New York, 1998), pp. 64, 96.

with a rise in serial killings becoming a staple among Hollywood plot devices.[108] However that may be, it is clear that with such claims, serial killers are treated as a group of individuals affected by social conditions. The generalization is quite different with white racists who stereotype blacks as untrustworthy, or with black racists who stereotype whites as social predators. Were blacks taught to believe that justice was only for whites? Were whites taught to believe their racial superiority consequently had a right to land-grabs? With stereotyping, such questions are irrelevant. Stereotyping, in one stroke, nullifies the relevance of cause and effect. By contrast, with civil hatred, the family of the victim of a serial killer may demonize the killer and fantasize, or, perhaps even take revenge brutally. But the hatred still extends to the individual, and is connected with the serial killer's individual deeds and history. It presumes a particular spatio-temporal context for specific acts and their causes and effects. Contrastingly, monolithic group hatred, by stereotyping, targets not the specific person nor his or her deeds, but a cluster of motives, manners, habits, facial expressions, values and sensibilities that are imposed, whole cloth, upon the hated group.

The reasons for civil hatred are also different from those of monolithic group-hatred. Civil hatred has some claim to legitimacy in that it outstrips norms requisite for, or supportive of, human coexistence. It is just such considerations that lead philosophers such as Locke and Kant[109] to argue that certain types of behavior are necessarily antagonistic to civil society. Slander, for example, is anti-social in civil society. It undermines trust by misrepresenting another's behavior. The public's hatred of a slanderer who intentionally ruins an individual's career through false 'murmurs' has a different basis from monolithic group-focused hatred that, as we've proposed, involves the contrivance of 'home' and 'alien' groups in necessary opposition. In fact 'the oppositional *or*' develops differently in civil hatred. The person who targets another with civil hatred sequesters the malfeasor into a group of liars, renegades, outcasts, misfits, reprobates, social menaces, and so on. But, the 'us' side of the 'oppositional *or*' is not an idealized home-group, but civil society at large, with a very loose extension of boundaries extending beyond one's 'home-group'. Regardless of their criminality in *de facto* legal codes, child molesters are conceived as hateful in civil society worldwide.

Philosophic misanthropy, arguably, is a second type of benign hatred. Here the target of hatred is human behavioral traits in general. Such hatred exhibits a very peculiar, and in a sense, advanced development of the exclusive '*or*'. As with civil hatred, it serves to make repugnant socially harmful types of behavior, but in the case of philosophic misanthropy, it's universal human traits that are reprehensible.

---

108 Roy F. Baumeister, *Evil: Inside Human Violence and Cruelty* (New York, 1999), pp. 277–81.

109 Of course, Locke and Kant come to a similar conclusion by different sorts of arguments. Locke argues from the notion of a 'law of Nature', and Kant from the foundations of the idea of morality itself. But both in fact conclude that a civil society self-destructs without the observance of basic moral principles. See John Locke, *An Essay Concerning the True Extent and End of Civil Government* (Chicago, 1952), Chapter II, 'Of the State of Nature'; and, Kant, *Groundwork of The Metaphysics of Morals*, in *The Cambridge Edition of the Works of Immanuel Kant: Practical Philosophy* (Cambridge, 1996), Section II, 'Transition from Popular Moral Philosophy to Metaphysics of Morals'.

Among the classical models, Diogenes the Cynic is exemplary. When asked where in Greece he saw good men, he replied, 'Nowhere.'[110] To be 'thrice human' is to be 'thrice wretched'.[111] Even so, Diogenes does not exploit an opposition between an ideal home-group and a loathed alien-group. He does not pit master against slave, Greek against barbarian, nor rich against poor, and so on. His hatred is civil hatred taken to the extreme of conceiving humanity at large at fault.

The exclusive '*or*' appears through an animal *versus* human opposition. Diogenes played at shuffling off his human role. He would be a hound: 'I fawn on those who give me anything, I yelp at those who refuse and I set my teeth in rascals.'[112] He learns how to adapt to circumstances by watching a mouse.[113]

Among philosophers Nietzsche is brother to Diogenes in railing against the all-too-human. Nietzsche, like Diogenes, will prefer the animal to the human. In 'On the uses and disadvantages of history for life' Nietzsche writes: 'If happiness, if reaching out for new happiness, is in any sense what fetters living creatures to life and makes them go on living, then perhaps no philosopher is more justified than the Cynic: for the happiness of the animal, as the perfect Cynic, is the living proof of the rightness of Cynicism.'[114] Nietzsche too expressed hatred of human hypocrisy passionately: 'Oh this insane, pathetic beast – man! What ideas he has, what unnaturalness, what paroxysms of nonsense, what *bestiality of thought* erupts as soon as he is prevented just a little from being a *beast in deed*!'[115]

Philosophical misanthropy, inasmuch as it targets humanity in general, deserves to be called benign if indeed, as in Diogenes' cynicism, there is a remonstrance of human hypocrisy, but not the wholesale dismissal of woebegone human creatures. Diogenes, himself, reveled in deprecating human hypocrisies, but he did not speak ill of life itself. 'When some one declared that life is an evil, he corrected him: Not life itself, but living ill.'[116] Philosophic misanthropy is benign, as civil hatred is benign, inasmuch as it generalizes human nature but does not stereotype it. As with Nietzsche, Diogenes' ridiculing human hypocrisy never was the end of the story about humanity. 'When Plato styled him a dog, "Quite true," he said, "for I come back again and again to those who have sold me."'[117] The Athenians accordingly maintained him as a kind of public watchdog. 'At all events, when a youngster broke his tub, they gave the boy a flogging and presented Diogenes with another.'[118]

---

110 Diogenes Laertius, 'Diogenes', in *Lives of the Eminent Philosophers*, Book I (Cambridge, MA, 1925), VI.27, p. 29.

111 Diogenes Laertius, Ibid., VI.47, p. 49.

112 Diogenes Laertius, Ibid., VI.60, p. 63.

113 Diogenes Laertius, Ibid., VI.22, p. 25.

114 Friedrich Nietzsche, 'On the uses and disadvantages of history for life', in *Untimely Meditations*, (Cambridge, 1983), p. 61.

115 Nietzsche, *On the Genealogy of Morals, Ecce Homo*, (New York, 1989), II.22, p. 93.

116 Diogenes Laertius, Ibid., VI.55, p. 57.

117 Diogenes Laertius, Ibid., VI.40, p. 41.

118 Diogenes Laertius, Ibid., VI.43, p. 45.

Conclusion

The Logical Underpinnings
of Love and Hate

Man does not know what love is, or hate, and both of these in his eyes are vanity.

(Ecclesiastes, 9:2)

As we have considered, personal love, sexual love and hatred have distinct logical components. Personal love discerns the uniqueness of the beloved in conjoining empathies, one after another; sexual love fixates upon sexual 'parts' and reorders the mapping of loved's body according to tactile space and temporality; and hatred, even in its less developed forms, generalizes and exclusively separates the culpability of the hated person from oneself. Reviewing the manner in which the logical components are 'underpinnings', we may summarize by considering the various senses of the term. The logical complements of personal love, sexual love and hate, 'pin together' beliefs, emotions and decisions, fastening distinct shapes, as papers or pieces of cloth might be pinned together. They also guide the development of love and hate, figuratively stated, as pin-pricks. So personal love urges on the discovery of the beloved as a source of incomparable value; sexual love conflicts with personal love, in the special case of parent-child personal, and arrives at the intolerable counter-purposes of sexual love and parent-child love; and, hatred maximizes generalization and the 'us-them' opposition in violent group-focused hatred. Finally, the logical complements of love and hate are also underpinnings in the principal architectural sense of the term, that is, as foundations that support and strengthen a building. So, the logical foundations of love and hate, at least in the mind of the lover or hater, validate the desires and choices made in loving and hating, by grounding these passions in worldly facts.

Those familiar with Husserlian phenomenology will likely detect that the notion of 'underpinnings' fits with the Husserlian doctrine that 'reason' (*Vernunft*) and 'unreason' (*Unvernunft*) are part of the constitution of objects. Husserl, in *Cartesian Meditations*, hardly could be more emphatic: '*Reason is not an accidental de facto ability*, not a title for possible accidental matters of fact, but rather a title for an *all-embracing essentially necessary structural form belonging to all transcendental subjectivity.*'[1] When for example, I see a white stone on a trail, which turns out to be just a patch of sunlight, as a perceiving subject, I enact, pre-reflectively, an 'exclusive disjunction', as Husserl puts it.[2] I see either the stone or the sunlight patch, but never

---

1   Husserl, *Cartesian Meditations: An Introduction to Phenomenology* (The Hague, 1973), §23, p. 57 [Husserl's emphasis].
2   Husserl, Ibid., p. 57.

both. 'Our perception is entirely dominated by a logic which assigns each object its determinate features in virtue of those of the rest, and which "cancel out" as unreal stray data; ...' as Merleau-Ponty states.[3] In proposing that there are 'logical underpinnings' to love and hate we are describing a special case of how reason plays 'an essential and necessary structural role' in the constitution of objects.

Aligning emotions with cognitive distinctions is not new in the history of philosophy and psychology. It appears quite early. Plato, in the *Philebus*, in an effort to show that knowledge is superior to pleasure, has Socrates catalog the emotions of anger, fear, longing, lament, love, emulation and envy, as mixed pleasures of the soul.[4] Then, by considering how we speak of true and false emotions, Plato focuses on the cognitive aspects of these emotions. And surely some fears at least (a phobic response to cats or the number thirteen) rely on false beliefs.

Aristotle takes matters further. Aristotle, in his analysis of emotions in the *Rhetoric* offers a demonstration of how emotions are cognitive.[5] He argues that the emotions, inasmuch as they are based in beliefs, and not merely in physiological disturbances, are open to reasoned persuasion.[6] Nor is the primacy of the rational component of emotions lost on modern philosophers. Philosophers such as Robert C. Solomon, for example, in his study *The Passions* makes rationality central to his discussion of the passions. He debunks 'the Myth of the Passions' which presumes that emotions are: 'irrational forces, beyond our control, disruptive and stupid, unthinking and counterproductive, against our "better interests", and often ridiculous.'[7]

But Husserl takes matters further by proposing that reason is woven into the very manner in which objects are structured and maintain their appearance. He goes so far as to assert that logical categories, in some primitive sense, play into our pre-predicative strivings in general. For example, in *Experience and Judgment*, a work published shortly after Husserl's death (1938), Husserl declares:

> With this [the apprehension of sense-forms], we are at the *place of origin of the first part of the so-called 'logical categories.'* It is true, we can only begin to speak of logical categories in the proper sense in the sphere of predicative judgment, as elements of determination

---

3   Merleau-Ponty, *Phenomenology of Perception* (London, 1989), p. 313.

4   Plato, *Philebus* (Cambridge, MA, 1925) p. 47E.

5   Aristotle's analysis of the emotions is particularly astute inasmuch as it determines cognitive aspects of emotions as necessary conditions. In the *Rhetoric*, for example, Aristotle defines anger as a desire for revenge accompanied by pain on account of an apparent slight to oneself or one's own, the slight being unjustified, (Aristotle, 1984, *Rhetoric*, 1387a30–32). In so saying, Aristotle makes the efficient cause of the component of anger a necessary condition. Anger *requires* the belief that an outrage has been experienced. The colleague who mocks my reading of current politics, say, provokes a sense of slight through his belittlement. My anger cannot be removed from my colleague's unkind remarks. Without the belief that my colleague had unjustifiably judged my politics, my anger would dissolve for, as Aristotle well understood, someone cannot be angry when he thinks himself treated justly. In effect then Aristotle supplies necessary conditions for the intentionality of anger, an exactitude of definition seldom accomplished by current psychology.

6   W.W. Fortenbaugh, *Aristotle on Emotion* (New York, 1975), pp. 16–18.

7   Robert C. Solomon, *The Passions: Emotions and the Meaning of Life* (Indianapolis/Cambridge, 1993), p. 181.

which belong necessarily to the form of possible predicative judgments. But all categories and categorial forms which appear there are erected on the prepredicative syntheses and have their origin in them.[8]

If Husserl is correct that logical distinctions, even logical categories, appear in 'prepredicative syntheses', that is, in a human being's passive nonreflective strivings and endeavorings,[9] we'd expect, then, emotional reactions to be affected by this cognitive development. The question is how? There is little question that Husserl himself thought the relationship between emotions and cognitive development was profound. In *Ideas I*, for example, Husserl provocatively connects 'plural judgments', in the logical sense, with personal love:

> For example: the mother who looks lovingly upon her flock of children, embraces each child singly, and all together in *one* act of love (*in einem Akte der Liebe*). The unity of the collective act of loving is not a loving and, in addition, a collective objectivating, even if it is attached to the loving as its necessary foundation. Loving, instead, is itself collective; it is, similarly, as many-rayed as the objectivating and perhaps plural judging 'underlying' (*'unterliegende'*) it. We should speak of a plural loving in precisely the same sense as we speak of a plural objectivating, or judging. The syntactical forms enter into the essence of the emotional acts themselves, namely into the positional stratum peculiar to them.[10]

But how do 'syntactical forms enter into the essence of the emotional acts themselves?'[11] We'll consider further personal and sexual love and hatred individually in this regard.

---

8   Husserl, *Experience and Judgment* (Evanston, 1973), p. 115.

9   Husserl's writings concerning the genesis of logical distinctions are voluminous and extend from early on in his career to the end of his career. The genetic phenomenological account of the constitution of objects, concepts and logical categories appears, in particular, in three works. First, in a series of lectures presented three times in the 1920s: the winter semester of 1920/21; the summer semester of 1923, and the winter semester of 1925/26. These lectures are published in *Analysen zur passiven Synthesis*, Husserliana XI; English trans: *Analyses Concerning Active and Passive Synthesis* (Dordrecht/Boston/London, 2001). The second main text is *Formal and Transcendental Logic*, appearing in 1929, reprinted as *Formale und transzendentale Logik*, Husserliana XVII, (Den Haag, 1974); English trans. *Formal and Transcendental Logic*, (Den Haag, 1969). Husserl did not live to see the publication of the third work, *Experience and Judgment*, but due to Ludwig Landgrebe's editorial efforts, it appeared shortly after Husserl's death. Not appearing in the Husserliana series, it is published as *Erfahrung und Urteil* (Hamburg, 1986); English translation: *Experience and Judgment* (Evanston, 1973).

10 Husserl, *Ideas Pertaining to a Pure Phenomenology and to a Phenomenological Philosophy, First Book* (Den Haag, 1982), §121, p. 289.

11 [Die syntaktischen Formen gehen in das Wesen der Gemütsakte selbst ein, nämlich in die ihnen spezifisch eigentümliche thetische Schicht.] Husserl, *Ideen zu einer reinen Phänomenologie und Phänomenologischen Philosophie, Erstes Buch* (Den Haag, 1976), §121, p. 279.

The Logical Complement of Personal Love, its Perfections and Perils

Love does not seek equals; it creates them[12]

Turning to the 'syntactical forms'[13] that enter into personal love, as quoted, Husserl tells us that: '... there is besides the doxic "and" (the logical "and") an axiological and practical "and".'[14] Love, in particular, accommodates a manner of affective conjunction. Love, he says, 'is itself collective; it is, similarly, as many rayed as the objectivating and perhaps plural judging "underlying" it.'[15] '... The mother who looks lovingly upon her flock of children, embraces each child singly, and all together in *one* act of love.'[16] How shall we understand this?

Returning to our analysis of personal love as based in 'contact' and inter-empathetic *Nachverstehen*, in fact the core of the idea of love's 'emotional and practical *and*' is already present in the manner in which *Nachverstehen* arrives at the uniqueness and incomparable value of the beloved.

To begin with there is the 'emotional and practical *and*' which operates in the relation between the loving person and the beloved. From the very beginning, personal love weaves one's own self into the life of the beloved, even if only as an anonymous benefactor. Without love's 'emotional and practical *and*' the uniqueness of the beloved would not be accomplished for it requires that one's own reactions are collated with the strivings of the other. Say I pass by a mannequin in a store window. Gazing at the lifeless figure, I am an anonymous spectator. But suppose, by chance I happen to see through the store window the woman I love. I am immediately *with* her, not as a double or shadow, but as a companion, a cohort, a partner. This linkage appears whether she recognizes that I'm there or not.

But conceptualizing this partnership is elusive. No sooner do I state the duality between myself and my beloved that I say too much or too little. In commenting on the passage from Husserl on the 'emotional and practical *and*' quoted above, Paul Ricoeur notes that there is a conjunctive 'ray' that the lover extends to the beloved.[17] But, once we put the matter into words, we build upon the structure of the objective world because our subject/predicate statements arise from judgments that presuppose the objective world.[18]

---

12 'L'amour/Fait les égalités et ne les cherche pas.' Stendahl (Marie-Henri Beyle) has Julien Sorel recall this epigram of Corneille as he sets out to capture Mme de Rênal's affections. Stendahl, *Le Rouge at Le Noir* (Paris, 1964), Book I, Chapter xiv, p. 107.

13 Husserl, *Ideas, First Book*, §121, p. 289, quoted above.

14 Husserl, Ibid., p. 289, quoted above.

15 Husserl, Ibid., p. 289, cited above. [Sondern das Lieben selbst is kollektives, es ist ebenso vielstrahlig wie das ihm 'unterliegende' Vorstellen und ev. plurale Urteilen.] Husserl, *Ideen, Erstes Buch*, §121, p. 279.

16 Husserl, Ibid., p. 289, cited above.

17 Husserl, Ibid., §121.

18 Paul Ricoeur explains the passage from *Ideas I* cited above, pointing out that loving itself does not require objectification, but its (verbal) expression requires a shift to the 'doxic' (perceptual/cognitive) mode. That objectifies the expression. He writes: 'The "syntax" of "and," "or," etc., is therefore as well suited to love and to evaluation as it is to representation.'

The curious elusiveness of the lover/beloved partnership is conveyed in quirks of grammar. A great variety of languages maintain a *dual* number, in addition to a *singular* and *plural*. Inuktitut, the language of the Inuit people of the Eastern Arctic, along with Hebrew, modern Arabic as well as earlier forms of Indo-European languages, make use of the dual number along with the singular and plural. In these languages, people can refer to people or things in terms of 'twosomes'. Many of these languages inflect the dual number in nouns, adjectives, pronouns, and verbs as well. In Sanskrit and in Homeric Greek,[19] for example, there are single words that mean, *the two* of us, *the two* of you, or *the two* of them and nouns and verbs that are inflected accordingly.

You see the curious inability to express the intrinsic duality of partnership in subject/predicate form in the absence of certain dual forms in Homeric Greek.[20] An episode from the *Odyssey* helps to illustrate.

As every reader of the epic knows, after ten years of wandering, Odysseus returns to Ithaca disguised as a beggar. Throughout some six books of the *Odyssey*, Odysseus keeps secret his identity from Penelope, making especially climactic the moment when Penelope finally recognizes him. In the Greek text, to convey the love that follows, Homer repeatedly employs the dual number: 'They [the Greek text has the dual form for 'the two'], when they were gladdened [Greek text: dual inflection of 'made glad'] by the joy of love, they took delight in recounting tales to each other, [Greek text: dual form for 'both recounting'].'[21] This repeated usage of dual forms is especially poignant since it underscores how, after Odysseus' and Penelope's long-suffering separation, they, reciprocatively, as a twosome, finally renew their love for each other. But, some fifty lines later, Odysseus himself shifts to direct address and declares to Penelope: 'Now since we both have come to the much-loved bed ...'[22] In so saying, Homer drops the dual number. Indeed he must. There are no dual grammatical forms for the *first person*. The gap in grammar, in fact, recapitulates a gap in reflective consciousness. Odysseus cannot refer to their love in the dual, because, to put matters phenomenologically, in shifting to the first person, Odysseus' speech presumes a position-taking consciousness that 'objectifies'. Homer can convey Odysseus' and Penelope's love as a twosome, because his identity is hidden through the point of view of an anonymous spectator. But, once Odysseus

---

"Syntaxes" are thus not doxic de jure. This conclusion is in conformity with what we already know about the "thetic": namely, that the thetic is broader than the "doxic" but can only be expressed by objectifying itself in the doxic thesis.' Paul Ricoeur, *A Key to Edmund Husserl's Ideas I* (Milwaukee, 1996), p. 153.

19 The dual number was part of standard usage in Homeric Greek. It became increasingly infrequent in Attic Greek, until it faded altogether from active usage by the 3rd century BC.

20 Herbert Weir Smyth, *Greek Grammar* (Cambridge, MA, 1920), §954, p. 263: 'The first person dual [of a subject] agrees in form with the first person plural [of the verb].'

21 Homer, *The Odyssey* (Cambridge, MA, 1995), Book XXIII, lines 300–1: τὼ δ᾽ ἐπεὶ οὖν φιλότητος ἐταρπήτην ἐρατεινῆς / τερπέσθην μύθοισι, πρὸς ἀλλήλους ἐνέποντε. In these lines, 'τὼ' is a pronoun, 'ἐταρπήτην' a verb, and 'ἐνέποντε' a participle, all in the dual number.

22 Homer, Ibid., Book XXIII, line 354: νῦν δ᾽ ἐπεὶ ἀμφοτέρω πολυήρατον ἱκομεθ᾽ εὐνην.

directly addresses Penelope, he is no longer part of a 'we' that is genuinely dual. He is rather the Odysseus who reflects on his and Penelope's love, *from his point of view*. Similarly, in ordinary English, a loving partner who declares *vis-à-vis* his beloved, 'We love each other', however true the statement may be, conveys a sense of usurping his beloved's point of view. True loving partnership resists first person description.

Husserl's own account of the pairing relation establishes it as pre-predicative. Husserl sees the apprehension of *pairs* as a 'primal form' of passive synthesis.[23] The apprehension of a pair is prior to the apprehension of two objects as a sum or as one object apprehended after another.[24] In a manuscript dated February 1927, Husserl explains that the passive synthesis of pairing is accomplished on an affective level: 'an arousal goes from one to the other. One [member of the pair] affects me, so the affection crosses over to the other, so that they reinforce and reverse the other's affections.'[25] Without reflecting upon the transition, we are drawn from (attracted, thus 'affected by') one element of the pair to the other, to the extent that if we 'objectify' one of the pair, we do so from a preceding givenness of the twosome.

The 'emotional and practical *and*' of personal love, accordingly, is already prepared by especially fundamental ways of organizing the world. Its 'logic' is a possibility that arises with primitive cognitive syntheses, which are, from the beginning, imbued with an affectivity. The growth of personal love, it would seem, builds upon this foundation.

Further, the 'emotional and practical *and*' of personal love appears in the fundamental ways of constituting an individual. Marguerite Duras, speaking of seemingly widely diverse characters in her films, remarked incisively of their love: 'To love one child and to love all children, whether living or dead – somewhere these two loves come together. To love a no-good but humble punk and to love an honest man who believes himself to be an honest man – somewhere these, too, come

---

23 'Pairing is a *primal form of that passive synthesis* which we designate as "*association*", in contrast to passive synthesis of identification. In a *pairing association* the characteristic feature is that, in the most primitive case, two data are given intuitionally, and with prominence, in the unity of a consciousness and that, on this basis – essentially, already in pure passivity (regardless therefore of whether they are noticed or unnoticed) – as data appearing with mutual distinctness, they *found phenomenologically a unity of similarity* and thus are always constituted precisely as a pair.' Husserl, *Cartesian Meditations*, p. 112. See also Husserl, *Analyses Concerning Active and Passive Synthesis*, p. 179; and *Zur Phänomenologie der Intersubjektivität, Zeiter Teil*, Husserliana XIV, p. 530.

24 'Looking into the matter more closely, the act of representation (A, B) has priority over the act of collection (A + B), in which the *sum* is the object. That is, in order that the sum may be given, in order that it may be apprehended in self-givenness and contemplated as such, we must apprehend the A and B together; in the unity of this apprehension of two objects, the new object is preconstituted as its result, so to speak, as something which we now apprehend as one and which we can explicate in the individual apprehension of A, B ...' Husserl, *Experience and Judgment* (Evanston, 1973), pp. 245–6.

25 Husserl, *Zur Phänomenologie der Intersubjektivität, Zeiter Teil*, Husserliana XIV, p. 530: [Affiziert mich das eine, so geht die Affektion in der Art auf das andere über, dass sie des andern Affektion verstärkt und umgekehrt.]

together.'[26] It is a mainstay of Husserlian, as well as post-Husserlian, phenomenology that we perceive objects in the context of internal and external horizons.[27] The mannequin I see in a store window may be made of plastic or plaster, but whatever its material, in seeing it I also sense its 'insides' as 'being there'. I don't know for sure what I'll find if I crack open the mannequin, but I'm sure there will be something, plaster, a metal frame, and so on. The indeterminate co-present insides of the object, phenomenologically speaking, are its 'internal horizons'. I also accept as 'there' the indeterminate background of the mannequin, say, the indefinite bridal scene in which the window dresser has ensconced the mannequin. The background scene, in phenomenological terms, is part of the object's 'external horizons'.

The presence of internal and external horizons has special characteristics in the case of the beloved, which are in keeping with the emotional and practical '*and*'. Unlike the mannequin, the beloved's internal horizons, promise a shared inter-empathetic history. There is an incorporation of an inter-empathetic 'story' within the very presence of the beloved. In subtle implications, the beloved's presence conveys a litany of interactions, countless squabbles, reconciliations, and makings-up, which no more add up into a single set of qualities, than a Mozart string quartet is summed up with a single chord. The inter-empathetic 'emotional and practical *and*' incorporates the shared experiences to the extent that it should be no surprise that the beloved is a source of meaning. The 'emotional and practical *and*' of personal love brings with it a collage of 'means-ends' experiences. Innumerable little Ithacas concatenate to make the beloved a wellspring of meaning and value.

What is true of the interior horizons of the beloved also is true of her or his exterior horizons. As mentioned before, in passing by the mannequin in a store window, without occasion to reflect I am no more than an anonymous spectator. But if I see through the store window the woman I love, I am immediately with her, not as a double or shadow, but as a companion or partner. In the external horizon of the woman I love, I am there as a silent comrade. And hence in spite of all the perfidies, jealousies, longings and despair inspired in Charles Swann by Odette de Crécy, once Odette settles into an abiding affection for Swann, Proust is right to have her say to M. Verdurin when asked how she can be with Swann when he's a thousand miles away: 'Nothing is impossible to the eye of a friend.'[28]

If we follow Husserl in his account of extraordinary possible external horizons of personal love, we enter into his reflections on its perfection as 'ethical love'. Husserl describes an 'empathy horizon'.[29] Personal love, through its inherent 'emotional and

---

26 The interview appeared in *Le Monde* in 1977. Duras was referring to Vera Baxter in *Baxter, Vera Baxter* and the identityless woman in *Le Cammion*. The interview, reprinted and translated as 'The Path of Joyful Despair', appears in Marguerite Duras, *Outside* (Boston, 1986), p. 142.

27 See esp. Husserl, *Experience and Judgment*, pp. 104–6 for a full description of internal and external horizons.

28 Marcel Proust, *Swann's Way* (New York, 1989), p. 409.

29 '... within the vitally flowing intentionality in which the life of an ego-subject consists, every other ego is already intentionally implied in advance by way of empathy and the empathy horizon.' Husserl, *Crisis of European Sciences and Transcendental Phenomenology* (Evanston, IL, 1970), p. 255.

practical *and*', promises the progress of building upon the inter-empathetic relation with others arriving at 'ethical love'.

Ethical love, Husserl writes, is neither instinctual nor natural. It requires a 'conversion of original instincts'.[30] It is wholly attentive to the individual and apprehends each individual as unique and exceptional.[31] He returns to the paradigm of motherly love:

> The children are a mother's children, not as objective states of affairs, rather for her, they have their worth in their individuality, and in relation to the individuality of the mother. And as to their worth, for the mother all the children are equal; there is not a question of different perspectives, for example the perspective of their aptitudes, by which the mother determines more or less worth, and, if such should be the case, to all both more and less. The 'equivalence' of worth for the mother is not a question of more and less. On the contrary, they are equal in that, as their worth is individual, they are beyond comparison ...[32]

As in personal love, with ethical love there is no question of objective traits. There are not 'objective states of affairs', as he states. The children 'have their worth in their individuality, and in relation to the individuality of the mother'. This suggests the notion of *Nachverstehen* and its capacity to find uniqueness in the beloved by virtue of the uniqueness of the empathetic overlayering. But the model takes us further. It is no longer a question of discerning the uniqueness of *an* other; now the field of others is open. Even so, it is not a group or collectivity that is loved, but individual 'unicities', each unique enough to make comparisons, and therefore generalizations, inappropriate.

Ethical love in the full sense requires self-forgetfulness (*Selbstvergessenheit*). In a manuscript written in the early 1930s, Husserl distinguishes three types of self-forgetfulness. A first type is instinctual self-forgetfulness and it leads to taking immediate action, say, to helping somebody in distress. With this first type of self-forgetfulness, there is action, but little self-consciousness.[33] In a second type of

---

30 Ms. E III 4, p. 21:19: '... als Umwendlung ursprünglicher Instinkte.'

31 E III 9, p. 51: '[Ethical love] is not a general love for humanity, but rather my love finds in this individual person something that is unique and exceptional.' [Das is nicht allgemeine Menschenliebe, sondern als meine Liebe zu diesem individuellen Menschen etwas ganz Einziges, Ausgenommenes.] Cited by René Toulemont, *L'essence de la société selon Husserl* (Paris, 1962), p. 254.

32 E III 9, p. 49. [Die Kinder sind die Kinder dieser Mutter, nicht als objektive Tatsachen, sondern für sie in ihrer Individualität Werte und zurückbezogen auf die Individualität der Mutter. Der Mutter stehen alle ihre Kinder als diese Werte gleich – nur aus anderen Gesichtspunkten kann sie z. B. hinsichtlich der Begabung das eine Kind höher werten, das andere weniger hoch und ev. beide gleich. Die «Gleichstellung» aller Werte ist für die Mutter keine Wertvergleichung nach mehr oder minder. Sondern sie sind darin gleich dass sie als Individualwerte über alles Vergleichen erhoben sind.] Cited by Toulemont, Ibid., p 254.

33 A V 24, p. 29:4–8, dated January 1932: 'Most notably: the other is "here and now" in danger, or he is treated shockingly unfairly by a third [person], and one jumps immediately to his aid, what this forebodes for oneself, overall remains not at issue, one does not think of the damage to oneself.' [My trans.] [Am auffälligsten: der Andere ist *hic und nunc* in

self-forgetfulness, a person centers upon the welfare of another person, and when one's own interests come to mind, one dismisses them from consideration. Self-consciousness makes an appearance but efforts are taken to keep it from becoming a concern.[34] In a third type of self-forgetfulness, there is full consideration of one's own interests, answered by a choice to act solely on behalf of the friend or beloved.[35]

Finally, Husserl postulates a love that is 'infinite, absolute and universal' [*Diese ist unendlich ist absolut und universal ...*]. It is an absolute limit of the possibility of love. With an Anselm-like turn of argument, he considers a love compared to which one cannot imagine a greater version. This limiting case of love must be distinguished from doctrinaire varieties of love, which would imbue it with denominational, and *tant pis*, sacramental legitimation. Understanding this unconditional love, he writes, is 'impeded by superstitions and traditionalisms'.[36]

His line of thought may be reconstructed as follows: Ethical love is grounded by personal love, which, as we discussed in Part One, is based in the empathetic response to another's *striving*. 'As I love someone who takes the trouble to strive, in loving him I love the idea of the good, and so for humanity.'[37] Ethical love, then, does not depend upon an *a priori* inference based in a deduction from moral rules as with, for example, Kant's Categorical Imperative. Rather, as a perfection of personal love, it arises affectively, from the empathetic caring for the beloved. Because we love a person who 'takes the trouble to strive', we also love the idea of the good manifested in the person. Since this love focuses on the uniqueness and the exceptionality of the loved, one person is not rated more worthy than the next. As with the paradigm of motherly love, one child is not worth more than another since they are beyond comparison. Ethical love extends to a collectivity, but the collectivity remains non-generalizable. The goodness of the group is thereby articulated according to its

---

Lebensgefahr, oder er wird empörend unbillig von Dritten behandelt, und man springt ganz unmittelbar ihm bei, was immer man für sich vorhat, bleibt überhaupt unbedacht, ev. unter Eigen-Schädigung, an die man nicht denkt.]

34 A V 24, p. 29:8–12: 'But one can also think of oneself, one can have a thematic consciousness of oneself, but in such a manner that "self"-interest does not bring into consideration "one's" interest. One's interests may enter into the field of attention, but one separates oneself immediately from them. They are not part of the conversation.' [Aber man kann auch an sich denken, man kann sich mit thematisch haben, aber so daß man das 'Selbst'-Interesse, 'sein' Interesse nicht in Rechnung zieht, nicht in Erwägung, um sich erst dann zu entscheiden. Tritt es in den Blick, so mag es ohne weiteres ausgeschieden werden. Es hat nicht mitzusprechen.]

35 A V 24, p. 29:12–16: 'Finally, also a consideration and overview of one's own interest may take place, and then in the decision-making a pure behavior on behalf of the interest of the other.' [Endlich kann auch die Erwägung statthaben und der Versicht auf das eigene und dann in der Entschiedenheit ein reines sich-Verhalten im Interesse des Anderen ...]

36 Ms. E III 4, p. 19:1–2: 'All ethical life is absolute in its limits – it can be impeded by superstitions and traditionalisms.' [Absolut is jedes ethische Leben in seinen Grenzen, es kann behaftet sein mit Superstitionen, mit Traditionalismen.]

37 Ms. E III 4, p. 20: [Aber wie ich den einzelnen Menschen, 'der streben sich bemüht', liebe und, ihn liebend, in ihm die Idee des Guten, seines Guten, liebe, so für die Menschheit.]

members indefinitely. As such, it extends to what is 'fine and good *in infinitum*' [*schönes und gutes in infinitum*].[38]

Husserl also considers an absolute limiting act of ethical love. It is marked by what Husserl refers to in manuscripts as an unconditional 'act of life' [*Lebensakt*]. The unconditional act of life consists in the decision to offer one's life for the sake of the goodness of others. This marks the limiting case of the third type of self-forgetfulness. Husserl writes in a manuscript dated Summer, 1930: 'If one sacrifices one's life to the communality or to the authentic love of one's neighbor, one loses one's worldly life, but one gains one's true life, because in the decision of sacrificing oneself is consummated an act of life [*Lebensakt*] which necessarily loves and wills life absolutely.'[39] To the extent that one's will aims at such a love, one's motivation is absolute.[40]

It is difficult not to see as prototypical the sacrifice of Jesus Christ. But one must understand that for spiritual leaders of the likes of Gandhi, in making such an allusion, one is pointing to 'the enshrinement of an eternal law'. Gandhi writes in the newspaper *Harijan*, 27 October 1946:

> But whether the Jesus tradition is historically true or not I do not care. To me it is truer than history because I hold it to be possible and it enshrines an eternal law – the law of vicarious and innocent suffering taken in its true sense.[41]

And we should also recall that thinkers and leaders who precede or identify themselves outside the Christian tradition conscript intimations of such sacrifices. The first century Jewish leader, Johanan ben Zakkai, enabled the Jewish tradition to survive by accepting the futility of violently opposing the catastrophe of the burning

---

38 Ms. E III 4, p. 21: 'And at once with that, one affirms the life of humanity as a life unconditionally needed, fine and good *in infinitum*.' [Und in eins damit bejaht er das Leben der Menschheit als ein absolut gefordertes, schönes und gutes in infinitum.]

39 Ms. E III 4, pp. 20:25–21:2: [Opfert er sein Leben der Gemeinschaft, oder aus echter Nächstenliebe, so verliert er sein irdisches Leben, aber er gewinnt sein wahres Leben, weil in der Entscheidung für das Opfer ein Lebensakt vollzogen ist, den er absolut lieben und wollen muß.]

40 Ms. E III 9, p. 20: 'This love is infinite, is absolute and universal, it is of such a kind that it is not possible to conceive what I could love more, in the sense that I could sacrifice what I love thus. If I live a life where my will is so oriented, if I live as an individual, according to a will that aims at an authentic life and, as a member of humanity, according to a will aimed at humanity progressing towards authenticity, then this will is motivated unconditionally.' [Diese Liebe ist unendlich, ist absolut und universal, sie ist von einer Art, daß ich nichts denken kann, was ich mehr lieben könnte, nämlich in einem Sinn, daß ich um dessentwillen das Geliebte preisgeben könnte. Lebe ich in diese Willensrichtung, lebe ich für mich in dem Willen zu meinem echten Leben und als Menchheitsglied im Willen zu einer werdenden echten Menschheit, so ist dieser Wille absolut motiviert.]

41 M.K. Gandhi, *Non-violence in Peace & War*, vol. II (Ahmedabad-14, 1949), p. 160. In the same edition of his newspaper, *Harijan*, 27 October 1946, Gandhi refers to Christ's sacrifice as a 'perfect act': 'A man who was completely innocent, offered himself as a sacrifice for the good of others, including his enemies, and became a ransom of the world. It was a perfect act. "It is finished" were the last words of Jesus' Gandhi ...' Ibid., p. 160.

of the Temple and the fall of the Jewish state in 70 ACE. By transmogrifying its material manifestations into intellectual and spiritual ones, he kept Judaism alive, making the Bible itself into a kind of portable fatherland. He did not react to violence with counter-violence, but retained the moral law in view of the sacrifice of worldly manifestations. Among so-called pagans, Aristotle surely had more than an inkling of the enormous worth extended to those who sacrifice themselves for the good of another: 'Now those who die for others doubtless attain this result [one great and noble action]; it is therefore a great prize they choose for themselves.'[42] In speaking of 'one great and noble action' Aristotle derived, what Christ embodied, ben Zakkai instituted, and Husserl determined, namely, that the absolute limit of personal love is marked by the decision to guide one's life upon a sacrifice of one's own life for the life of others. Such a sacrifice has the following features: 1) it ranks *the worth* of the personal beloved's life beyond the limit of one's own life inasmuch as the sacrifice of one's own life is deliberately offered to preserve the beloved (self-forgetfulness #3); 2) it attests that the beloved is loved, since the act is performed for the sake of the other; and 3) it suggests that the beloved is loved 'absolutely' inasmuch as one is willing to give up one's own life for the other. This 'act of life' [*Lebensakt*], so Husserl speculates, renders ethical love absolute and unconditional.

Perhaps it comes as a surprise that Husserl, the founder of phenomenology who strove to make it rigorous science (*strenge Wissenschaft*), would be occupied with such issues. But in manuscripts dating from the summer of 1930, we find as much. Husserl assigns to the philosopher, and in particular to the transcendental phenomenologist, the role of explaining the constitution of the absolute limits of the ethical life, which relocates the transcendental Ego within an ultimate limit of a field that 'embraces all co-subjects'. These subjects, he says, are: 'in the field of my ethical solicitude ... their true good and bad concerns me and, inversely, mine concerns them ...'[43]

---

42 Aristotle, *Nicomachean Ethics*, IX, 1169a25–6.

43 Ms. E III 4, p. 19:2–15: 'The awakening of philosophy signifies the awakening of an absolute, a truly absolute and universal autonomy, as a life, an existence, which can respond absolutely on its own in every regard, and even which can be, through and through, a unity of an absolute life, which can be constituted from the unity of a personal absolute and a communal absolute, a life absolute in its relativity. And this universality signifies also that it embraces all co-subjects. If I have become an absolute ethical subject, these subjects are for me not only subjects thought *sub specie* authenticity, as subjects thought of regarding their true self-preservation, subjects for the exigency of their own autonomy. Rather, they are also for me as co-subjects, subjects in the field of my ethical solicitude; their true good and bad concerns me and, inversely, mine concerns them, in the measure to which they have understood their significance and form.' [Das Erwachen der Philosophie besagt Erwachen einer absoluten, und zwar absolut universalen Autonomie, als Sein und Leben, das sich in jeder Hinsicht absolut verantworten kann, das eben durch und durch Einheit eines absoluten Lebens sein will, in dem Einheit der absoluten Personalität in der absoluten Gemeinschaft sich konstituieren kann, absolut in seiner Relativität. / Und diese Universalität bedeutet auch die alle Mitsubjekte umgreifende. Diese sind, wenn ich absolutes ethisches Subjekt geworden bin, für mich selbst nur sub specie der Echtheit, als Subjekte wahrer Selbsterhaltung gedacht, unter der Forderung dieser selben Autonomie. Aber sie sind auch für mich Mitsubjekte als

In one remarkable passage Husserl describes the ethical love for others as an analogue of the transcendental reduction itself! As the phenomenologist puts objects 'out of action' in the phenomenological reduction, with ethical love, they analogously suspend the thematic interests extended to another person. The other person is no longer someone with whom I have an agenda of any sort. This analogue of the *epochē* uncovers persons as occupied in their own strivings. As such, the transcendental connection to the other, as a 'responsive alter Ego' appears. This means that we allow ourselves to accept others in their uniqueness, a transcendental condition for personal love. Finally, uncovered is a permanent, yet worldly, union with the other's individuality.[44]

Along with the perfection of personal love, we might add a consequent peril that follows upon it. As we have considered, hatred, by its nature, is devoted to the general case. In its especially virulent form it rests upon pseudo-essential generalizations. As William Hazlitt put it, 'We can scarcely hate anyone we know.'[45] 'It is the mask that we dread and hate: the man may have something human about him!'[46]

A consequent peril of personal love arises when it totters on the possibility of generalizing people into types, for as we have considered this is a precondition of hatred. E.M. Forster understood the weakness of group-directed love. Forster writes in *Two Cheers for Democracy*: 'The idea that nations should love one another, or that business concerns or marketing boards should love one another, or that a man in Portugal should love a man in Peru of whom he has never heard – it is absurd, unreal, dangerous.'[47] Forster argues that love is a great force in private life, but that it does

---

Subjekte in meinem ethischen Fürsorgefeld, ihr wahres Wohl und Wehe geht mich selbst an, und meines geht, wofern sie den Sinn ihrer Form erfaßt haben, umgekehrt sie an.]

44 Ms. E III 4, p. 12:5–8: 'It [phenomenology] shows that, with authentic love of one's neighbor, the other is not an object in the world, as natural reality, which is taken as a theme, but rather the other is a responsive-Ego [Gegen-Ich]; it shows that it produces rather a transcendental personal love, that is, a permanent union as also worldly and simultaneous in its manifestations.' [Sie (die Phänomenologie) weist auf, wie in der echten Nächstenliebe nicht der Andere als Weltobjekt, als Reales thematisch ist sondern der Andere als Gegen-Ich und wie in der Liebe transzendental personale, *d. i.* bleibende Einigung statthat, wie sehr zugleich verweltlicht erscheint.]

45 William Hazlitt, *The Complete Works of*, vol. VIII, *Table-Talk* (1826) (London, 1931), Essay xxvi: 'Why Distant Objects Please', p. 262.

46 Hazlitt, William, Ibid., p. 263.

47 Edward M. Forster, 'Tolerance', in *Two Cheers for Democracy* (New York, 1938), p. 45. Forster is making a fairly recurrent observation about the limits of compassionate love. Consider Adam Smith's statement in the *Theory of Moral Sentiments*: 'Let us suppose that the great empire of China, with all its myriad of inhabitants, was suddenly swallowed up by an earthquake, and let us consider how a man of humanity in Europe, who had no connexion with that part of the world, would be affected upon receiving the intelligence of this dreadful calamity. He would, I imagine, first of all, express very strongly his sorrow for the misfortune of that unhappy people, he would make many melancholy reflections upon the precariousness of human life, and the vanity of all the labours of man, which could thus be annihilated in a moment... And when all this fine philosophy was over, when all these humane sentiments had been once fairly expressed, he would pursue his business or his pleasure, take his repose or his diversion, with the same ease and tranquility, as if no such accident happened. The most

not work in public affairs. He cites glaring cases of its repeated failure as a political program.[48] Forster's point is worth serious consideration inasmuch as personal love is directed towards unique individuals, and resentment and hatred, towards generalizations. A club, company, corporation, or nation cannot have 'personal love' for humanity *en masse*. A club or community may be interested in helping the unemployed, the homeless, or the mentally ill. Such motivations require, either from one's own direct experience, or from empathy-producing biographies and stories, an empathetic contact with someone who's striven to find work, shelter, or grappled with retaining sanity. Blanket attitudes toward groups, even attitudes that are at first apparently loving, through their generalizing introduce one of the conditions of resentment, and perhaps, down the road, of hatred. Recall Dante places Brutus and Cassius in the lowest circle of Hell because they chose to betray Julius Caesar, their friend, rather than their country. Leaving aside Dante's doctrinaire depiction of hell, Brutus' and Cassius' interest in the 'the future of Rome' could hardly have been motivated by personal love. But, their betrayal consisted in a treachery of personal love. As has often been stated, the same Germans who were impassive or even laughed when forced to see the Holocaust victims' mass graves wept upon seeing *The Diary of Anne Frank*. The political and spiritual leaders who make compassion a guiding principle for political action have understood the problem. Gandhi proposed the solution succinctly: '... if one takes care of the means, the end will take care of itself.'[49]

The Logic of Wholes and Parts and the 'Scandal' of Sexual Love

We have proposed that sexual love takes as its object sexual parts, especially as co-founded with other parts, in the creation of tactile-kinesthetic wholes. We have employed the whole/part distinction to describe the profound difference between sexual love and personal love. Perhaps it comes as no surprise that the whole/part distinction plays an originary role in the genesis of logical distinctions. It provides the conceptual underpinning of especially primitive stages in the genesis of logical distinctions. Husserl returns to the whole/part distinction to found, among other basic

---

frivolous disaster which could befal himself would occasion a more real disturbance. If he was to lose his little finger to-morrow, he would not sleep to-night; but, provided he never saw them, he will snore with the more profound security over the ruin of a hundred millions of his brethren, and the destruction of that immense multitude seems plainly an object less interesting to him, that this paltry misfortune of his own.' Adam Smith, *The Theory of Moral Sentiments* (Oxford, 1973), p. 136.

48 Forster asks us to consider the Christian civilizations of the Middle Ages and the secular movement in the French Revolution that asserted the Brotherhood of Man.

49 Gandhi, M.K., 'Working of Non-Violence', *Harijan*, 11 February 1939, in *Non-violence in Peace and War*, vol. I (Ahmedabad-14, 1942), p. 212.

logical distinctions, the 'universal relation of containment'[50] the notion of substrate[51] and of quality.[52]

How does one talk about the world of pre-predicative, pre-reflective experience? Husserl himself sometimes reverts to such terminology as pre-reflective 'unities' or 'homogenities'. But this phraseology leaves out a feature of pre-reflective life that is essentially relational. When we attend to the rustle of curtains, the page fallen from the book or the gleam of a sapphire ring, there is an non-deliberative interest in the successive 'determinations' of these 'unities' or 'homogeneities'.[53] Looking for language to describe how the glance passes from the gleam of the sapphire to other features of the ring, we may have recourse to the terms, 'determinations' and 'unities' or 'homogeneities'. But the whole/part distinction has advantages. It conveys both the unity of the pre-reflective 'thing', while at the same time accommodates the primary phenomenological insight that things are always perceived along with their 'internal and external horizons'.[54] From the beginning, we presume that the gleam of the sapphire that catches our eye promises an annulated band of some sort, and so we are drawn to discern the white-gold ring that holds the gem, although we never see it whole. Our vision, attracted to the gleam of the sapphire, immediately presumes it to be part of a whole, which we increasingly, but never completely, fill out. This is not to presume that the whole/part distinction is innate or for that matter especially chronologically formative in the cognitive development of children. It is enough that it has the functional value of founding the genealogy of logical distinctions. That warrants its value for describing sexual love. It would be a curious lover indeed, who, in the throes of passion, dwelt consciously upon the whole/part distinction. But this only confuses dwelling on an idea with its *de facto* application. We *do* become fascinated with sexual parts in love-making. And the primitive role of wholes and

---

50 Consider for example: 'As you see, the universal *relationship of part and whole* and *vice versa* (or better, the universal relationship of containment and of what is contained, or part to part, and much else) naturally belongs in this realm of the most *general, formal universality*, a realm contained in itself.' Husserl, *Analyses Concerning Active and Passive Synthesis*, p. 346:3–7.

51 'First let us mention what follows from this for the *concept of a whole*. For possible internal determination, every substrate can be regarded as a *whole* which has *parts* in which it is explicated.' Husserl, *Experience and Judgment*, p. 141.

52 'We can thus *define* a quality as an *immediate dependent moment of a whole* or as an immediate part of a whole, a part for which there are not any other immediate parts with which it might be "connected".' Husserl, *Experience and Judgment*, p. 148.

53 As presented in this book's Introduction, Husserl scholar, Donn Welton, maintains that perhaps Husserl's most influential contribution is the notion of the 'world' as 'horizonal'. But the horizonality of the world cannot be conceived without presuming a passive explorative tendency, a 'being there' of an object's backsides and undersides which are given as undetermined yet for which at the same time we harbor anticipations and which our interest in the object leads us to increasingly fill out. See Donn Welton (ed.), *The New Husserl: A Critical Reader* (Bloomington, IN, 2003), p. 223.

54 For an account of the primacy of internal and external horizons, see Husserl, *Experience and Judgment*, pp. 32–3.

parts in the genealogy of logic goes a long way in explaining how such a fascination would seem to overturn our social inter-personal world, at least in the throes of sex.

Raw talk of sex is jarring, not just because it sometimes involves a disrespect for persons, for it just as often involves adoration. It is jarring because it easily manages to deflate existential pretenses. It wrenches us away from an objective world shared by anyone with the 'normal' capacity to perceive. Consequently, we surely are loath to introduce, in public address, raw reference to sexual parts. In the middle of *Tropic of Capricorn*, Henry Miller writes: 'This is all a figurative way of speaking about what is unmentionable. What is unmentionable is pure fuck and pure cunt: it must be mentioned only in *de luxe* editions, otherwise the world will fall apart ... But *fuck*, the real thing, *cunt*, the real thing, seems to contain some unidentified element which is far more dangerous than nitroglycerin.'[55] Even in quoting Miller's words, 'fuck' and 'cunt', there is likely a sense that the rules of scholarly discourse have been suspended. Similarly, the world of sexual love brings with it a kind of existential snap. There is always a scandal involved. And that word 'scandal', in its roots tells a story. Shared by modern Western languages in meaning 'unseemly conduct' its cognates in Latin and Greek[56] and even further in the surmised Indo-Germanic, as **skand*, indicates its development from a spring or a jump that leads to capture. And there is in lovemaking a captivating jump or spring from the mundane, habitual, world of objects that we presume in everyday life. This snap or spring from mundanity makes bathetic, and sometimes ludicrous, that world which we temporarily leave behind, a world in which we never doubt that the sunset viewed is the same one seen by everyone. The sexual world is always scandalous. Not only are parts strangely no longer sustained in their familiar milieu and as such are 'pre-predicative',[57] the sexual world, as we've considered, privileges the contact senses, smell, taste and touch, over the distant senses, hearing and vision. Thus, it is doubly disruptive. That world must remain hidden, or, perhaps more often, simply lied about. It's not just a matter of threatening 'morality' and 'decency'. The turnabout goes deeper. Ancient philosophers recognized that they could teach virtue through the enactment of tragedies. But in the world of sex it is the satyr who reigns. He cares little for the

---

55 Henry Miller, *The Tropic of Capricorn* (London, 1964), p. 174.

56 French has *scandale*; German, *Skandal*, and Spanish, *escándalo*. The Latin and Greek roots trace the metonymy out of which the word developed. The Latin *scandalum*, that is, a cause of disgrace or stumbling, is related to *scandere*, to climb. The Greek, σκάνδαλον, means a moral stumbling, but its earlier usages, as in σκανδάληθρον, connect it to the spring of a trap. And here we see the odd metonymy upon which the word developed, that is, from the notion of a *spring* or *leap*, which entraps.

57 That sexual love itself is strangely separate from discursive description has often been reflected upon by novelists. Consider E.L. Doctorow: 'You can't remember sex. You can remember the fact of it, and recall the setting, and even the details, but the sex of the sex cannot be remembered, the substantive truth of it, it is by nature self-erasing, you can remember its anatomy and be left with a judgment as to the degree of your liking of it, but whatever it is as a splurge of being, as a loss, as a charge of the conviction of love stopping your heart like your execution, there is no memory of it in the brain, only the deduction that it happened and that time passed, leaving you with a silhouette that you want to fill in again.' E.L. Doctorow, *Billy Bathgate* (New York, 1989), Chapter 16.

pretense of worldly happenstance. And this dispensation is not only liberating, it has its truth, since it unfastens the false, and even self-servingly arrogant, belief in our one and only visually-organized objective world.

The Confinement of Hatred into the Logic of an Exclusive 'Either/Or'

Hate traps us by binding us too tightly to our adversary[58]

In the conclusion to personal love, we quoted Husserl's statement in *Ideas I*: '...there is besides the doxic "and" (the logical "and") an axiological and practical "and".'[59] Consider now the appended statement: 'The same holds for the "or" and all the syntheses belonging here.[60] It should come as no surprise that hatred exploits an exclusive '*or*'. From the beginning, as the principle of blame would indicate, hatred denies the hater's culpability while coolly affirming it of the hated. A clear line is drawn between who deserves to be blamed and who does not, with the hater, or the hater's home-group excluded from the equation.

Hardly unusual, yet exemplary are statements made by Wahhabi cleric, Shaikh Saad Al-Buraik in exhibiting the axiological and practical '*or*'. His statements were recorded on tape in 2002 as Al-Buraik presided over a fund-raising telephon:

> I am against America until this life ends, until the Day of Judgment; I am against America even if the stone liquefies. My hatred of America, if part of it was contained in the universe, it would collapse. She is the root of all evils, and wickedness on earth. Who else implanted the tyrants in our land, who else nurtured oppression?[61]

The cleric's violent hatred expresses an exclusive either/or in its America *versus* the universe opposition. Al-Buraik says: 'My hatred of America, if part of it [his hatred] was contained in the universe, it [the universe] would collapse.' This statement, extremely hyperbolic, conveys how Al-Buraik conceives the size of the stakes involved. According to Al-Buraik, American culture and politics has so fomented hatred that it threatens to destroy the universe. The 'them or us' is not between America, 'the root of all evils' and the Wahhabis, the Saudis, or Islam. According to Al-Buraik, the opposition is between America and the universe.

The statements of Al-Buraik also exemplify the 'affective and volitional *or*' as it arises in the 'generativity' of the ideal home-group versus the ideal alien-group. As we've considered, the constitution of 'the homeworld' depends on a sense of tradition and history. And, for a tradition to be maintained it must be capable of repeating itself; it must contain 'generative' practices and beliefs. One need not look

---

58 Milan Kundera, *Immortality* (New York, 1991), Part One, 'The Face', p. 26.

59 Husserl, *Ideas, First Book*, p. 289, cited above.

60 Husserl, Ibid.

61 Saudi Information Service, 2002, published as 'Saudi Telethon Host Calls for Enslaving Jewish Women', in *National Review*, 26 April 2002. During the two-day long telethon $109 million were raised. On the tape, Al-Buraik said that the money raised would go to Palestinian fighters.

far into Al-Buraik's indictments to find the generative aspects of the 'home-group' and how its generativity is threatened. Al-Buraik says:

> People should know that Jews are backed by the Christians, and the battle that we are going through is not with Jews only, but also with those who believe that Allah is a third in a Trinity, and those who said that Jesus is the son of Allah, and Allah is Jesus, the son of Mary.

Al-Buraik tells his audience that Allah, the Creator, is equated with, and thereby displaced by, Jesus, the son of Mary, a flesh and blood female. As we have explained in the part on hatred, violent group hatred presumes that the generativity of the home-group is at stake. Al-Buraik's Allah is surely an unsurpassable principle of generativity. He sees US Christians, in particular, as demoting Allah by equating Allah's godly status with a mere human female's progeny (Jesus). The generativity of the home-group is thereby undone. It should not be surprising that this prospect marshals the fear of a group whose identity and salvation lies in submission to the will of the incomparably powerful and merciful Allah.

Al-Buraik's beliefs also exhibit the exclusive 'or' in its *volitional* expression. As indicated, Al-Buraik's speech prompts the fear that one's identity and salvation is imminently threatened. Two groups are polarized and his listeners must choose. He thrusts an either/or choice upon his audience:

> Which is a better choice, to die on your bed, or to die perseverant, fighting, not retreating? Which is better to suffer long before death many days, or taste death quickly? Which is better to suffer a slow death, or die as a martyr in your way to heaven. A death that you will be forgiven on the first drop of your blood.

Choosing, deciding or willing some action (the volitional attitude), unlike desiring, aspiring, or hoping for an action, presumes that practical means are at hand. And, Al-Buraik assures his listeners that practical means are indeed readily available. On the same tape, Al-Buraik states that the staggeringly large amount of funds collected from the two-day telethon ($109 million) will support Palestine fighters.[62]

Al-Buraik's statements also exemplify the 'affective and volitional *or*' as it enters into (hyper)generalization. Recall that violent group hatred not only essentializes, but also stereotypes the target of its hatred. Beyond making the loathsome traits *necessary*, the differences between individuals count for little to nothing. As we've considered, when persons, in hatred, stereotype the hated group, they are blind to the group members' individuality as well as to their membership in the human species. They saturate their enemy with a collection of slurs and negative caricatures. Calling members of the hated group, 'cockroaches', 'scum', 'vermin', and so on, imposes not only universally pejorative traits, individuality is also excluded. Cockroaches, scum, vermin, and so on, have neither positive traits nor significant differences.

In the history of twentieth century philosophy, the grave social, political, and philosophical errors arising from bifurcating an essence and its individual instance

---

62 The dollar amount is taken from the *National Review* report cited above, Saudi Information Service, 2002.

is perhaps most associated with American pragmatism. John Dewey, in particular, called the 'problem of the relation of the ideal and the real' 'the standing problem of life'.[63] The solution to the problem as Dewey saw it was not to dispense with ideals, but to 'have the right ideals'. And the right ideals are based in a systematic understanding of reality.[64] The idealizing of the home-group into a pure genetic or theological union, or both, as with Aryanism, White-supremacy, Islamic-supremacy, Zionist-supremacy, Japanese *Nihonjinron* supremacy, and so on, clearly imposes the wrong ideals. In fact, there is typically a recurrent political pre-occupation between those who qualify for the true home-group and those who are lapsed, reluctant, dissident, or sham members of the group. Hutu Power racist propagandist Hassan Ngeze, a journalist who goaded the 1994 Tutsi genocide, insisted that true Hutus must be unforgiving and eliminate Tutsi-loving or lapsed Hutus.[65] Pierce, in his hate-mongering fable, *The Turner Diaries*, rants on about the need to separate 'true Whites' from the merely apparent Whites.[66] Thus we have yet another tessellation of the exclusive '*either-or*'. Here it appears in the opposition between true Aryans, Hutus, Bosnian Serbs, and so on and their counterfeits, who are only nominally members of the idealized group.

But if there is an exclusive 'either-or' political tension between those who qualify for the home-group and those who do not, it is relatively mild compared with the 'either-or' opposition that pervades the generalization of the hated alien-group. As 'scum' or 'vermin', the hated aliens barely qualify as objects. Like dust or dirt, they are nameless and typeless, merely suitable for being washed away. The either-or contrast resorts to the most unindividualized metaphysical entity conceivable, a loathsome undifferentiated mass.

The 'Either/Or' Logic of Hatred Suggests a Threefold Approach to its Abatement

This reflection on violent eidetic hatred as framing beliefs, feelings, and volitions according to an exclusive '*or*', thankfully also suggests a format for sorting out various releases from its entrapment. As quoted at the head of this section, Milan

---

63 John Dewey, *Reconstruction in Philosophy* (New York, 1937), p. 130. The hitherto incomparably violent conflict he was privy to (World War I) Dewey states was, 'carried on for purely ideal ends:– for humanity, justice and equal liberty for strong and weak alike.' Dewey, Ibid., p. 128.

64 Dewey's full statement runs: 'It is false that the evils of the situation arise from absence of ideals; they spring from the wrong ideals. And these wrong ideals have in turn their foundation in the absence of social matters of the methodic, systematic, impartial, critical, searching into "real" and operative conditions which we call science and which has brought man in the technical realm to the command of physical energies.' Dewey, Ibid.

65 Philip Gourevitch, *We wish to inform you that tomorrow we will be killed with our families: Stories from Rwanda* (New York, 1998), p. 88.

66 'It was no longer sufficient to be merely White; in order to eat one had to be judged the bearer of especially valuable genes.' William L. Pierce, *The Turner Diaries* (Fort Lee, NJ, 1996), p. 206. 'As the war of extermination wore on, millions of soft, city bread, brainwashed Whites gradually began to regain their manhood. The rest died.' Pierce, Ibid., p. 207.

Kundera observed: 'Hate traps us by binding us too tightly to our adversary.'[67] We have argued that hatred, along with personal and sexual love, come to their full expressions, when guided by the emotional and volitional analogues of their logical underpinnings. We can sort out, then, the loosening of the entrapment of violent group hatred according to the underpinnings of its belief-based (in phenomenological terms, its 'doxic') affective and volitional logic.

First, as to the *belief-based* aspects of malevolent hatred, we have argued that extreme violent hatred builds on the belief that there is an idealized home-group pitted against an alien-group. This extreme version of hatred, along with its lesser forms, makes the alien-group wholly responsible for whatever misfortunes of the home-group (the principle of extra-vituperation). One principal counter-measure, then, involves assuming personal responsibility for the harm the home-group has caused to the alien-group. From a political perspective this countermeasure becomes especially effective when issued from leaders, but it applies to hatred in general inasmuch as it alters the identification of the person who hates.

It is remarkable how effective a weakening of the home-group idealization can be even when the disavowal, repentance or acceptance of responsibility is grossly separated in time and place from the original offense. Consider the extreme case of an apology for a religious campaign, coming some 800 years after the fact: the capture and pillage of Constantinople by the pilgrims of the Fourth Crusade in 1204. It is easily overlooked that the divisiveness it instituted continued to insinuate itself into Western European, Balkan and Russian politics for centuries. Even, today it provides propaganda for Middle East terrorism.

In Constantinople in 1204 the typical lines were drawn between the idealized home-group and the demonized alien-group. Robert of Clari, a pilgrim present at the sack of Constantinople, in April of 1204, records the sermons made by the Christian bishops who mobilized the Crusaders to sack the Christian 'new Rome'. Robert of Clari writes:

> Then the bishops preached to the army, the bishop of Soissons, the bishop of Troyes, the bishop of Havestaist, master Jean Faicette, and the abbot of Loos, and they showed to the pilgrims that the war was a righteous one; for the Greeks were traitors and murderers, and also disloyal, since they had murdered their rightful lord, and were worse than Jews. Moreover, the bishops said that, by the authority of God and in the name of the pope, they would absolve all who attacked the Greeks. Then the bishops commanded the pilgrims to confess their sins and receive the communion devoutly; and said that they ought not to hesitate to attack the Greeks, for the latter were enemies of God.[68]

According to the bishops and abbots, by joining in the slaughter, the pilgrims entered the hallowed ranks of true Christian soldiers, that is, the idealized home-group. The Byzantines, to a man, woman and child, became spiritual enemies. No matter that their doctrinal beliefs, literally, differed by only an iota from the Crusaders.

---

67 Kundera, Ibid., p. 26, cited above.

68 Dan Carlson Munro (ed.), 'The Fourth Crusade', *Translations and reprints from the Original Sources in European History*, vol. III, no. 1 (Philadelphia, PA, 1907), pp. 13–14.

More than eight hundred years later, John Paul II apologized for the April 1204 slaughter. An apology, if understood as sincere, by its nature assumes taking responsibility and taking responsibility breaks the encapsulation of the alien-group's unworthiness.

But what possible good could come from an apology made over 800 years after the offense? In fact the apology was efficacious because it bore symbolically upon current home-group's beliefs, which arise in a multitude of Balkan/Latinist conflicts. Such conflicts abetted the propaganda used in the Bosnian War of the 1990s. The late pontiff's apology even had some pertinence to current terrorism. Osama bin Laden and members of Al Qaeda repeatedly refer to the US, and to 'the West' in general, as 'crusaders'. The dissemination of Pope John Paul II's apology in the minds of those who assume the rigidity of official Catholic doctrine, deflates, if not absolves, this part of Osama bin Laden's rhetoric.

Pumla Gobodo-Madikizela writes, drawing upon her immediate experience with South Africa's Truth and Reconciliation Commission:

> When criminal offenders, even of the most egregious kind, show contrition and apologize, they are, quintessentially, acting as human beings.[69]

By 'acting as human beings', the worst of the idealized home-group cracks the shell of the closed-off identification with the ideal home-group and the demonization of the alien-group.

On 25 March 1998 President Clinton and Madeleine Albright visited Rwanda. Clinton reiterated Albright's apologies made in mid-December 1997 for refusing to intervene during the 1994 Tutsi genocide. To many, Albright's and Clinton's apologies came too late. Indeed, they were too late if one considers the conflict to be a momentary tragic episode of history. But as with the late Pope's apology for April 1204 in Byzantium, such 'moments' are easily absorbed into the background beliefs that make up national legends and as such continue to frame ethnicities long after the event.

Obviously, personal apologies and expressions of regret and remorse fail to alter the fact of past evils. Hannah Arendt observes in *The Human Condition* that 'radically evil' acts 'transcend the realm of human affairs'.[70] They are consequently neither punishable or forgivable. Arendt's point is well-taken. Punitive justice requires that the punishment match the crime. There are no punishments that match the crimes of Adolf Hitler, Pol Pot, Idi Amin, Slobodan Milosevic, Saddam Hussein, and so on. Gourevitch, reflecting on the Rwandan genocide, arrives at the same truth: '... a true genocide and true justice are incompatible.'[71] Further, forgiveness is meaningless if the act of forgiveness implies that it undoes the injustices done to the victims of the mass murderers.

But what often is left out in claims about the ineffectiveness of retrospective responsibility-taking is that the psychological machinery that creates mass hatred often remains dormant for the right demagogue to fire up again long after the

---

69 Gobodo-Madikizela, *A Human Being Died That Night* (Boston, 2003), p. 127.
70 Hannah Arendt, *The Human Condition* (Chicago, 1998), p. 241.
71 Gourevitch, Ibid., p. 249.

egregious offense. In fact the Hutu-supremacist killings of Tutsis did not end in 1994. The killings continued into the late 1990s and beyond. There is no changing the past, but when key representatives of idealized groups sincerely take responsibility for previous offenses, the psychological machinery they rely upon weakens. In a sense, such regrets put the beliefs founding violent group hatred 'in reverse'. Instead of idealizing the home-group and making the alien-group sub-human, they humble the home-group and elevate the alien-group, guaranteeing its worth of respect.

What about the loosening of the entrapment of 'us-them' hatred from the perspective of the *affective* oppositional '*or*'? Emotions, feelings, and the sense of values they instill, are at issue. Herein lies the role of empathy. Personal love individualizes. It is antithetical to violent group-targeted hatred. Empathy in general, insofar as it requires a sense of a person's strivings and endeavors, emerges from a sense of the life of an individual. We need to see, hear, or read about the individual and understand their strivings, hopes, and dreams to feel empathy.

To forestall the possible use of empathy, as itself a reason for further retaliatory hostility, empathy especially counteracts 'us-them' opposition when it is *double-sided*. Images of bomb-maimed children induce empathy for the nearby parents struck dumb by grief. But, these same images can easily justify the victims' cause. The image of maimed body of the dead Israeli child makes the Palestinian suicide bomber inhuman. But the image of the lifeless mutilated Palestinian child makes the Israeli soldier equally inhuman. The goal is to acknowledge that the home group and the alien-group have *both* suffered immeasurably. Since the suffering on both sides is immeasurable, comparisons as to which side has suffered more are pointless.

Recall the humanization of the victims of 11 September by the *New York Times*, 'Portraits in Grief'. Kenneth Jackson, director of the New York Historical Society, understood the power of the recurrent short biographies:

> The particular genius of it was to put a human face in numbers that are unimaginable to most of us ... As you read those individual portraits about love affairs or kissing children goodbye or coaching soccer and buying a dream house ... it's so obvious that every one of them was a person who deserved to live a fully successful and happy life. You see what was lost.[72]

But this empathy, even so, was one-sided. As far as Al-Qaeda operatives were concerned, its one-sidedness was perhaps justified. But its extension to Afghanis in general was not. Immediately post 9/11 few US newspapers dared put a human face upon the suffering of Afghanis, even if they had nothing to do with the Taliban's politics. The Boston Globe was an exception. They published an account of an intensive care unit at Jalalabad Public Hospital, which was filled with casualties from the American bombings:

> In one bed lay Noor Mohammad, 10, who was a bundle of bandages. He lost his eyes and hands to the bomb that hit his house after Sunday dinner. Hospital director, Guloja

---

72 Janny Scott, 'Closing a Scrapbook Full of Life and Sorrow', *New York Times*, 31 December 2001, p. B6.

Shimwari shook his head at the boy's wounds. 'The United States must be thinking he is Osama,' Shimwari said. 'If he is not Osama, then why would they do this?'[73]

Hospital director, Shimwari, was right. Recall in violent group hatred, there are no traits of the hated alien-group that are not hateful traits. Individuality is eclipsed. Just as there are no significant differences between vermin or cockroaches, when hatred has progressed to its full-blown generalization, there are no significant differences between members of the Al Qeada, the Taliban, and even the progeny of possible associates of the Taliban. In Scheler's terms, hatred 'radiates'. From the perspective of fully fomented group-hatred, the ten year-old Noor Mohammad was an extension of Osama bin Laden.

In fact Husserl's account of the basis of empathy as relying on a pairing with another person directly applies to the individualizing effect of empathy.[74] Empathy arises especially when the bodily presence of another is before us. The empathy engendered by the tragedy of the ten year-old Noor Mohammad emerges as we see the effects of hatred written 'on his flesh'. It's impossible to divorce his mutilations from their effects on his future. Victims of such mutilations are personalized by their sufferings. Ten year-old Noor Mohammad's life is removed from generalization altogether. Like ourselves in our own bodily existence, he is an individual. He suffers as an individual, and his life-plans are altered individually.[75]

---

73 John Donnelly, 'Unintended Victims Fill Afghan Hospital', *Boston Globe*, 5 December 2001, p. A1.

74 Husserl, *Cartesian Meditations* (Den Haag, 1973), §51.

75 Not surprisingly, after the Vietnam War in the US strategies were developed to curtail the reporting, and especially the *photographic* reporting, of war zones. Consider the 1983 invasion of Grenada. For days the nation's press corps was denied access to the island. Armed forces prevented reporters' access to the island by boat or small plane. No journalists succeeded in stationing themselves in Grenada to document the invasion. Reporters finally gained unlimited access to Grenada but, by then, the invasion had already been deemed a success.

Controlling the press's access to a war zone became known as preventing the so-called 'Vietnam syndrome'. Throughout the Vietnam War, combat coverage came straight from the battlefield to the homes of the US public. It became so commonplace that political strategists assumed that this was a main cause for the increasing unpopularity of the Vietnam War in the US.

Among the especially influential images communicated to the US public during the Vietnam War was one caught by the Vietnamese photographer Nick Ut. In June 1972, Nick Ut photographed a naked nine-year-old girl, Kim Phuc, fleeing her village after a napalm attack. Kim, at the center of the photograph, runs naked, her badly burned chest and arms bare. Next to Kim runs her older brother. On her right runs her younger brother looking back to the black smoke. Holding hands and running behind her on the left are two other family members. The specter of desperation conveyed by this picture, shown in the US, China and Vietnam, among other places, won Nick Ut a Pulitzer prize. It also made many question the US military presence in Vietnam.

Like the verbal image of ten-year-old Noor Mohammad, the picture of nine-year-old Kim Phuc, naked, her arms out-stretched, running in terror, her young body expressing outrage seemingly by itself, simply is incompatible with the condition of the stereotyping whereby

But the suspension of the affective oppositional 'or' by empathy, even by 'double-sided' empathy, has its shortcomings. The intensity of the empathy may lead to a suspending of the 'them-us' opposition. It may lead to doubting or dismissing the 'them-us' dichotomy. But still people may *do* little. They may love, fear, envy, regret, or feel remorse about having hated somebody because they're a member of a group and still not take action. The suspension of the affective '*or*' surely makes it more likely action will follow, but it does not ensure it. 'Tears show their love, but want their remedies.'[76] For action, we need consider the *volitional* 'or'.

In developing a theory of action, Husserl appropriates William James' notion that decision-making and willfulness depends upon a '*fiat*', a 'let it be done'.[77] For Husserl, the 'fiat' is a type of judgment whereby an agent constantly affirms 'the strived for' in every phase of its aiming towards some goal. There is an essential difference, for example, between *deciding* to go to Istanbul, say, and *wishing* to go to Istanbul. The decision to go to Istanbul contains a 'let it be done', whereby the agent affirms taking steps to achieve the goal, even if those steps are unknown as yet. As such, it is impossible to decide to go to Istanbul, without believing that the steps along the way are practically possible.[78]

In manuscripts dating from the end of the war years to the early 1920s, Husserl further considers actions that arise from *communal* volition:

> Specifically, as far as action is concerned, my will can direct itself to another; I might have ordered him to do something, and I might view him as acting by my orders. I might have willfully determined his actions in other ways. He does something which is practically wanted by me. His action is then indirectly also my action ...[79]

The scenario mentioned above concerns an agent acting upon the command of another, either through explicit command, or, implicitly, in the belief that the commander 'practically wants the action'. Examples of those who act on violent 'us-them' hatred bear witness to this condition. To his death, Timothy McVeigh claimed that his attack on the Oklahoma City Federal Building was motivated by the federal government's mishandling of two alleged anti-American insurrections: the 1992 standoff at Ruby Ridge, Idaho which resulted in the death of the wife and son of

---

each member of the alien-group possesses all the hated traits. We, creatures of flesh and bone, subject to mutilations, burnings, and maimings, and to bodily expressions of joy and love as well, are not a 'them'.

76 Shakespeare, *Richard II* form *The Complete Works of* (London, 1980), III, iii, 204.

77 For James' discussion of the 'fiat' see section William James, *The Principles of Psychology* (Chicago, 1952), 'Ideo-Motor Action', pp. 790ff.

78 Consider for example *Ideas II*, '... in activity, I am "into" the thing in a practical way; in the "*fiat*" I am first of all engaged in setting the scene; the action which now unfolds is constituted as having happened according to my will, as happening through my agency as a freely willing being; I am constantly there as bringing about the strived for, as aiming in will. And every phase of the aiming itself is such that in it the pure willing subject "attains" the willed as such.' Husserl, *Ideas Pertaining to a Pure Phenomenology and to a Phenomenological Philosophy*, Second Book (Dordrecht, 1989), p. 104.

79 Husserl, *Zur Phänomenologie der Intersubjektivität, Zeiter Teil*, Husserliana XIV, p. 193 [my trans.].

white separatist, Randy Weaver; and, the 1993 siege of the Branch Davidian building near Waco, Texas that ended in the death of seventy-five members of the religious group. Even so, these events could not have adequately prepared McVeigh's 'fiat', in the James/Husserlian sense, to bomb the Oklahoma City federal building. As far as the judgment, whereby McVeigh committed himself to the bombing of the federal building, McVeigh needed at his command the practical steps to the goal. More likely, then, *The Turner Diaries* written by neo-Nazi, William L. Pierce was decisively formative.[80] With this book, Pierce placed in McVeigh's hands the wherewithal for McVeigh's 'fiat'. Pierce supplied the practicality for the bombings, the ingredients and chemistry of the explosives as well as the violently white-supremacist ideology that 'justified' McVeigh's actions.[81]

But the 'fiat', the awareness of requisite practicalities that allow one to say of the action, 'let it be done', unfortunately come from both deleterious and beneficent sources. The commanding agent, who provides the 'fiat', may be a deity. Notwithstanding the professed beliefs, that deity, at least in the mind of the believer, may justify malevolent actions. Innumerable agents of violent eidetic hatred profess acting in accordance with the will of a deity. Saad Al-Buraik, the Wahhabi cleric cited before, leads his telethon audience to violent action by asserting they are following the will of Allah:

> Muslim Brothers in Palestine, do not have any mercy neither compassion on the Jews, their blood, their money, their flesh. Their women are yours to take, legitimately. God made them yours.[82]

The terrorist's chanting of 'Allah Akbar' (God is great) upon detonating bombs is well-known. Osama bin Laden is quoted as saying shortly after 11 September: 'I'm fighting so I can die a martyr and go to heaven to meet God. Our fight now is against the Americans.'[83]

Of course, Islam has no monopoly on fanaticism. The bishops who mobilized the pilgrims in the Fourth Crusade appealed to the will of God, a familiar rallying cry for the Crusades. The battle cry of the First Crusade, promulgated by pope Urban II himself, was '*Deus vult*' – God wills it. Nor need we turn back history much to find 'us-them' hatreds, abetting crimes against humanity, allegedly enacted according to the will of God. Hitler writes in *Mein Kampf*: 'Hence today I believe that I am acting

---

80 The will of a 'commander' is sickeningly replete in *The Turner Diaries* itself. Although never mentioned by name, 'the Great One', whose posthumous volition the racist protagonist of *The Turner Diaries* implements, is undoubtedly Adolf Hitler. The dream of a White world becomes a certainty in 1999, 110 years 'after the birth of the Great One'. Hitler was born in 1889. Pierce, Ibid., p. 210.

81 Pierce specifies: 'ammonium nitrate fertilizer ... sensitized with oil and tightly confined.' This matches the explosives McVeigh placed in the truck next to the Oklahoma City federal building. Pierce, *The Turner Diaries*, pp. 35–6.

82 Cited above: 'Saudi Telethon Host Calls for Enslaving Jewish Women', *National Review*, 26 April 2002.

83 Osama bin Laden, quoted in CBS News, 'Bin Laden: I Didn't Do It' (12 September 2001).

in accordance with the will of the Almighty Creator: by defending myself against the Jew, I am fighting for the work of the Lord.'[84]

The commander one follows, mortal or divine, also may be one who thematically chooses to demonstrate and overcome the conditions of 'us-them' hatred. The names of Lincoln, Gandhi, and Martin Luther King need hardly be cited. And one may surely appeal to Judaic, Christian, Islamic, Hindu, Buddhist, Confucian, and Taoist, scriptures[85] that present the will of God, or enlightened being, in profound opposition to 'us-them' hatred.

But Husserl's theory of action also includes communal actions that arise from group interaction. Here the 'fiat' arises by acknowledging the resources provided by the group.

... if the relationship is interactive, then my action and his activity for me is a simultaneously complex action, which is done and only done immediately one part by him and one part by me. The entire action and achievement is my action and his action also ...[86]

Here, we find the volitional conditions that are more especially suited to taking action in opposition of 'them-us' hatred. Such actions do not rely on the bestowal of a 'fiat' from a commander's order, mortal or divine, and consequently do not engage their possible misuse.[87]

Interactive volitions, in the conflict resolution literature, often go under the name of 'joint projects'. Joint projects may have humble goals. They may involve building houses, schools, parks, and hospitals that have positive value for the conflicted groups. Even such simple shared tasks as carrying heavy objects can help. In Bosnia, the cooperative rebuilding of houses by Croats and Muslims, destroyed during the Bosnia War shows what can be accomplished when former enemies work together in mutually beneficial cooperation.[88] These shared projects break down 'us-them' oppositions and provide material goals. 'Us-them' opposition thrives upon the separation between the groups. The immediate interpersonal interaction between people working on the same project makes people question the relevance of their acquired beliefs and induces degrees of empathy. For merely egotistical reasons, former hatreds get in the way, when a previous enemy helps in realizing the goal. Also, these shared projects may be designed to bring people of similar ages, vocations, or family roles together so as to further promote the

---

84 Adolf Hitler, *Mein Kampf* (Boston, 1998), vol. I, Chapter 2, last sentence.

85 Consider Zechariah, 8:17; Isaiah, 2:4; Matthew, 5:9; Matthew, 5:43–46; Luke, 6:27–8; *Koran*: Surah 5, verse 45; *Koran*: Surah 2, verse 190; *Bhagavad Gita*: Chapter 16; *Dhammapada*: I, verse 5; *Dhammapada*: XV, verse 201; *Analects*: 12.19; *Tao-Te Ching*: Chapter 63.

86 Husserl, *Zur Phänomenologie der Intersubjektivität, Zeiter Teil*, Husserliana XIV, p. 193 [my trans.].

87 '... my action and his activity for me is a simultaneously complex action, which is done and only done immediately one part by him and one part by me.' Husserl, Ibid.

88 Bruce Hemmer, 1997, 'Bottom-up Peace Building in Bosnia', PARC News, Spring, 1997, pp. 4, 8; Peace Watch, 'Bringing Croats and Muslims Together', *United States Institute of Peace*, II, 2, February 1996, p. 4.

empathy between the participants.[89] The Galilee Bilingual School in Israel, for example, brings together Arab and Jewish children in classes, all of which have both an Arab and Jewish teacher.[90]

Shared projects may also take on multi-national proportions. The European Union dates from the end of World War II. To the extent that Europeans accept it as a joint project, and especially in as much as they see its individual members as carrying their own weight, centuries old ethnic and national European conflicts become irrelevant.

The capacity of athletic contests to break down 'us-them' conflict has longstanding proven usefulness. The spectators engrossed in an international Olympic event, for example, know from the beginning that competitors are people from various national groups. But through the competition, they see more than an Australian, Japanese or Nigerian competing. They see an individual athlete striving for excellence. And the standards for excellence are directly designed to make national or ethnic distinctions irrelevant.

The success of black athletes, such as Jackie Robinson, Arthur Ashe, Michael Jordan, Magic Johnson and Tiger Woods has reduced racial stereotypes and hatred. Sports have special advantages for overcoming 'us-them' conflicts. First, the players, the playing fields, and the playing times are relatively arbitrary and changeable as compared with the neighborhoods, regions, nations and histories from which such hatreds rise. Further, the rules of the games, the goals and the athletes' interactions are conspicuous and relatively easily monitored for impartiality. This makes the prominence of 'us-them' conflicts capable of fairly direct treatment, not only for the team players, but also for the spectators.

Team sports are effective since they rely on roles, for example, quarterback, pitcher, goalie, and so on that demand their cooperative interaction. Participation relies on a degree of shared beliefs and one-on-one empathy. To cheer on a team is to crack the shell of 'us-them' oppositions. The JAMAA project, for example, has sponsored soccer games made up of young players in Burundi, both Hutus and Tutsis.[91] The organization is well named. The word, 'jamaa' in Swahili means 'family member' or 'friend'.

---

89 This is not to suggest that shared projects are a cure-all for 'us-them' hatred. Greg Brown, Program Officer for the International Rescue Committee (IRC), notes the various ways in which shared projects are less successful at reducing conflicts. The project may be poorly organized, so that one side feels that it will benefit more than the other. When joint projects are conceived of and organized by third parties, such as Non-Governmental Organizations (NGOs), participants from conflicting groups may lack a necessary ownership. But, these problems amount to ways that shared projects are something short of just that, *shared projects*, that is, projects that involve the fair and interactive participation of individuals. Greg Brown, 'Joint projects' (Conflict Research Consortium, University of Colorado, 2003), http://www.beyondintractability.org/m/joint_projects.jsp.

90 Gil Sedan, 'In One Bilingual Galilee School, Students Seek Out Common Ground', Common Ground News Service (CG News), 27 May 2005.

91 As sponsored by JAMAA, in December 1999, young people in Bujumbura and Ngozi, townships in the central east African nation of Burundi, participated in the first soccer

Whether it is on a sports field, or in constructing a school or homes, however, especially powerful are those shared projects whose participants have experienced similar heavy personal losses, such the death of a child. These sufferings cut through the overlay of ethnic pride and reveal the universality and commonality of human needs and grief.[92] Chris McMorran of the Conflict Research Consortium at the University of Colorado sums up the power of joint projects for conflict resolution:

> Although joint projects are certainly not a panacea for highly escalated, intractable inter-group conflicts, they are one element in a variety of peacebuilding activities that are absolutely essential to bring about eventual conflict transformation and stable peace.[93]

For the purposes of undoing that concoction of inexperience, fallacious-thinking and scapegoating that hides personal self-doubts, fears and humiliations, and that is called violent group-targeted hatred, it is clear that shared projects especially serve in undoing the volitional '*or*'. They supplant a destructive volition with a constructive one. They unlock oppositional beliefs and feelings through practices that repeatedly expose the ignorance upon which this type of hatred is based.

Goethe famously remarked: 'Hatred is something peculiar. You will always find it strongest and most violent where there is the lowest degree of culture.'[94] In one sense of 'high' and 'low' culture, Goethe's remark is surely mistaken. After all, Austria's early twentieth century culture was home to painter Gustav Klimt, playwright Arthur Schnitzler, poets Stefan Zweig, Georg Trakl, and Rainer Maria Rilke, psychologists Brentano and Freud, scientists Mach and Pauli and, philosophers Carnap, Neurath, Popper, Wittgenstein and, of course, Husserl. Vienna seemed a paragon of 'high culture'. Nonetheless, in spite of this cultural flourishing came the *Anschluss*, Austria's nearly unanimous vote for its annexation to Hitler's Germany.

Goethe surely had a piece of the truth, however. 'High' also suggests a greater elevation from which one can descry not just one's immediate surroundings but also

---

tournament in an ethnically conflicted district. The soccer tournament and week-end camp took place every four months and included an evening dialogue and roundtable discussion.

92 Chris McMorran, writing on behalf on the Conflict Research Consortium at the University of Colorado, underscores the characteristics of joint projects that are especially successful for conflict resolution: 'Ideally, individuals who are members of conflicting groups cooperate to organize joint projects. For example, academics, religious leaders, or parents who have lost children to the conflict have begun joint projects. These joint projects begun by individuals close to the conflict tend to have the most promise of success, due to the sense of project ownership and the direct transformation that tends to occur as the projects are undertaken.' Chris McMorran, *Intractable Conflict Knowledge Base Project* (Conflict Research Consortium, University of Colorado, 2003), http://www.beyondintractability.org/m/joint_projects.jsp.

93 Chris McMorran, Ibid.

94 Johann Wolfgang Goethe, *Conversations of Goethe with Eckermann and Soret*, (London, 1883), Supplement to Monday, March 14, 1830, p. 457. [Überhaupt», fuhr Goethe fort, «ist es mit dem Nationalhaß ein eigenes Ding – Auf den untersten Stufen der Kultur werden Sie ihn immer am stärksten und heftigsten finden.] J.W. Goethe, 'Gespräche mit Goethe', *Gedenkausgabe der Werke, Briefe und Gespräche*, vol. XXIV (Zürich, 1949), pp. 733–4.

distant places. The *Iliad* may have for centuries inculcated in Greek schoolboys that the majority of the Olympian gods were on their side. Even so, Homer, if anything, portrayed the Trojans as more noble than the Greeks. The dialogue between Achilles and Priam at the end of the epic attests to Priam's greater moral depth. Even more significantly, what the epic surely does not hide is the enormous suffering that took place on *both* the home-group's and the alien-group's sides. It becomes moot whose culture was more deserving and whose leaders made better decisions. It is perhaps not so bizarre, as Martha Nussbaum notes, that the *Iliad*, even with its relentless anatomically precise description of battle wounds and maiming, was used in therapeutic programs for disturbed Vietnam veterans suffering from post-combat stress syndrome.[95]

Like shared-work, cultures, 'high' not in their artistic and scientific élitism, but in their humanistic breadth, foster cooperative efforts and reconcile differences. Shared activities between conflicted peoples become a repeated source of welcome discovery.

---

95 Martha C. Nussbaum, *The Therapy of Desire* (Princeton, NJ, 1996), p. 404, note #2.

Bibliography

Source of Husserl's Manuscripts

Unless otherwise indicated in footnotes, all references to Husserl's unpublished manuscripts arise from consulting the Husserl Archive at The New School for Social Research, New York City during the summer of 2000. I am grateful to Professor Gail Soffer for permission to conduct research at the archive.

General Bibliography

Abramson, Paul R. and Pinkerton, Steven D., *With Pleasure; Thoughts on the Nature of Human Sexuality* (Oxford: Oxford University Press, 2002).

Ackerman, P. and Duvall, J., *A Force More Powerful: A Century of Nonviolent Conflict* (New York: Palgrave, 2000).

Adams, M.S., and Neel, J.V., 'Children of Incest', *Pediatrics*, 40 (1967): 55–62.

Adamson, P.B., 'Consanguineous Marriages in the Ancient World', *Folklore*, 93, i, (1982).

Allport, Gordon W., *The Nature of Prejudice* (Garden City, NY: Doubleday Anchor Book, 1958).

Apuleius, *The Golden Ass, Being the Metamorphoses of Lucius Apulieus*, W. Adlington, trans. (London: William Heinemann, 1915).

—— *The Transformation of Lucius Otherwise Known as the Golden Ass*, Robert Graves, trans. (New York: Farrar, Straus and Giroux, 1951).

Arendt, Hannah, *The Human Condition* (Chicago: University Press, 1998).

Arens, William, 'Incest taboos', in *The Dictionary of Anthropology*, T. Barfield (ed.) (Oxford: Blackwell, 1997).

Aristotle, *The Complete Works of Aristotle*, The Revised Oxford Translation, Jonathan Barnes (ed.) (Princeton, NJ: Princeton University Press, 1984).

Augustine, 'Reply to Faustus the Manichaean', Stothert trans., *St. Augustin: The Writings Against the Manichaeans and Against the Donatists*, in *The Nicene and Post-Nicene Fathers*, vol. IV (Grand Rapids, MI: Wm. B. Eerdmans Publishing Co., 1956).

Bai, Matt, 'Anatomy of a Massacre', *Newsweek*, 3 May 1999, pp. 25–31.

Baird, P.A., and McGillivray, B., 'Children of Incest', *Journal of Pediatrics*, 101 (1982): 854–7.

Baumeister, Roy F., *Evil: Inside Human Violence and Cruelty* (New York: W.H. Freeman, 1999).

—— 'Violent Pride', *Scientific American*, 284, 4 (April 2001): 96–101.

Bhagavad Gita, Part I: Text and Translation, F. Edgerton, trans. (Cambridge, MA: Harvard University Press, 1944).

Boyle, Kay, *Words That Must Somehow Be Said: Selected Essays of Kay Boyle* (San Francisco: North Point Press, 1985).

Brown, Greg, 'Joint projects' (Conflict Research Consortium, University of Colorado, 2003) http://www.beyondintractability.org/m/joint_projects.jsp.

Byron, Lord (George Gordon), *The Works of*, vol. VI, 'Don Juan' (London: William Blackwood and Sons, 1906).

Cairns, Dorion, *Guide for Translating Husserl, Phaenomenologica*, 55 (The Hague: Martinus Nijhoff, 1973).

Callimachus, *Fragmenta*, vol. 1, (*Fragmenta incertae sedis*), R. Pfieffer (ed.) (Oxford: Clarendon Press, 1949).

Carter, C.O., 'Risk to offspring of incest', *Lancet*, 1 (1967): 436.

Catullus, 'The Poems of Gaius Valerius Catullus', in *Catullus, Tibullus and Pervigilium Veneris*, Cornish, trans. (Cambridge, MA: Harvard University Press, 1962), pp. 7–8.

Chang, Iris, *The Rape of Nanking: The Forgotten Holocaust of World War II* (New York: Basic Books, 1997).

Chekhov, Anton, *The Portable Chekhov*, Constance Garnett, trans. (New York: Penguin Books, 1977).

Cleckley, Hervey M., *The Mask of Sanity* (St. Louis: C.V. Mosby, 1941).

Clement of Alexandria, *Butterworth*, trans. (Cambridge, MA: Loeb Classics, 1919).

Darwin, Charles, *The Expression of the Emotions in Man and Animals*, 3rd edn (Oxford: Oxford University Press, 1998).

Davidson, L. and Cosgrove, L., 'Psychologism and Phenomenological Psychology Revisited, Part II: The Return to Positivity', *Journal of Phenomenological Psychology*, 33, 2 (2002).

Day, R. and Wong, S., 'Anomalous Perceptual Asymmetries for Negative Emotional Stimuli in the Psychopath', *Journal of Abnormal Psychology*, 105, (1996): 648–52.

Derrida, Jacques, *Speech and Phenomena*, Allison and Garver, trans. (Evanston: Northwestern University Press, 1973).

Dewey, John, *Reconstruction in Philosophy* (New York: Henry Holt and Company, 1937).

Dilthey, Wilhelm, 'Über das Studium der Geschichte der Wissenschaften vom Menschen, der Gesellschaft und dem Staat', (1875), in *Gesammelte Schriften*, vol. V, (Stuttgart: B.G. Teubner, 1924), pp. 36–41.

Diogenes Laertius, 'Diogenes', in *Lives of the Eminent Philosophers*, Book I, Hicks, trans. (Cambridge, MA: Loeb Classics, 1925).

—— 'Zeno', in *Lives of the Eminent Philosophers*, Book II, Hicks, trans. (Cambridge, MA: Loeb Classics, 1929).

Doctorow, E.L., *Billy Bathgate* (New York: Random House, 1989).

Donnelly, John, 'Unintended Victims Fill Afghan Hospital', *Boston Globe*, 5 December 2001.

Dostoyevsky, Fyodor, *Brothers Karamazov*, Garnett, trans. (New York: Random House, 1955).

——— *Notes From Underground*, Coulson, trans. (London: Penguin Books, 1972).

Douglas, Frederick, *Narrative of the Life of Frederick Douglas*, Gates (ed.) (New York: Dell Publishing, 1977).

Dozier, Rush W. Jr., *Why We Hate* (Chicago: Contemporary Books, 2002).

Drake, Monica, 'Sex: Fiction's Hamburger Helper: How Authors Wrestle with Sex on the Page', *The Portland Mercury*, 2, 20 (2001), 18 October 2001.

Duras, Marguerite, 'The Path of Joyful Despair', Goldhammer, trans., in *Outside* (Boston: Beacon Press, 1986).

Durkheim, Emile, *Incest: the Nature and Origin of the Taboo* (New York: Lyle Stuart, 1962) [La Prohibition de l'incest et ses origines, *l'Année Sociologique*, 1897].

Eliot, George (Cross, Marian Evans), *Daniel Deronda* (London: John Murray, Albemarle Street, 1903).

Eliot, T.S., *The Family Reunion* (New York: Harcourt, Brace & World, 1939).

——— *The Complete Poems and Plays (1909–1950)* (New York: Harcourt, Brace and Co., 1952).

Engels, Friedrich, *The Origin of the Family, Private Property and the State* (Chicago, IL: Kerr, 1920) [Ursprung der Familie, des Privateigentums und des Staats, Zurich, 1884].

Euripides, 'Medea', *Euripides in four volumes*, vol. IV (Cambridge, MA: Loeb Classics, Harvard University Press, 1912).

Evans, J. Claude, *Strategies of Deconstruction* (Minneapolis: University of Minnesota Press, 1991).

Fanon, Franz, *The Wretched of the Earth*, Farrington, trans. (New York: Grove Press, 1963).

Fine, Kit, 'Part-whole', in *The Cambridge Companion to Husserl* (Cambridge: Cambridge University Press, 1995).

Forster, Edward M., 'Tolerance', in *Two Cheers for Democracy* (New York: Harcourt, Brace and Company, 1938).

Fortenbaugh, W.W., *Aristotle on Emotion* (New York: Harper & Row, Inc., 1975).

Foucault, Michel, 'La maison de fous', Franco Basaglia and Franca Basaglio-Ongaro (eds), *Les criminels de paix* (Paris: 1980), pp. 145–60.

Frazer, James, *Totemism and Exogamy* (London: Macmillan, 1910).

Freeman, Derek, *Margaret Mead and Samoa: The Making and Unmaking of an Anthropological Myth* (Cambridge, MA: Harvard University Press, 1983).

Frege, Gottlob, 'On Sense and Reference', in *Translations from the Philosophical Writings of Gottlob Frege*, Geach and Black (eds) (Oxford: Basil Blackwell, 1960).

Freud, Sigmund, *Totem and Taboo: resemblances between the psychic lives of savages and neurotics* (New York: Moffat, 1918) [Totem and Tabu, Leipzig, 1913].

——— *The Major Works of Sigmund Freud*, in *Great Books of the Western World*, vol. LIV (Chicago: Encyclopaedia Britannica, Inc., 1952).

——— *Introductory Lectures on Psychoanalysis*, vol. XVI in the *Standard Edition of the Complete Works of Sigmund Freud*, 24 vols, James Strachey (Gen. ed.) (London: Hogarth Press and the Institute for Psycho-Analysis, 1953–74).

Gandhi, M.K., *Non-violence in Peace and War*, vol. I (Ahmedabad-14: Navajivan Publishing House, 1942).

—— *Non-violence in Peace and War*, vol. II (Ahmedabad-14: Navajivan Publishing House, 1949).

Gaylin, Willard, *Hatred: The Psychological Descent into Violence* (New York: Public Affairs Books, 2003).

Gibbs, Nancy and Roche, Timothy, 'The Columbine Tapes', *Time*, 20 December, 1999, pp. 40–56.

Gilligan, Carol, *The Birth of Pleasure: A New Map of Love* (New York: Random House, 2002).

Gobodo-Madikizela, Pumla, *A Human Being Died That Night* (Boston, MA: Houghton Mifflin Company, 2003).

Goethe, Johann Wolfgang, *Conversations of Goethe with Eckermann and Soret*, Oxenford, trans. (London: George Bell & Sons, 1883).

—— 'Gespräche mit Goethe', *Gedenkausgabe der Werke, Briefe und Gespräche*, vol. XXIV (Zürich: Ernst Beutler, 1949).

Goldberg, Jeffrey, 'Among the Settlers', *The New Yorker*, 31 May 2004, pp. 47–69.

Gourevitch, Philip, *We wish to inform you that tomorrow we will be killed with our families: Stories from Rwanda* (New York: Farrar, Straus and Giroux, 1998).

Green, Jonathan, *The Cassell Dictionary of Slang* (London: Cassell, 1998).

Gutman, Yisrael, 'On the Character of Nazi Antisemitism', in Shmuel Almog, *Antisemitism Through the Ages*, Nathan Eisner, trans. (Oxford: Pergamon Press, 1988).

Hadreas, Peter, 'Phenomenology and the Incest Taboo', *Journal of Phenomenological Psychology*, 33, 2 (2002): 203–22.

Hamilton, D.L., Gibbons, P.A., Stroessner, S.J. and Sherman, J.W., 'Language, intergroup relations and stereotypes', in G.R. Semin & K. Fiedler (eds), *Language Interaction and Social Cognition* (London: Sage, 1992), pp. 102–28.

Harrison, Faye, 'race', in *The Dictionary of Anthropology*, Thomas Barfield (ed.), (Oxford: Blackwell, 1998).

Harrison, William, *The Description of England* (Ithaca, NY: Cornell University Press, 1968, rpt. of original 1587 folio).

Hart, James G., 'Husserl and Fichte: With special regard to Husserl's lectures on 'Fichte's ideal of humanity'', in *Husserl Studies*, 12 (1995): 135–63.

Hazlitt, William, *The Complete Works of*, vol. VIII, *Table-Talk* (1826) (London: J.M. Dent and Sons, Ltd., 1931).

Heidegger, Martin, *Being and Time*, Macquarrie and Robinson, trans. (New York: Harper & Row, 1962).

—— *Sein und Zeit* (Tübingen: Max Niemeyer Verlag, 1973).

Hemmer, Bruce, 'Bottom-up Peace Building in Bosnia', *PARC News*, Spring, 1997.

Hitler, Adolf, *Mein Kampf*, Ralph Manheim, trans. (Boston, MA: Houghton Mifflin, 1998).

Homer, *The Iliad*, in two volumes, A.T. Murray, trans. (Cambridge, MA: Loeb Classics, Harvard University Press, 1924).

—— *The Odyssey*, in two volumes, A.T. Murray, trans.; Dimock rev. (Cambridge, MA: Loeb Classics, Harvard University Press, 1995).

Honig, Jan Willem and Both, Norbert, *Srebrenica: Record of a War Crime* (New York: Penguin Books, 1997).

Horace, *Odes and Epodes*, Shorey and Laing (eds), (New York: University of Pittsburgh Press, 1910).

Hrdy, S.B, 'The primate origins of human sexuality', in R. Belling and G. Stevens (eds), *The Evolution of Sex* (San Francisco: Harper & Row, 1988).

Hume, David, *A Treatise of Human Nature* (Oxford: Clarendon Press, 1888).

Hurley, Patrick J., *A Concise Introduction to Logic*, 5th edn (Belmont, CA: Wadsworth, 1994).

Husserl, Edmund, *Erfahrung und Urteil: Untersuchungen zur Genealogie der Logik*, L. Landgrebe (ed.) (Prague: Academie-Verlag, 1938).

—— *Ideen zu einer reinen Phänomenologie und Phänomenologischen Philosophie, Zweites Buch, Phänomenologische Untersuchungen zur Konstitution*, M. Biemel (ed.) Husserliana, vol. IV (Den Haag: Nijhoff, 1952).

—— (*Die*) *Krisis der europäischen Wissenschaften und die transzendentale Phänomenologie, Eine Einleitung in die phänomenologische Philosophie*, Walter Biemel (ed.), Husserliana, vol. VI (Den Haag: Martinus Nijhoff, 1954, rpt. 1962).

—— *The Paris Lectures*, Peter Koestenbaum, trans. (Den Haag: Martinus Nijhoff, 1964).

—— 'Phenomenology as Rigorous Science', in *Phenomenology and the Crisis of Philosophy*, Quentin Lauer, trans. (New York: Harper & Row, Publishers, 1965).

—— *Analysen zur passiven Synthesis: Aus Vorlesungs- und Forschungsmanuskripten 1918–1926*, Margot Fleischer (ed.), Husserliana, vol. XI (Den Haag: Martinus Nijhoff, 1966).

—— *Phänomenologische Psychologie, Vorlesungen Sommersemester 1925*, Walter Biemel (ed.), Husserliana, vol. IX (Den Haag: Martinus Nijhoff, 1966).

—— *Formal and Transcendental Logic*, Dorion Cairns, trans. (Den Haag: Martinus Nijhoff, 1969).

—— (*The*) *Crisis of European Sciences and Transcendental Phenomenology: An Introduction to Phenomenological Philosophy*, David Carr, trans. (Evanston, IL: Northwestern University Press, 1970).

—— *Cartesian Meditations: An Introduction to Phenomenology*, Dorion Cairns, trans. (The Hague: Martinus Nijhoff, 1973).

—— *Cartesianische Meditationen und Pariser Vorträge*, Stephan Strasser (ed.), Husserliana, vol. I (Den Haag: Martinus Nijhoff, 1950, rpt. 1973).

—— *Experience and Judgment*, Churchill, trans. (Evanston, IL: Northwestern University Press, 1973).

—— *Zur Phänomenologie der Intersubjektivität, Texte aus dem Nachlass, Zeiter Teil: 1921–1928*, Iso Kern (ed.), Husserliana, vol. XIV (Den Haag: Martinus Nijhoff, 1973).

—— *Zur Phänomenologie der Intersubjektivität, Texte aus dem Nachlass, Dritter Teil: 1929–1935*, Iso Kern (ed.), Husserliana, vol. XV (Den Haag: Martinus Nijhoff, 1973).

—— *Formale und transzendentale Logik, Versuch einer Kritik der logischen Vernuft*, Paul Janssen (ed.), Husserliana, vol. XVII (Den Haag: Martinus Nijhoff, 1974).

—— *Logische Untersuchungen, Ersten Band, Prolegomena zur reinen Logik*, Elmar Holenstein (ed.), Husserliana, vol. XVIII (Den Haag: Martinus Nijhoff, 1975).

—— *Ideen zu einer reinen Phänomenologie und Phänomenologischen Philosophie, Erstes Buch, Allgemeine Einführung in die reine Phänomenologie*, Husserliana, vol. III, 1–2, Karl Schuhmann (ed.) (Den Haag: Martinus Nijhoff, 1976).

—— *Phenomenological Psychology: Lectures, Summer Semester, 1925*, John Scanlon, trans. (The Hague: Martinus Nijhoff, 1977).

—— *Shorter Works*, McCormick and Elliston (eds), Palmer, trans. (Notre Dame, IN: University of Notre Dame Press and Harvester Press, 1981).

—— *Ideas Pertaining to a Pure Phenomenology and to a Phenomenological Philosophy, First Book, General Introduction to Pure Phenomenology*, Fred Kersten, trans. (Dordrecht: Kluwer, 1983).

—— *Logische Untersuchungen, Zweiter Band, Untersuchungen zur Phänomenologie und Theorie der Erkenntnis*, Ursula Panzer (ed.), Husserliana, vol. XIX, 1–2 (Den Haag: Martinus Nijhoff, 1984).

—— *Aufsatze und Vortrage (1922–1937)*, Thomas Nenon and Hans Rainer Sepp (eds), Husserliana, vol. XXV (Dordrecht: Kluwer Academic Publishers, 1989). This volume includes 'Philosophie als strenge Wissenschaft', *Logos*, I (1910–11).

—— *Ideas Pertaining to a Pure Phenomenology and to a Phenomenological Philosophy, Second Book, Studies in the Phenomenology of Constitution*, Richard Rojcewicz and Andre Schuwer, trans. (Dordrecht: Kluwer, 1989).

—— *Briefwechsel* (Husserliana Dokumente III), Karl Schumann in collaboration with Elisabeth Schuhmann (eds), in ten volumes (Dordrecht/Boston/London: Kluwer Academic Publishers, 1994).

—— *Analyses Concerning Active and Passive Synthesis*, Lectures on Transcendental Logic, Anthony J. Steinbock, trans. (Dordrecht/Boston/London: Kluwer Academic Publishers, 2001).

—— *Logical Investigations, Vol. I & II*, J.N. Findlay, trans., preface by M. Dummett, Dermot Moran, (ed.) (New York: Routledge, 2001).

James, William, *The Principles of Psychology*, in *Great Books of the Western World*, vol. LIII (Chicago: Encyclopaedia Britannica, Inc., 1952).

Jaspers, Karl, *Psychologie der Weltanschauungen* (Berlin: 1919).

Johnston, V.S. and Franklin, M., 'Is beauty in the eye of the beholder?' *Ethology and Sociobiology*, 14, (1993): 183–99.

Kant, Immanuel, *Critique of Judgement*, in *Great Books of the Western World* (Chicago: Encyclopaedia Britannica, Inc., 1952).

—— *Anthropology from a Pragmatic Point of View*, V.L. Dowdell, trans. (Carbondale, IL: Southern Illinois University Press, 1978).

—— *Groundwork of The Metaphysics of Morals*, in *The Cambridge Edition of the Works of Immanuel Kant: Practical Philosophy* (Cambridge: Cambridge University Press, 1996).

—— *Critique of Pure Reason*, Paul Guyer and Allen W. Wood, trans. (Cambridge: Cambridge University Press, 1999).

Kierkegaard, Søren, *Training in Christianity*, Lowie, trans. (Princeton: Princeton University Press, 1967).

Kosir, Beth Marie, 'Fifteenth-Century Life: Modesty to Majesty: The Development of the Codpiece', accessible on-line from ORB: The Online Reference Book for Medieval Studies, http://www.r3.org/life/articles/codpiece.html.

Kristeva, Julia, *About Chinese Women*, Barrows, trans. (New York: Marion Boyars, 1968).

—— *Tales of Love*, Roudiez, trans. (New York: Columbia University Press, 1987).

Kundera, Milan, *Immortality* (New York: HarperCollins Publishers Inc., 1991).

Lacan, Jacques, *Écrits: A selection*, Alan Sheridan, trans. (New York: W.W. Norton, 1977).

Leibniz, G.W., *New Essays on Human Understanding* (Cambridge: Cambridge University Press, 1996).

Lévi-Strauss, Claude, *The elementary structures of kinship* (Boston, MA: Beacon, 1969) [Les structures élémentaires de la parenté, Paris, 1949].

Lewis, C.S., *Till We Have Faces* (New York: Harcourt Brace Jovanovich, 1956).

Locke, John, *An Essay Concerning the True Extent and End of Civil Government*, in *Great Books of the Western World*, vol. XXXV (Chicago: Encyclopaedia Britannica, Inc., 1952).

Lukacs, G., *The Destruction of Reason* (London: Merlin, 1980).

Lykken, David T., 'A Study of Anxiety in the Sociopathic Personality', *Journal of Abnormal and Social Psychology*, 55 (1957): 6–10.

Maass, A., Montalcini, F., and Biciotti, E., 'On the (dis-)-confirmability of stereotypic attributes', *European Journal of Social Psychology*, 28 (1998): 383–402.

MacDonald, Andrew (pseudonym). *See* Pierce, William L.

Maryanski, A. and Turner, J., *The Social Cage* (Stanford, CA: Stanford University Press, 1992).

McCabe, J., 'FBD marriage: Further support for the Westermarck hypothesis of incest taboo?' *American Anthropologist*, 85 (1983): 50–69.

McMorran, Chris, *Intractable Conflict Knowledge Base Project*, Conflict Research Consortium, University of Colorado, 2003, http://www.beyondintractability.org/m/joint_projects.jsp.

Mead, Margaret, *Coming of Age in Samoa: A Psychological Study of Primitive Youth for Western Civilisation* (New York: Morrow, 1928).

Melle, Ulrich, 'Husserl's Phenomenology of Willing', in J.G. Hart and L. Embree (eds), *Phenomenology of Values and Valuing* (Dordrecht: Kluwer Academic Publishers, 1997).

Mensch, James R., 'Freedom and Selfhood', *Husserl Studies*, 14 (1997): 41–59.

—— 'Instincts – A Husserlian Account', *Husserl Studies*, 14 (1998): 219–37.

—— *Postfoundational Phenomenology: Husserlian Reflections on Presence and Embodiment* (University Park, PA: Pennsylvania State University Press, 2001).

(The) *Merck Manual of Diagnosis and Therapy*, 17th edn (Whitehouse Station, NJ: Merck Research Laboratories, 1999).

Merleau-Ponty, Maurice, 'Eye and Mind', in *The Primacy of Perception*, Dallery, trans. (Evanston, IL: Northwestern University Press, 1964).

—— *The Visible and the Invisible*, Lingis, trans. (Evanston, IL: Northwestern University Press, 1968).

—— *Phenomenology of Perception*, F. Williams, trans. and rev. (London: Routledge, 1989 reprint).

Michel, Lou and Herbeck, Dan, *American Terrorist: Timothy McVeigh and the Oklahoma City Bombing* (New York: HarperCollins, 2001).

Miller, Henry, *The Tropic of Capricorn* (London: John Calder, 1964).

Money, John, *Gay, Straight, and In-Between: The Sexology of Erotic Orientation* (Oxford: Oxford University Press, 1988).

Montaigne, Michel de, *The Essays*, in *Great Books of the Western World*, vol. XXV (Chicago: Encyclopaedia Britannica, Inc., 1952).

—— *Œvres completes* (Paris: Gallimard, 1962).

Moore, Barrington, Jr., *Privacy: Studies in Social and Cultural History* (Armonk, NY: M.E. Sharpe, 1984).

—— 'Privacy', *Society*, 35, 2 (1998): 287–300.

Morgan, Lewis Henry, *Ancient Society* (New York: Holt, 1877).

Morris, Desmond, *The Naked Ape: A Zoologist's Study of the Human Animal* (New York: McGraw-Hill Book Co., 1967).

Moynihan, Daniel, 'The Negro Family: The Case for National Action', in L. Rainwater and W.L. Yancey (eds), *The Moynihan Report and the Politics of Controversy* (Cambridge, MA: MIT Press, 1967).

Mulligan, Kevin, 'How not to Read: Derrida on Husserl', *Topoi*, 10 (1991): 199–201.

Munro, Dan Carlson (ed.), 'The Fourth Crusade', *Translations and Reprints from the Original Sources in European History*, III, 1 (Philadephia, PA: University of Pennsylvania, 1907); Original found in Robert de Clari, Old French, ch. lxxii, lxxiii, in Hopf: *Chroniques*, p. 5758.

Nietzsche, Friedrich, 'On the uses and disadvantages of history for life', in *Untimely Meditations*, Hollingdale, trans. (Cambridge: Cambridge University Press, 1983).

—— *On the Genealogy of Morals, Ecce Homo*, Walter Kaufmann, trans. (New York: Random House, 1989).

Nussbaum, Martha C., *The Therapy of Desire* (Princeton, NJ: Princeton University Press, 1996).

Ovid, (Publius Ovidius Naso), *The Art of Love, and Other Poems*, J.H. Mozley, trans. (Cambridge, MA: Loeb Classics, Harvard University Press, 1929).

Pascal, Blaise, *Pensées* (Paris: Garnier-Flammarion, 1976).

Patrick, C.J., Bradley, M.B., and Lang, P.J., 'Emotion in the Criminal Psychopath: Startle Reflex Modulation', *Journal of Abnormal Psychology*, 102 (1993): 82–92.

Peace Watch, 'Bringing Croats and Muslims Together', *United States Institute of Peace*, II, 2 (1996): February.

Philipse, Herman, 'Transcendental Idealism', in *The Cambridge Companion to Husserl*, Smith and Smith (eds) (Cambridge: Cambridge University Press, 1995).

Pierce, William L., *The Turner Diaries*, 2nd edn (Fort Lee, NJ: Barricade Books, 1996).

Plato, *Phaedo*, Fowler, trans. rev., vol. I (Cambridge, MA: Loeb Classics, Harvard University Press, 1914).

—— *Philebus*, Fowler, trans. vol. XII (Cambridge, MA: Loeb Classics, Harvard University Press, 1925).

Plotinus, *Enneads, Plotini opera*, vol. III, P. Henry and H.-R. Schwyzer (eds) (Leiden: Brill, 1973).

Plutarch, 'Of Envy and Hate', *Moralia*, vol. VII (Cambridge, MA: Loeb Classics, Harvard University Press, 1959).

Proust, Marcel, *Swann's Way*, Moncrieff and Kilmartin, trans. (New York: Vintage, 1989).

Rich, Adrienne, *Necessities of Life, Poems, 1962–1965* (New York: W.W. Norton & Company, 1966).

Ricoeur, Paul, 'Sur la phénoménologie,' in *A l'école de la phénoménologie* (Paris: J. Vrin, 1987).

—— *A Key to Edmund Husserl's Ideas I*, Harris and Spurlock, trans. (Milwaukee: Marquette University Press, 1996).

Roosevelt, Theodore, 'The Winning of the West', in *The Works of Theodore Roosevelt*, vol. 9 (New York: Scribner's, 1926).

Russell, Bertrand, *The Autobiography of Bertrand Russell, 1872–1914* (Boston: Little, Brown & Co, 1951).

Saint-Exupéry, Antoine, *Wind, Sand and Stars*, Galantière, trans. (New York: Harcourt Brace & Co., 1992) [French title: *Terre des hommes.*]

Sartre, Jean-Paul, *Anti-Semite and Jew*, Becker, trans. (New York: Schocken Books, Inc., 1948).

—— *Being and Nothingness* (New York: Washington Square Press, 1966).

Saudi Information Service, 'Saudi Telethon Host Calls for Enslaving Jewish Women', in *National Review*, 26 April 2002.

Scheler, Max, *The Nature of Sympathy*, Heath, trans. (Hamden, CN: Archon Books, 1970).

—— *Ressentiment*, Coser and Holdheim, trans. (Milwaukee, WI: Marquette University Press, 1998).

Scott, Janny, 'Closing a Scrapbook Full of Life and Sorrow', *New York Times*, 31 December, 2001.

Sedan, Gil, 'In One Bilingual Galilee School, Students Seek Out Common Ground', *Common Ground News Service* (*CG News*), 27 May 2005.

Seemanová, E., 'A study of children of incestuous marriages', *Human Heredity*, 21 (1971): 108–28.

Seebohm, Thomas M., 'The Apodicity of Absence', in *Derrida and Phenomenology*, W. McKenna and J. Evans (eds) (Dordrecht: Kluwer, 1995), pp. 185–200.

Seneca, *Ad Lucilium Epistulae Morales*, Gummere, trans. (Cambridge, MA: Loeb Classics, Harvard University Press, 1917).

Shakespeare, William, *The Complete Works of*, The Cambridge Text, Wilson, John Dover (ed.) (London: Octopus Books Ltd, 1980).

Shepher, J., *Incest* (New York: Academic Press, 1983).

Slackman, Michael, 'Arabs See Jewish Conspiracy in Pokémon', *Los Angeles Times*, 24 April 2001, pp. A1, ff.

Smith, Adam, *The Theory of Moral Sentiments* (Oxford: Clarendon Press, 1973).

Smith, Barry, 'Book review of Husserl's correspondence', *Husserl Studies*, 12 (1995): 98–104.

Smyth, Herbert Weir, *Greek Grammar*, Messing, rev. (Cambridge, MA: Harvard University Press, 1920).

Solomon, Robert C., *The Passions: Emotions and the Meaning of Life* (Indianapolis/ Cambridge: Hackett Publishing Co., 1993).

—— *About Love: Reinventing Romance for Our Times* (New York: Madison Books, 2001).

Spinoza, Benedict de., *Ethics*, in *Great Books of the Western World*, vol. 31 (Chicago: Encyclopedia Britannica, Inc., 1952).

Steinbock, Anthony J., 'Generativity and generative phenomenology', in *Husserl Studies*, 12 (1995): 55–79.

—— *Home and Beyond: Generative Phenomenology after Husserl* (Evanston, IL: Northwestern University Press, 1995).

Stendahl (Marie-Henri Beyle), *Le Rouge et Le Noir* (Paris: Garnier-Flammarion, 1964).

Stoddard, Lothrop, *The Rising Tide of Color against White World-Supremacy* (New York: Charles Scribner's Sons, 1920).

Thompkins, Peter, *Secrets of the Great Pyramid* (New York: Harper and Row, 1978).

Thucydides, *History of the Peloponnesian War* (Cambridge, MA: Loeb Classics, Harvard University Press, 1920).

Toulemont, René, *L'essence de la société selon Husserl* (Paris: Presses Universitaires de France, 1962).

Twain, Mark, *The Adventures of Huckleberry Finn* (New York: Signet Classic, 1952).

Tyler, Edward Burnett, 'On a method of investigating the development of institutions', *Journal of the Royal Anthropological Institute*, 18 (1889): 245–69.

Virgil, *Eclogues*, vol. 1, Fairclough, trans. (New York: G.P. Putnam's Sons, 1930), pp. 74–5.

Walter, A., 'The evolutionary psychology of mate selection in Morocco', *Human Nature*, 8 (1997): 113–37.

Welton, Donn (ed.), *The New Husserl: A Critical Reader* (Bloomington, IN: Indiana University Press, 2003).

Wickler, Wolfgang, 'Socio-Sexual Signals and Their Intraspecific Imitation among Primates', in *Primate Ethology*, Desmond Morris (ed.) (Chicago: Aldine Pub. Co., 1967).

Wistrich, Robert S., 'The Devil, the Jews, and Hatred of the "Other"', in *Demonizing the Other*, Wistrich (ed.) (Jerusalem: Harwood Academic Publishers, 1999).

Wittgenstein, Ludwig, *Philosophical Investigations*, Anscombe, trans. (New York: Macmillan Publishing Co. Inc., 1953).

Wolf, A., and Huang, C.S., *Marriage and Adoption in China, 1845–1945* (Stanford, CA: Stanford University Press, 1980).

Yeats, W.B., *The Collected Works of*, vol. I., *The Poems* (New York: Macmillian Publishing Company, 1989).

Yutang, Lin, *The Wisdom of Confucius* (New York: Modern Library, 1994).

Zahavi, Dan, *Husserl's Phenomenology* (Stanford, CA: Stanford University Press, 2003).

Index